14 Day

Budapest

HUNGARY

Varna

Belgrade

Corfu   Salonika Kavela

Athens

Crete

GREECE

FRESH FROM THE LAUNDRY

Ilka Chase

With 24 pages of photographs by Dr. Norton Brown

Venturing behind the Iron Curtain may not be everyone's bowl of sour cream, but armchair travelers will delight in the adventures of Ilka Chase and her husband, Dr. Norton Brown, on their amusing, sometimes frustrating foray to the Communist countries of Hungary, Bulgaria, Romania, Czechoslovakia, Yugoslavia, and to definitely non-Communist Greece. Here, in her fourth travel book, Miss Chase gives humorous advice on how to cope with bugged hotel rooms, interminable passport examinations, "People's State" plumbing, low-wattage light bulbs, and phones inexplicably out of order. She also gives many valuable tips on where to stay and what to see and do in these fascinating countries not yet commonly visited.

After a few days in Germany, Miss Chase and her husband went to Prague, with its quaint opera house (where, she says, snowcaps nearly

(continued on back flap)

Books by Ilka Chase

FRESH FROM THE LAUNDRY

SECOND SPRING AND TWO POTATOES

ELEPHANTS ARRIVE AT HALF-PAST FIVE

THE CARTHAGINIAN ROSE

THREE MEN ON THE LEFT HAND

THE ISLAND PLAYERS

NEW YORK 22

FREE ADMISSION

I LOVE MISS TILLI BEAN

IN BED WE CRY

PAST IMPERFECT

ALWAYS IN VOGUE (with Edna Woolman Chase)

ILKA CHASE

PHOTOGRAPHS BY NORTON BROWN

Fresh from the Laundry

1967

DOUBLEDAY & COMPANY, INC., GARDEN CITY, NEW YORK

CONTENTS

CONTENTS

FRESH FROM THE LAUNDRY

CHAPTER ONE

Wiesbaden   Prague

It all came about because of Greece . . . the rest of the journey I mean. Greece and, I suspect, a sliver of annoyance on the part of the doctor.

I was about to write jealousy, but that is too heavy a word and besides, if I use it, my husband utters a sound between snort and sneer which I interpret as non-complimentary.

He utters it because in the spring of the year, although I knew he could not get away at the time, I announced that I had an urge to make a quick trip to Paris and certain environs like Antibes and Mallorca. I had received invitations from old friends and wanted to accept them.

"I cannot think," said my dear husband as my plan unfolded in simple splendor, "that this trip is necessary." It was his wartime training, but I was the lady of the jingle:

"Mrs. Dick was very sick and nothing would improve her except to see the Tuileries and gallop through the Louvre."

I departed, I was cured, I returned, and it was then that Norton attached himself with more dedication than he had heretofore shown, to planning a mutual trip for the autumn.

We knew definitely we would be in Greece. We had been there before, and it had won our hearts, so, since we would be in that part of the world in any event, might we not, he suggested, embrace adjacent territory? With my example of Antibes and Mallorca, why weren't countries like Czechoslovakia and Romania and Bulgaria adjacent?

As far as I was concerned they were. I would consider Katmandu adjacent and hope he will someday come home with our tickets.

Actually, his scheme did seem the soul of simplicity. One evening, when he had locked up the comics for the day and was relaxing, cocktail dividend in hand, waiting for dinner to be served, I approached him with the planet earth; our small portable plastic one. "You see, lovey, this is how it will work." I spun the globe from the Marshall Islands, where it had stopped in its last revolution and which were opposite his nose, across the Pacific, across North and South America and the bulge of Africa and halted at approximately eastern Libya. From eastern Libya moseying north, crossing the Mediterranean in a trice, you arrive, barely panting, at the Peloponnesus. Once there in half a trice the eye encompasses the Balkans. "There you are and you're right," I said. "Adjacent. Why *not* visit those Balks? So they're Communists, but maybe they're human too, and I believe there's no difficulty any more about getting passports. Shall I go ahead?"

"Go," said he, "tell me what you find out."

What I found was that not only are passports to that part of the world easily obtainable—the U. S. State Department is beginning to see the light—but that those countries themselves are eager to welcome tourists. Possibly they might prefer the Yankee dollar minus the Yankee—a large part of the world has become accustomed to the long-distance handout—but they are realists. If they can't have one without the other, they settle for the source of supply in person. Besides, they are probably as curious to see the horns of the Capitalist devils as we are to see the tails of the Communist.

As often happens the people are way out in front of the

leaders. The individuals we were to meet in eastern Europe were unfailingly polite and hospitable, quick to offer friendship and understanding.

Actually the co-operative attitude started on our own shores, especially in the person of Mr. Joseph Policano, who handles public relations for Czechoslovakia, Romania, and Bulgaria and who proved a tower of knowledge, patience, and efficiency. He, Mr. Stojan Pudar of the Yugoslav Travel Service, and Mr. Yanko Karayanev of the Bulgarian not only briefed us on points of interest and native ways but alerted their respective countries to our arrival. "We've told them about you," they said.

For some reason they reminded me of an eerie little exchange I had with a lady I met at the Lido in Venice a few years ago. I had been invited to lunch in the cabaña of an Italian friend, the Contessa Anna Maria Cigone, but when I arrived my hostess was swimming far out beyond the breakers, and the only sign of life around the cabaña was a recumbent female sunning herself on a cot, a parasol held over her face. Her eyes were tightly closed, yet, given the pose it seemed unlikely she was asleep. I tentatively cleared my throat. "I'm sorry to disturb you," I said, "my name is Ilka Chase. I've been invited for luncheon."

With enviable control of her stomach muscles the lady raised herself upward, legs straight out in front of her, parasol still in hand, eyes still closed. "Oh yes," she murmured, "Anna Maria warned me you were coming." Warned. Oh dear, oh dear. The lady, it later turned out, was Miss Nancy Mitford, but odd as her remark might have sounded, she acted as a true friend, offering to lend me a bathing suit so that I too might swim and sun myself.

Whether the Messrs. Policano, Karayanev, and Pudar were warning their Balks I did not know; only time would tell.

In any event, as a result of their efforts and our own involved preparations, since the doctor wished to take no chances with traffic on the Labor Day weekend, we arrived one Friday at Kennedy Airport three hours and fifteen minutes early for TWA's evening flight to Frankfurt. What a happy waiting period it was! We had all *sorts* of fun.

We bought Deutchemarks—one mark equals twenty-five cents—and a Berlitz German phrase book. The little professor is still with us, seeming, not unnaturally, more appropriate to Germany than to Italy or Spain. The books are helpful but they could afford to cut down on those phrases for customs; in most parts of the world through which we have traveled customs are moribund, the officials having apparently discovered that not enough travelers are smuggling dope or diamonds to make surveillance worthwhile.

Also waiting in the TWA lounge was the luscious Miss Arlene Dahl garbed in yellow and blue and wearing absolutely sensational make-up. Eye shadow professionally applied and out to here, mascara, glossy lipstick, every auburn tress burnished. I felt like a sparrow, an exhausted sparrow. I was in easygoing wool and cashmere, anticipating a restless all-night flight, and as a result of the vagaries of television and a series in which I was then working, I had been up at five-thirty three mornings running.

Miss Dahl was en route to Hollywood where she would be arriving in a few hours bright as a button, a refreshment to the eye, while the poor Frankfurters would have to take what they got; an unshaven medic and his rumpled wife.

We were flying TWA because that line has a crush on Greece and speedy service to and from and we would be coming back with them direct from Athens, but since we were to begin our Communist-bloc tour with Czechoslovakia we decided to begin a little to the west of it with a trip up the Rhine. Hence the Frankfurt airport and a couple of days in Wiesbaden.

Once airborne we were served a long, leisurely, sumptuous dinner, and then came the movie. It was my maiden voyage with a movie and I had always wondered what one did if wanting to close one's ears to it. It's simple. You don't hear a thing. Even with the ear plugs you don't hear much, because of the engines. Oh, you get the dialogue all right, but there is certainly no dinning.

I am not like my husband, I do not feel superior to movies—he hates them—whereas I thoroughly enjoy a good one; but unfortunately *Shenandoah*, Mr. James Stewart's space vehicle, was not in that category. I gave up after the first five minutes, consoling myself with the thought that on the return flight we would undoubtedly hit the jackpot. We did not. The return goody was *Ghenghis Khan*. Condolences to one and all.

We and the dawn arrived at Frankfurt simultaneously, approaching over rolling fields and great patches of woodland, which I hoped was the Black Forest; I was geographically askew; that is farther south.

I was wrong about our hotel in Wiesbaden too, the Nassauer Hof, which I promptly associated with Nasser, but it has to do with the former duchy of Nassau, northeast of the Main River. These are the little pointers one picks up in a life of travel.

The hotel has an old-fashioned *gemütlich* atmosphere, and after we had removed the enormous wedge-shaped pillows between the box springs and the mattress the beds were quite comfortable. The room keys were formidable, as heavy as revolvers and of approximately the same shape and size but with a complicated arrangement of shafts, handles, and shields. There's a management that will never have guests walking off inadvertently with the hotel hardware!

After breakfast and a brief nap we strolled around the town, which is prettily laid out with parks and gardens and terraces. Wilhelmstrasse, the main street, is lined with well-stocked stores on one side and a big park across the way. In dress and physiognomy the people looked provincial, but they appeared prosperous and were certainly well fed. There were many pastry shops in one of which we bought delicious cookies, a triumphant alliance of chocolate, orange peel, and nuts. There were many book shops too and, unexpectedly, a number of places selling Persian rugs. Wiesbaden is decidedly bullish on oriental carpeting, yet it is perhaps not surprising that their interests are wide-ranging.

The locality was settled by the Celts in the third century B.C. and those greatest bathers of them all, the Romans, stopped marching around Europe long enough to enjoy the saline baths for which the town is still renowned.

Today, Wiesbaden's nearby neighbor, Frankfurt, counts among its Auslanders 30,000 American troops who are stationed in the city. I was wondering aloud how the Germans liked the idea. "I wouldn't worry," Norton said, "it's a great shot in the arm for the economy, and they probably like it better than the Russian troops who would be the alternative."

Returning to lunch at the hotel we were felled by the enormous helpings of smoked pork, sausages, sauerkraut, and mashed potatoes set before us but balanced it with a dinner of lighter weight which we ate that night in a restaurant called Mutter Engel. Mum's atmosphere is pleasant but I should say costly for what we got. The bill was $26, and German red wine is a mistake. Stick to white or beer.

Our luncheon, however, sustained us through the afternoon, which we spent visiting one of the world's best zoos. Driving away from the airport in the morning we had seen enormous cutouts of wild animals and I remembered then that the Frankfurt zoo is the justified pride of its distinguished director, Dr. Bernard Grzimek. Those who have read *Serengeti Shall Not Die* will remember that it was Dr. Grzimek and his son, Michael, who were making a count of animals in the Ngorongoro Crater in Africa when the boy's plane crashed and he was instantly killed.

In warm weather the Frankfurt zoo tenants have a semblance of freedom for there are comparatively few cages or bars. They are confined to their open areas by moats, or a

fence which insures the safety of the people while the
animals have room to move about.

Yet for the beasts of Africa sojourning in any zoo must
be a poignant exile because for the most part the skies of
the great cities where they are incarcerated are gray in
winter and the atmosphere either cold or dismal. The zoo
of San Diego, in California, is a rare exception because of
sunshine and the balmy climate.

The Frankfurt zoo's building known as the Exotarium is
exactly that and impressive. Exotic creatures are on display. Fish and reptiles and crocodiles sleep their sluggish
lives away in the warm, moist, tropical atmosphere that
has been created for them. The penguins fare pretty well
too in their man-made refrigerator where their bottoms are
as cold as in Antarctica.

We wished, the next day, for a little man-made sunshine. In two months in Europe we had only two days of
rain but one of them, with a diabolic sense of timing, was
the Sunday we steamed up the Rhine.

The morning, though gray, was not wet, so we started off
optimistically. There was, after all, a chance that it might
clear, the skies *could* lighten rather than darken. They
could, but they weren't in the mood. Still, en route to
Coblenz, we were able to admire the countryside unveiled
by rain. Neat forests without underbrush, old churches on
mountain sides, clanging bells, and the attractive town of
Schlangenbad. We passed Bad Ems too on the Lahn River.
If they avail themselves of nature's amplitude in the matter
of baths, the Germans in that district must be notably
clean and, I would imagine, content, for they are surrounded by pine forests, flowers spill from every window
box, cows graze in the fields, and there are few people.
Very pleasant.

Driving along I was leafing through a motor glossary with
columns of words giving driving terms in four or five lan-
guages when, under Tools, I came upon the German
word for spanner or wrench. *Schraubenschlüssel.* I was

crazy about it. It sounded like a hair-raising Teutonic oath straight out of *Götterdämmerung,* an invective which, hurled at the opponent, would rot the eyes in his head. "Speed limit" is pretty good too. *Geschwindigkeitsgrenze.* And, this being Germany, there were *verbotens* galore.

We arrived in Coblenz at lunch time. In 9 B.C. the site of today's city was a Roman military encampment called Confluentes because it is here that the Rhine and Mosel meet. A peninsula juts out into the confluence of the two rivers and on it has been erected Deutsches Eck, a large ugly monument to the German dead of World War I. I am sure that their women and their children mourned them but it is hard for me to feel compassion for Germans. They go out of their way to earn their destiny.

After luncheon we boarded the *Lorelei,* one of the roomy, comfortable Rhine steamers that can accommodate 3400 passengers. There were several restaurants and much open deck space but the clouds had lost control and the deck glistened like a lake of ice under rain.

It didn't obscure the view too much, however, and we now know that Rhine wine is authentic. Mile after mile the vineyards border the river, the vines planted almost always perpendicularly. Conscious of contour farming and the need to contain water, the system surprised me, but the scientific Doc opined that the vintners probably wanted the water to run off, and I believed that too much sogginess can indeed prove disastrous to a grape harvest.

Despite the chilly gloomy weather we passed a good many racing kayaks and thought them very sporting. Viewed through a microscope the waters of the Rhine may be polluted but with the exception of one empty crate we saw no garbage or debris in the five hours the voyage lasted.

At intervals, as we sat huddled on the lee side or, if the rain slackened, ventured out on deck for a few minutes, a voice over the loud-speaker indicated in French, German, and English, sites and sights of particular interest along the historic shores. Most of the castles are little more than ruins, but they form picturesque silhouettes for photographing and inevitably prompt the inquiries "Why?" "How?". The massive piles would seem as indestructible as the rock from which they rise, but the answer is simple; man made them and man destroyed them.

Since Roman times the Rhine Valley has been a vital communications route, and the castles were built in the Middle Ages by feudal lords equally desirous of protecting their lands from marauders and of gathering in the loot; those rich tolls extracted from every passing ship. From Bingen to Coblenz the river is comparatively narrow, and along the thirty-five-mile stretch there are more castles than in any other river valley in the world.

The first onslaught against the strongholds came in the thirteenth century with the robber-knights making hay and attacking The Establishment in the troubled times before a League of Rhenish Cities had been formed and before Rudolph of Hapsburg was elected King of Germany in 1273, when most of the marauders' own castles were destroyed.

The Thirty Years' War, 1618–48, raged intermittently all over Germany, involving the Catholic versus the Protestant States of Europe. It saw Frenchmen, Spaniards, and Swedes battling for the strategic key position which the castles afforded and inevitably ruining a good many of them in the process.

In 1688 and 1689 Louis IV of France, having gained sovereignty over Alsace, sent troops as far as the Rhine to protect his forces from the rear and any protesting centers were demolished. Over one hundred years later, in 1792, Prussian armies under the Duke of Brunswick were defeated at Valmy by the French who forced them to withdraw behind the Rhine, and those castles that had been rebuilt were again attacked and their defenders scattered.

Today they stand melancholy, moribund dinosaurs of architecture and of another age. As the boat glides past

them or the sites on which their proud turrets once rose,
the Voice over the loud-speaker imparts their story and the
legends that are so much a part of German folklore.

Usually the comments were informal but as we approached the most famous of the landmarks there was a
hush, the canned music ceased and in accents befitting the
solemnity of the revelation the Voice intoned, "Ladies
and Gentlemen, the rock of the Lorelei."

As far as I was concerned the rock was a big bluff in
both senses. I had always imagined it being in the middle
of the Rhine, a real menace to navigation, and upon
it a fair creature, very like the White Rock sprite of my
childhood, lured strong men to their doom.

Actually it is part of the shore line, a high bluff or pali-
sade, and I should think one would have to be a deplorably
poor navigator to make lethal contact with it even on a
stormy night. Not according to the legend though. According to that the Lorelei, a hybrid minx—voice of nightingale,
hair of gold, form of moonlight, and eyes of stars—had
caused the death of half the ship-borne males in the kingdom; as they panted toward her, forgetting to steer, their
frail barks were shattered upon the rock.

Eventually this lamentable magnet disappeared but only
after causing the destruction of Ronald, the son of the
Palatinate Count and the covey of stout-hearted men who
went in search of him.

Ronald was obsessed by the thought of the enchantress.
Sighting her one night through the mist, hearing the
voice more melodious than the angels, and watching her
combing her hair like one of the seven Sutherland sisters,
he leapt from his boat; but as he would scramble ashore
he gave a blood-curdling cry and the waves washed over
him. He was a *corpse*.

Those who went to avenge him fared little better. Seeing
them approach, the mocking siren pulled a string of pearls
from her appetizing décolletage and wound them around
her head (I see Beatrice Lillie in the part), crying as she

did so, "What are the weak sons of earth seeking up here on the heights?" As if she didn't know! "You sorceress, we will dash you into the river below," cried the leader, but she trilled a silvery laugh, which must have been infuriating under the circumstances, and sang a little ditty:

> Haste thee, haste thee, oh father dear!
> Send forth thy steeds from the water clear.
> I will ride with the waves and the wind!

Dad did as requested. The Rhine, for it was he, rose in howling thunder and driving rain, two white combers like snow-white steeds billowed upward, Lorelei slipped onto them, and they went roaring off into legend.

The story that I liked better, one can lick one's chops over the ending, is the one about the Mouse Tower, a stronghold on an island in the Rhine. It was built by Hatto, Archbishop of Mainz, and vicious was he; greedy, cruel, and with a coarse sense of humor.

The tower was a toll gate and every passing ship was obliged to fatten the archbishop's already ill-gotten hoard. That was bad enough, but what happened afterward was even more heinous. A cycle of drought and hail had destroyed the crops and such little corn as was available from the previous year had, you may be sure, all been snatched up by old horror puss, and stored away in his own granaries. The people were starving. One day, as the archbishop and his equally depraved companions were sitting down to a sumptuous feast the wretched villagers came pouring into his castle. With a demoniacal smile the fiend invited them to the barn where the corn was stored. "Help yourselves, help yourselves," he urged cordially, but once they were within, he ordered the doors locked and set fire to the building.

The shrieks of the victims reaching the palace caused even some of the bishop's perfidious guests to blanch, but Hatto shrugged it off. "Ha, ha, ha, ho, ho, ho," quoth he.

"Hear how the mice are squeaking in the corn." Well! Did *he* get his comeuppance!

Mice there were, by the hundred thousands. They came streaming from the burning barn, and Robert Southey in his poem, *God's Judgment on a Wicked Bishop* tells what happened next.

> Bishop Hatto fearfully hastened away,
> And he crossed the Rhine without delay,
> And he reached his tower and barred with care
> All the windows and doors and loopholes there.
>
> He laid him down and closed his eyes
> But soon a scream made him arise:
> He started and saw two eyes of flame
> On his pillow from whence the screaming came.
>
> He listened and looked—it was only the cat,
> But the bishop grew more fearful for that,
> For she sat screaming mad with fear,
> At the army of rats that was drawing near.

They swarmed into the tower. Nearer they came and nearer, the ferocious ravening legions, and they tore the flesh from the wicked man's bones and devoured him down to the last eyelash and hangnail and left tooth marks on his golden rings. The people were avenged!

I consider that a good story, though I have been told, and alas fear it to be true, that the tale is apocryphal. Hatto of Mainz did exist, however; in fact, there were a couple of them, Hatto I and Hatto II, and although they apparently never burned down a barnful of people they still needed Madison Avenue, for their images were not sympathetic. They were tyrannical and treacherous and even though wealth accrued to the See because of them the country folk drew a breath of relief when they died, and murmured heartfelt things like "Good riddance" and "God be praised."

History frequently does have a deflating way with the

sails of legend, for the Hattos lived in the tenth century while the Mouse Tower was not constructed until the thirteenth or fourteenth, depending on what authority convinces you, and the word *Maeuseturm* is, in all likelihood a corruption of mautturm or toll tower. So much for tiresome old fact.

Continuing our rainy journey, as evening closed in, we went down to a cozy bar on the lowest deck for a bit of cheer and found ourselves in the middle of a large group of noisy students. Two or three girls wearing little plaid caps came in and although they were not very pretty they were instantly surrounded by attentive beaux, and we could see that life on the Rhine had its moments.

Night had fallen as we passed Bingen, but the town was swinging; lights, music, a merry-go-round. This was autumn, and the wine festival was in full tilt. The same was true of Rüdesheim where we disembarked to meet our chauffeur, Horst, and drive back to Wiesbaden. The boat goes there too, and one may stay on board until she docks, which, in the summer, would undoubtedly be the course to follow; but on a dark and rainy September evening with visibility zero the shorter quicker route seemed preferable.

The next morning we flew to Prague. Praha to the Czechoslovakians and a city of unparalleled beauty, but on arrival we met with a slight contretemps. The representative from Cedok, the Czech travel bureau who, we had been assured, would be there to meet us, had not turned up.

Fortunately their ambassador at the airport, an attractive young woman speaking perfect English, battled her native telephone system and emerging unscathed, suggested we take the bus into town. We could rely on someone meeting us at the terminal.

Passing through the suburbs we saw there was a good deal of building in progress; what we call low-cost housing and they refer to as workers' flats. The buildings were medium high-rise, the same boxlike architecture as our own, the same flimsy construction and tiny rooms, the only pleasant feature being a private balcony for every tenant, which many of our developments have too.

From lampposts along the way fluttered the red, white, and blue of the Czech flag and the red field with yellow hammer and sickle of the Russians. Since, once within the city limits, the flags disappeared we surmised they had been broken out for the cavalcade of an official visit.

Such symbols are what strikes one first when visiting the enemy, or more accurately, the opposition. In the United States a Russian flag would bring out the militia. There it is honored, as is the red star surmounting many public buildings in the Communist bloc.

Regardless of propaganda opposite numbers are the same everywhere and while there is such a thing as an unmoneyed society, whose members incidentally are struggling as hard as their regimes allow them to get out of that unpleasant condition, there is no such thing as a classless society. All over the world some people are more equal than others.

Crossing a river Norton and I wondered aloud which it might be and thought that a man on the seat behind us said it was the Volga. As a child in school I used to be rather good at geography, but that was a year or two ago, and although I was a little surprised by the information I did not seriously question it. Possibly the Volga had worn a new channel or had a far-wandering branch. I am now in a position to inform the equally ignorant that Prague is watered by the Vltava, also known as the Moldau, which is crossed by some of the world's most beautiful bridges.

Our young lady at the airport had spoken truly, and moments after we got out of the bus at the terminal Sonia Kopecka hurried up. Mrs. Kopecka spoke good English, but the news she imparted in that language aroused in us a faint foreboding. Unfortunately we could not get into the Hotel Jalta as planned. Even though reservations had been

requested quite a while ago they simply could not accommodate us.

This was our initiation into a situation we were to encounter wherever we traveled in central and eastern Europe. The hotels were filled to capacity. We had been,
I fear, a little smug in plotting our journey. It would be
autumn, Labor Day would be a thing of the past, and
that, as the whole *world* knew, heralded the close of the
tourist season. Americans went home. Hotels would be vying
for our trade. Who else was there?

Well, dear friends, for any of you contemplating a similar
trip at the same season that is not how things work out.
Who travels besides Americans? Germans, Russians, Chinese, Romanians, Bulgarians, Yugoslavs, Czechoslovaks,
Greeks, Hungarians, Africans . . . you name them. Furthermore their idea of prime time is September and October.
Bear it in mind.

We finally got a taxi, not too easy in central Europe
and the Balkans, where it always seems to be 4 P.M., the
hour every cab in New York City goes off duty, that
vacuum being followed by the Great Dearth, 8 P.M. or
theatergoing time, when hacks are either non-existent or
occupied.

Our destination was the Zlata Husa. Zlata Husa means
Golden Goose, but there was no shine upon the hotel.
Standing in the cramped dingy lobby with its stained walls
and ceiling and seedy-looking personnel, the doctor glanced
around and his reaction was succinct. "Fleabag."

Well, it was and it wasn't. The beds were uncomfortable,
but our room, while unpretentious certainly, was clean
and our private bath adequate. Right there we began to
realize that throughout the trip we would probably be
confronted with the same puzzlement. When things were
different or not to our liking was the difference attributable
to politics, economics, or race? Were they the way they
were because of Communism, of poverty—and if so, were
people poor because of the regime under which they

lived?—or were they differences of tradition? European, in this instance, eastern European, as opposed to American? It was a question not all of a piece but we tried solving, or at least understanding it, as we went along.

Also, it was there, at the Zlata Husa, our first Communist-bloc hotel that I began the detective work which I pursued diligently throughout our travels in the Communist countries—my search for hidden microphones. It consisted in peering behind the pictures on the walls or standing on chairs and running my fingers along the molding and it never failed to bring the same reaction from the doctor. "You are really nuts," he would say shaking his head.

"Why? In all probability there *is* a microphone. Look what they do to our embassies."

"Sweetie, the embassy is different. What do they care about casual travelers? But if there *are* mikes you may be sure we won't find them. They don't look like the ones at NBC, you know."

"Well, of course I know *that!*"

"They have them in light bulbs, behind the baseboard, in door knobs, in the mattresses."

"The mattresses!" My eyebrows must have risen very high, for the doctor grinned. "What do you care? We're married."

"Just the same, *that's* snooping." My husband seemed to find this quite comical, but I consider that there is orthodox and unorthodox spying, and, as we were shortly to learn, I wasn't the only who was worried about microphones.

We lunched that day at the Karvana, a restaurant adjoining the hotel, and experienced our first delicious local Pilsner beer. Afterward, going with Mrs. Kopecka to her Cedok office, we were enlightened as to Communist working hours. Seven A.M. to three-thirty, six days a week. We found that to be standard procedure throughout the Balkan countries too and decided the comrades do not fool around.

Understandably, since she must have been up since at

least six o'clock, if not earlier, our guide, having passed
on a few pointers for our sightseeing and entertainment,
left us on our own.

We strolled through the old part of the city and came
to an ancient astronomical clock tower she had mentioned.
Before it, in the square, a crowd had gathered and having been informed as to what we might expect, we joined
them and stood waiting.

As the chimes struck, two small doors high up on the
tower opened and a procession of twelve clockwork dolls,
the twelve apostles, marched by in jerky procession, turning
to face their public before they disappeared from view and
the little doors snapped shut. It was a modest display, but
it is extraordinary what people will stand in line for a long
time to see.

Moseying about in the shops it seemed to us that the
best buys were Bohemian glass, china, and drawn thread-
work. The first two unfortunately are not practical for air
travelers, but the designs done in drawn linen thread are
original and charming. I bought a beige horse with a spiked
white moon balanced on his back. The composition was
ingeniously framed between two sheets of glass, hanging
in one of those room-divider walls and visible from both
sides. There are any number of designs, they are inexpensive, weigh nothing, and may be laid flat or rolled up and
stuffed in a corner of a suitcase.

We had decided we would like to go to the opera that
night and Mrs. Kopecka having told us the curtain was
at seven we left our hotel early since walking was the only
means of locomotion. Taxis, as I have said, were few, but
even had they proliferated it would have done little good.
The street leading to the theater was so torn up as to be
impassable.

While it is true that the ancient buildings of Prague—
palaces, churches, bridges, are extraordinarily lovely, more
modern structures have a sad, down-at-heel appearance.
When we were there, although it was twenty years after

the war, they were only beginning to refurbish the city. Many façades were hidden behind scaffolding, and in certain streets the tram tracks lay like exposed skeletons, their accustomed fleshing out of cobbles and dirt having been removed preparatory to laying new pavement. Con Edison would have been in its element. Dig we must for growing Praha!

The evening being cool, I had put on my brief mink jacket.

"That," said Norton, eying it, "may be a mistake."

"I don't care," I said, "I want them to see what capitalists have," and in the same breath, "no, I don't, I don't. What a mean thing to say. How can the women help the kind of government they have, poor souls."

As it turned out neither of us need have fretted. In the darkened streets not a single person so much as glanced at us.

Since we had to buy our tickets and did not know the ropes, we arrived half an hour early to find the opera house as shuttered as the tomb and as dark. "But with a seven o'clock curtain, wouldn't you think they'd let the customers in?"

Two or three women were standing silently under the arches and I thought perhaps they might be streetwalkers, but they seemed a little old for the trade and withdrawn. We had not dined, and when we saw a restaurant across the street, I said to Norton, "Let's go over and have a drink and a sandwich."

"All right, but first let's try to find out when this place opens up."

We went around to a side entrance and discovered ourselves backstage with a few musicians just beginning to straggle in. With much pantomime, me opening my mouth and gargling fragments of French and German, we learned that the curtain was at seven-thirty.

We left, went over to the restaurant, and decided we must be crazy. The crowd of diners had vanished. At a few tables people were playing chess and drinking coffee, but food had been swept away and the best we could manage was a couple of beers which were a long time coming. We had become invisible. Waitresses passed but did not see us. Finally Norton asserted himself. *"Wo ist bier?"* *"Kommt bier,"* said the waitress. *"Yah, aber quand?"* said I who do not speak German. Throughout eastern Europe many people do, however. They learned it during the war and today, with so many East Germans traveling, it is a handy accomplishment. In the case of Czechoslovakia it is also traditional, for after the Czechs lost a battle to the Austrians in 1620 German was the official language for over two hundred years.

Seeing the lights come on in the lobby of the opera, we recrossed the street, but the doors were still not open. A couple of ushers in uniform appeared and there were obviously people in the box office. We could not understand their reluctance to sell tickets, although when we were finally admitted the reason for the casualness became obvious. The house was sold out. Oh, in the very highest gallery they did have maybe three or four places . . . if we wanted those . . . we did and began the ascension of Everest.

The Prague opera house is very very high and the wind whistled and little snow caps formed on our ears, but it was worth it. The seats were narrow and the backs uncompromising, but we could see and the acoustics would make the architects and engineers who are still struggling with Philharmonic Hall of New York's Lincoln Center groan and mutter in their sleep.

A nice usher handed me the best pair of opera glasses I have ever used and I had to exert a stern sense of discipline not to steal them. Norton has an elaborate pair from Japan which, when adjusted to a gnat's eyelash, both lenses and the thing in the middle for interpupillary distance precisely synchronized, brings the stage etching sharp right in front of your nose. But I am not good at the twiddling, and my only result as I try to sight the action is a sense of nausea. I think the Prague ones were nothing but strong magnifying glass, and they were big and easy and lovely.

It was interesting to see that while the audience were all in the proletarian attire appropriate to the Czechoslovak Socialist Republic every member of the orchestra was in white tie and tails.

The opera itself is not my favorite: Smetana's *Dalibor*. The tale it has to tell is more foolish than most operas— no mean triumph—but is supposedly based on legend based on a grain of truth from a historic episode. There once was a knight who was thrown into prison, but he played the violin so beautifully that people came from miles around to crouch near the barred window of his dungeon and listen to the sweet sounds.

His most prominent visitor the night we were there was a soprano of spacious proportions clad, for the sake of the plot, in boy's raiment, and no one suspected she was a girl. Her name was Milada Šubrtová and her singing was magnificent. She had a square jaw and broad Slavic cheekbones that gave great resonance to her voice and reminded me of a man to whom I was once married who hated tenors. "No wonder they can sing the way they do," he would mutter, "those great empty spaces in their skulls— superb echo chambers." To any intellectual tenors in the audience I apologize.

It had been suggested that we dine after the performance at the Opera Grill, but directions for finding it were not specific, and at night in a strange city, not speaking the language and with no taxis, getting around becomes involved.

In the course of trotting about during the day we had noticed a good many cafeterias or automats, but they did even less for gracious living than do American drugstores and short-order establishments. Customers serve themselves and then take their plates to very high tables where they stand eating, leaning on their elbows. When you have said the system is quick you have run the gamut of its charms.

We were not tempted and in the end returned to our hotel and the local Karvana which, by this time, we were beginning to know pretty well, having lunched and taken tea there.

At a table next to us a solitary Indian sat reading a newspaper. When we saw it was in English we asked him if he wouldn't join us. He was an interesting man, a patent lawyer, who travels all over the world in the course of business. He told us he had lunched with two Czech acquaintances and asked one of them if he wouldn't join him for dinner but the man had declined. "I'd better not," he said, "it might become embarrassing for both of us."

"But you've lunched with me."

"That's different. There are two of us. Believe me it is better if I do not see you alone." The government, I suppose, counts on friends informing on one another should the give and take between foreigners become too free.

We ourselves had a curious and rather unsettling experience. I have changed the names but the events actually happened. Czech friends of ours from London who had a sister still living in Prague arrived in New York for a visit shortly before Norton and I left for eastern Europe. I told them we were going there and asked if we might have a letter of introduction, as meeting the people of a country adds a great deal to one's enjoyment.

My friend said she would write her sister a discreet letter to sound her out. "It isn't that they don't like to see foreigners," she said, "but they might feel it wasn't wise to be in touch with you, although seeing someone who has just been with us would mean a great deal to Anna. To us too. Fancy, we have never met her new husband, you could tell us about him. Anyway, we'll write."

To our satisfaction a letter came back from Anna saying by all means please have us get in touch with her. Our friends had also asked if they mailed us a check would we give her the money, which we had naturally agreed to do.

We left sooner than they had understood, however, and the
check had not arrived.

When we got to Prague I rang the number they had
given us and asked if we might call. "No, no," Anna said
quickly, "I will come to your hotel, it is better." That
seemed a little odd, but we agreed, and shortly afterward she arrived, a pale, pretty woman in her early forties.
We greeted her warmly and told her we had all sorts of
messages from Madeleine and Stanislas. She looked happy
but apprehensive and, taking up a scratch pad and pencil
from the bedside table, she wrote, "There are microphones." I threw a triumphant look at Norton. "Bugged,"
I mouthed. Whether she was right or wrong there seemed
small point in taking chances so I suggested in clear bell-
like tones practically audible at headquarters without a
mike, "It's such a nice day, why don't we take a little
walk?" Anna instantly looked relieved and we went downstairs and out into the street. Outdoors, safely removed
from microphones, her eagerness was touching. "How are
they, Madeleine and Stanislas? How do they look? What
are they doing? Oh, how happy I am they got out of
Czechoslovakia." We gave her their news.

"But where is your husband?" Norton asked. "We want
so much to meet him and they're so anxious to know
what he's like."

She hesitated a moment. "I am sorry. To you it is probably not comprehensible but it is better he does not come.
When the Communists came to power he and his family
were in difficulty. They had a little theater where they
used to produce satirical reviews. Everyone thought them
funny, everyone but the new regime. Antonin was in jail
for three years. We are all right now. We think. But one
does not know. Something happens and the past is raked
up all over again."

Antonin's reluctance to be seen in the company of
foreigners was understandable. Even today their lives are
not easy. Anna and Madeleine have a brother living in

Vienna and Anna had been trying for eight months to get
a passport so she might visit him. So far it had been denied
her. "But why?" we asked. She shrugged. "Who knows?
That is how they are."

Throughout the following day we did not meet her, but
in the evening I called again. "We are leaving for Vienna
tomorrow," I said, "but we would so much like to see you
again. Would it be possible for you to come by?"

She came as we were in the middle of packing. Time was
running short, for a car was coming to pick us up and drive
us to the airport. I turned from the suitcases and we
talked quietly and noncommittally. Presently Anna asked,
and her voice was soft and trembling. "But is there *no*
other message? Nothing from Madeleine and Stanislas?"
Norton and I glanced at each other, we knew what she
meant. "Yes," I said, "there is. That's why I asked you to
come. They have sent you a check. I'll get it for you."

"No! Oh no," she said swiftly and, in a whisper, "no
check." I whispered back, "I don't mean a check, I'll get
the money but I must cash a traveler's check in order to
give it to you."

She led me to the window, pointed down the street and
around the corner. "There, there is a little pastry shop. I
will be waiting." Then she left us.

"This is crazy," Norton said, "I'm certain all this cloak
and dagger business is completely unjustified. Why would
the authorities care if she *does* get some money from
America? Simply brings more currency into the country,
and that's what they want."

I went close to him and whispered in his ear. "Maybe,
but it's her country and she's scared. After all her husband
was in jail and for some pipsqueak reason. That would
make anybody nervous. Where's a traveler's check? Madeleine and Stanislas want her to have fifty dollars and they'll
give it to us when we get back."

He signed a check and gave it to me. I took our passports
and went downstairs and into the lobby of the next hotel

where they changed the money, and while waiting for the ritual to be accomplished—I am certain that changing the wine into water took less time than changing dollars into crowns—I bought a couple of postcards. Then, adjusting my dagger securely in my garter and drawing my cloak about me, I went out the door, down the street, and around the corner to the pastry shop. Anna was waiting for me at a little table with a cup of tea in front of her. With the exception of a young couple and a mother and her little girl at two tables at the other end of the room, the place was empty. Nevertheless, Anna urged me to order something for the sake of appearances. I said I would take some tea too, and after the waitress had left, I drew from my handbag the sandwich I had made of the money and the two postcards. "I wonder if you'll be kind enough to mail these for me," I said, laying them in her lap under the table. The young couple engrossed in each other and the mother trying to persuade her reluctant child to finish its ice paid no attention to us. I doubt they were even aware we were there but having got into the charade I was determined to play it straight. Wildly improbable though it seemed, I couldn't *prove* we weren't being monitored.

Anna assured me the cards would be dropped in the post within the hour. She looked so happy and grateful that even if our behavior was totally nonsensical, I had a lump in my throat.

When we went outside she said, "May I kiss you?" She kissed my cheek. "This is for Madeleine." She kissed me again. "And for Stanislas." She looked at me and her eyes were wet. "And please, for you. You are good. If the security asks where I have been, I shall simply say the truth, with a friend of my sister and brother-in-law." I put my arms around her a moment and turned away.

Back at the hotel I found Norton in the lobby surrounded by luggage, and talking to our guide. He greeted me with suspicious bonhomie. "Ah, here you are at last! Berta was wondering where you'd got to." For a moment

I was taken aback. I had not counted on Berta or on making up some little story to cover my absence, but I underestimated the master. Norton dislikes movies and rarely goes but now and then he can be lured from the *Lancet* and the *New England Journal of Medicine* by a good spy thriller or a suspense yarn, and what he absorbs stays with him. Noting my vacant smile he leapt into the breach. "I told her you'd gone to look at the clock again."

"The clock?"

"Of course. The astronomical clock with the figures that come out. You were so crazy about it."

"Oh, *that* clock!" Since I had thought little of the jerky puppets, it took me a moment or so to get oriented, but I like to think I held up my end without overplaying. "So old, so heartwarming. Yes indeed, I'm in love with them."

To our relief at that moment the driver appeared in the doorway; we waved zestfully to Berta and took off for the airport.

I agreed with Norton that Anna had quite possibly overemphasized, if not entirely imagined, the surveillance she so obviously feared, but she and her family had suffered and we had not.

In the course of our journey we asked the foreign diplomats we met if they thought their hosts *had* concealed microphones in the offices and residences and from all of them we got the same reaction. A shrug and a "How can we tell? Maybe not, but it's possible. In any event what can we do about it? To begin with, no matter how hopeful they may be there isn't all that much 'top secret' stuff and when there is it's in code in the office, and we certainly don't blab about it at home."

All residencies have local staffs, and it is possible that one or two of the servants in each household are in the employ of the state, but as the diplomats said, what of it? Forewarned is forearmed, and reports, if any, filtering through to GHQ must inevitably be in the nature of trivia. Communist 007s are surely reserved for sterner stuff than the bridge and cocktail parties of foreign mission officials and their wives. In any event, Americans can ill afford holier-than-thouness in view of the bugging of telephones and the transistor spy market now flourishing in the United States through which any individual's privacy may be and frequently is violated and destroyed.

But to return to our arrival in Prague. As we had been driving into the city on the bus we read a pamphlet that had been handed us at the airport. According to it the economy is booming and I think there is little question that this is so, but they hand you a few statistics and leave you on your own. For example: "At the end of the year 1961 there was in the Czechoslovak Socialist Republic 1 electric washing machine per 5.7 inhabitants. 1 television set per 11.8 inhabitants and 1 radio set per every 3 inhabitants."

In the United States 98.2 per cent of the families own television sets. But are the Czech's figures good or bad for them? Do they consider that they have many or few appliances? And how many were there at the end of 1965? These details they do not give you.

But just as we claim that our great prosperity is only possible because of the capitalist system so do they say that their better life has come about solely because of Communism, or Socialism or Nationalization of the Country's Productive Forces, or whatever is the preferred phrase in a particular country. The truth, it seems to me, is that science and industrial progress and the changing philosophies of the twentieth century as such must all be credited or blamed rather than the particular regime in power in any one place.

When they say: "All working people receive medical attention free of charge. There is one doctor to every 554 inhabitants" they speak the truth, although they do not disclose their medical standards. However the quality of care that the children receive is good. Dr. Brown says he thinks the high standard of mother and child health quite possibly has something to do with physical characteristics. "Those broad-bottom Slavic types sneeze, and out comes the baby. It's easier for them than for linear women."

Yet it is true that great emphasis is placed on child welfare and they claim "that in 1961, thanks to perfect preventive measures not a single case of infantile paralysis was registered, that being something of which no other country in the world can boast."

The Czechs are also proud of their infant mortality rate, "23 per thousand, among the lowest in the world." But that is still trailing twelfth after Sweden, the Netherlands, Norway, Finland, Iceland, Denmark, Switzerland, New Zealand, Australia, England, Wales and Japan. The United States is rated fifteenth, coming after Czechoslovakia, France, and Canada. In 1964 our rate of infant mortality was 23.8 and in 1965, 24.4.

Propagandizing the good, sweeping that which is less desirable under the rug is by no means unique to Communism. Every country in the world does it, but to fool your own people, at any time or on any score whatever—war casualties or infant mortality or water shortages—is a shortsighted policy. An ignorant people is vulnerable.

On the other hand a certain cynicism about an "informed electorate" is understandable. Witness the reaction of the people of the rich, powerful, educated U.S.A. to the television coverage of the Gemini 8 spacecraft in March 1966. As some will recall, there was a serious malfunction in orbit and the two astronauts aboard, Mr. Neil Armstrong and Major David Scott were in peril of their lives. The networks did an admirable job of reporting a tense and thrilling true-life drama, and their reward was a deluge of phone calls from outraged viewers demanding that "Batman" and "The Virginian" be reinstated on the home screen. Bread and circuses still work pretty well.

Good things are unquestionably being done in the Communist-bloc countries. What is unfortunate is that they apparently do not believe they can achieve both improvement and freedom of speech, association and individual enterprise at the same time. Why don't they try it and see?

The guide who picked us up in the morning for our first really serious sightseeing was a dark, pretty young woman who took us to what had once been part of the ancient fortifications. The Powder Tower, restored in the early years of this decade but built in 1475 and adorned with Gothic stone figures, was slim and beautiful. We went also to the Jewish synagogue, the oldest in Europe, dating from 1270. It is a small Gothic building, one of the first erected in Prague, and on the inside walls are rows of words closely printed in varying hues of brown and beige and gray so that at first glance they appear to form a rather modernistic pattern. Then one looks more closely and becomes aware that the words are names followed by dates, and there are many thousands of them. "They are the names of Jews," said our guide, "Jews who were taken away by the Nazis. The numbers are the dates of their birth and the day they were taken. We do not know the actual date of death. There is my name," and she pointed to the name of a member of her family.

Among the thousands there were a few, a very few, erasures. "Those are people we thought had been killed, but they managed to escape the concentration camps and came back."

On the wall at one end of the synagogue was a double column of names: Dachau, Belsen, Ravenbrück, the whole infamous list of the Nazi extermination camps. Below them were heaped bouquets of faded flowers with red ribbons bearing in gold lettering the words NIE WIEDER. "That means 'never again' in German," our guide said. "But I don't know. I do not believe it, I suspect they would." And her young mouth twisted in an old bitter smile.

Adjacent to the synagogue, ancient stones still crowd

the graveyard. On some of them are small heaps of pebbles, symbolic of the piles of stones in the desert under which the Jews used to bury their dead to keep them from being disinterred by animals.

Leaving the chapel we walked along the streets toward the Charles Bridge. The sidewalks of Prague are charming, paved with small white and gray and pink cobblestones almost like mosaics. Charming to look at and rough on shoes.

The bridge was begun in early July 1357 during the reign of Charles IV, who entrusted it to Peter Palter, the twenty-seven-year-old architect of St. Vitus Cathedral. It is a beautiful structure spanning the Vltava with sixteen arches, enriched by thirty massive and elaborate statues that have been added from time to time through the centuries.

To bind his mortar the young architect decided to use eggs, and contemporary chickens must have worked overtime to provide the thousands needed. All the towns in the Kingdom of Bohemia were called upon to swell the quota. They responded, although with how much enthusiasm, one does not know. The community of Velvay, for example, sent its grosses hard-boiled, thus helping to build up the masons if not the mortar.

Whether they did it out of ignorance of the binding properties of raw eggs, or, because they were thumbing their noses at authority has never, I believe, been definitely established.

The oldest statue on the bridge is of John of Nepomuk, vicar-general of Bohemia who late in the fourteenth century tangled with King Wenceslaus in a political dispute and was tortured and tossed into the river in a sack. Another story has it that he was liquidated for refusing to betray the secrets confided to him by Queen Sophia in the confessional. The latter version gained such wide credence as to give rise to the speculation that possibly there were

two Johns of Nepomuk, both of whom proved distasteful
to the King, but it is all in the realm of guesswork.

That King Wenceslaus, by the way, was not the good
one who looked out. The looker lived about four hundred
years previously and was murdered by his brother, who,
being himself a free thinker and not caring for Wenny's
Christian piety, disposed of him about 936. It was many
centuries later that he achieved fame in the Christmas
carol.

A building which no traveler to Prague should miss is
the library of the Strahov Monastery-Church. In a city
where the Gothic is so superbly represented, the library,
despite the age of the complex which houses it, is a rococo
glory.

It was plundered in 1648 by the Swedes, who carted off
as the spoils of war nineteen enormous crates of priceless
volumes. It was started again from scratch, and because
the work of rebuilding was still in progress it was spared
by Joseph II, who in 1780 closed all the monasteries
which were not actively of cultural value.

Joseph, King of Bohemia and Hungary was the son of
Franz Stephan and Maria Theresa of Austria. He was an
ardent and revolutionary reformer and did a great deal to
improve life and increase happiness among the serfs. He
allowed them such novel privileges as marrying whom they
wanted to and the right to move about at will and to buy
from the nobility at moderate prices the land they cultivated.

Naturally he was hated by the nobles and by the clergy
too, being anti-clerical and holding the philosophy that
the contemplative orders controlled too much land and
contributed little to the public welfare.

He had another tiresome theory, which was that ability
and merit were more important than title and heredity, so
it is fortunate for posterity that the monks of Strahov were
beaver-busy during Joseph's energetic reign. The library itself—ignoring for the moment its contents—is extraordinary:

a very long room with a low vaulted ceiling of rich and
elaborate plaster carving, framing brilliantly painted frescoes, the books, 130,000 of them in superb vellum bindings,
standing in their stacks three deep.

There are all kinds of scholarly tomes, including a tenth-
century evangelical gospel. The Book of Kells in Trinity
College, Dublin, is older; it is thought to date from the
eighth century, but the tenth is venerable too.

Probably among the most curious and best-known books
of Strahov are the four volumes comprising the inventory
of the treasures of the Louvre which Napoleon had published and which Marie Louise gave to the monastery
when she stayed there in 1813. All was jingling along
merry as a marriage bell until assorted countries began
getting wind of the list and began clamoring for their
treasures that had been carried off to Paris by the Napole-
onic armies. The great soldier, code-giver, and arch-crook,
sheltering from the storm, hastily had it withdrawn from
circulation and the one at Strahov is one of the few extant
today.

There is another room in the same building that one
should not miss, the Philosophical Hall, a long narrow
immensely high apartment of great beauty with soaring
columns of fluted wood enhanced by gilded ornamentation.

Another treasure house in Prague is the Narodni Galerie,
the National Art Gallery. We were fortunate in having a
letter of introduction to Dr. Ladislav Kesner, the director,
which had been given us by Thomas Hoving. Mr. Hoving,
now the able and imaginative Commissioner of Parks in
New York City was, at that time, curator of medieval art
for the Metropolitan Museum, and his bailiwick was limited
to the Cloisters—not, incidentally, too mournful a limita-
tion.

I think one normally assumes curators of art will smack
of the venerable. We were therefore surprised to be welcomed by a savant who appeared to be on the sunny side

of thirty, although on second thought we decided our surprise was not justified, Mr. Hoving himself is scarcely a patriarchial type.

Mr. Kesner made me think of the time I received a letter from the redoubtable Christie's of London asking if I would allow a representative of theirs to come to look at one of our pictures the next time he was in New York. Flattered that Christie's knew or cared, the doctor and I said, "Of course, by all means." There followed intermittent bulletins reporting the progress of "our man." Months passed, nearer he came and nearer until one fine day I received a telephone call. "I am the man from Christie's. I am in New York, may I come to see the picture?"

"Certainly," I said graciously, "come along. Shall we say five o'clock?"

In my imagination I envisaged Commander Whitehead; graying, charming, distinguished. At five, the bell rang. I hurried to the door and opened it. There stood a little creature looking, I should say, all of twelve. "I am the man from Christie's," it said, and so, as matters turned out, it was. Furthermore it was knowledgeable. They start young in the art world.

Dr. Kesner invited us into his office for coffee. The coffee was excellent, and his office was furnished with three pieces of exquisite inlay work. There are certain virtues in living and working in a museum. A friend of mine, Ann Willan, once spent some time with the Van der Kemps. Monsieur Van der Kemp is the curator of Versailles. "And," said my friend, "it was really awfully nice. We'd keep switching the pictures around from the big galleries to the private apartments and there was always something lovely hanging on the walls."

There are pictures and sculptures from every period and from all over the world in the Prague gallery, but perhaps their most notable pieces are medieval and Gothic, which we expected, those eras being the Hoving forte and, one may suppose, responsible for the rapport between the two colleagues.

Its location and parks contribute greatly to the city's beauty but it is the spires and towers, 473 of them, castles and churches, the mingling of Gothic and baroque that make Prague unique. Its splendid age was the fourteenth century, when it had a larger population than London or Paris.

Charles IV (1316–78) was a passionate builder although the foundations of Hradcany Castle antedate him by some five hundred years. Still, once he got going his contribution was notable. He founded a university, and not only did he enlarge and modernize the palace, he built a city: churches and streets and squares. In these enterprises he was greatly aided by young Mr. Palter, the architectural genius who died in his twenties. The day we visited St. Vitus Cathedral we were in luck, for instead of churchly gloom, through which one can often only sense awestruck the architectural splendor, one of the most magnificent of the Gothic churches of Europe was brilliantly illuminated. Not by candlelight for a religious ceremony but by powerful electric lamps.

They were taping a performance of the Prague orchestra for television. The musicians stood on a carved balcony, tootling and fiddling under the direction of the cameraman and the electricians rather than the director. The brilliant floodlights enabled us really to see the details and richness of the carving. Behind an altar screen we saw too the tomb of Saint John of Nepomuk, for his followers fished him out of the river, after that awful King Wenceslaus had drowned him, and gave him Christian burial.

From the church we went to the castle, itself the size of a small town covering easily several acres. One of the most imposing apartments is Vladislav Hall, which used to serve as both throne room and tournament arena. A vaulted ceiling supported by slim arching ribs of stone in swirling patterns and tall French windows on either side give it a feeling of great elegance. There is also a broad shallow staircase for the tournament horses, and after the contests guests at the banquet were served by men on horseback. It must have taken considerable dexterity to be both waiter and equestrian at the same time, but if that was the In thing they probably carried it off with a flourish.

In another part of the castle the vast and elaborate Spanish Hall, a gold and white and crystal field day of eighteenth-century baroque with five square miles of parquet flooring was entirely reconstructed for the coronation of Franz Josef. After an army of carpenters, painters, glaziers, polishers, and chandlers had exhausted themselves in a frenzy of activity, the coronation was held somewhere else. There is an adjoining hall, companion acreage, called Rudolph's Gallery.

In 1922–23 both these huge apartments were completely refurbished and are used today by the Communist government for political sessions. If they have any sense of irony it must tickle them to find themselves ensconced in the luxury made possible by the derided monarchial and capitalist systems.

In this castle an incident occurred that touched off the Thirty Years' War and that is known as the Defenestration of Prague. In 1618 two envoys from the Catholic emperor in Vienna were tossed from a window by the Protestant Czechs who cared nothing at all for the high-handed maneuvers of the emissaries.

One might suppose that their necks would have broken but in actual fact, having been tossed, they landed in relative comfort on a huge pile of refuse and garbage which, accumulating over many months, rose nearly to the window sill. The two gentlemen dropped only a few feet and although they may have had to burn their clothes they scrambled away unhurt but the Thirty Years' War got under way just the same. It was the principle of the thing. The emperor felt his ambassadors should not have been tossed.

There were a few other reasons too. The Protestants were

incensed when the Catholics kept burning their churches, and the wretched conflict, or series of conflicts, starting over bitter religious differences soon became political, involved most of Europe and dragged on till the Peace of Westphalia in 1648.

The war began in Prague but ranged over Germany, as we have seen, and when it was over she was prostrate, her population reduced from twenty million to six million. Cities, towns and villages had been burned to ashes and hoards who had endured inconceivable cruelties at the hands of mercenaries roamed the devastated countryside at times resorting to cannibalism. It was not until the end of the Seven Years' War in 1763 and the rise of Prussia that Germany began once more to emerge as a European power.

One of the most prominent figures of the Thirty Years' War was General Albrecht Wenzel Eusebius von Wallenstein, later Duke of Friedland. He brought an army to the assistance of the Emperor Ferdinand, a dedicated Catholic, and secured for him many victories.

Wallenstein was a soldier, an administrator of outstanding ability and a man of enormous wealth, motivated by a passion for a united central Europe. His great palace in Prague, the Wallenstein, was only one residence, and his estates were the size of kingdoms.

The palace gardens are now used as a public park, and there is a fine aviary where we saw a Lady Amherst pheasant, a regal creature like a superb small peacock. The gardens, especially at twilight when we wandered through them, are a restful and charming memorial but the general came to uncharming end.

Ferdinand, victories or no victories, was none too sure where his general's allegiance lay. Sometimes he seemed to favor the Catholics, sometimes the Protestants.

Such capricious legerdemain, the emperor considered, showed a lack of conviction, and after the Battle of White Hill in 1620 (that was the one the Bohemians lost and had to speak German for two hundred years afterward), exulting in success and thinking he could stand alone, he fired Wallenstein. Was *that* a mistake! He was later obliged to call him back, naturally under terms galling to himself and extremely pleasing to the general, who, murmuring things like Revenge Is Sweet and aware he had Ferdinand over a barrel, demanded fantastic terms for his indispensable aid.

In the end however, the emperor and his advisers, leery he might turn his talents for belligerency against themselves, leaked the information that they would welcome his removal from the scene. A group of officers obliged. Wallenstein was speared to death in his bedroom at Eger by a Captain Devereux, and the gentlemen were handsomely rewarded for their thoughtfulness.

Unfortunately cruelty and perfidy did not end with the distant past. One afternoon we were driving past the Karl Borromaens Church and our guide told us of Jan Kubis and Joseph Gabeik, two Czech patriots who had hidden there. They had been with the free Czechoslovak army in England and had been parachuted into Prague from an RAF plane. On the twenty-ninth of May, 1942, they hurled a grenade into the car of Reinhard Heydrich, the sadistic Nazi general who was the Reichsprotektor for Bohemia and Moravia, and who was believed to be Adolf Eichmann's direct superior and responsible for the death of millions of Jews.

The car exploded under the impact of the grenade, the general's spine was shattered, and he died a few days later. The two Czechs fled to the church to hide. Our guide said that the German authorities in Prague were unable to force an entrance and because of the shape of the lower apartment in which the men were concealed they could not shoot them. They therefore brought water from the river and poured it through the barred window. The Czechs knew it was the end, and when the water reached their necks they shot themselves.

According to William Shirer, who gives a detailed account of the episode in *The Rise and Fall of the Third
Reich,* 120 members of the Czech resistance were sharing
the sanctuary at the time.

Shirer says they "were besieged by the S.S. and killed to
the last man" but he does not mention the water. He adds,
in a footnote, that the Gestapo were not aware "that the
actual assassins were among the dead in the church."

The German's revenge was wholesale but it did not stop
there. Three thousand Jews were sent east and exterminated, 500 of the few remaining Jews at large in Berlin
were arrested on June 4, the day of Heydrich's death, and
152 were subsequently executed.

To prove the sanctity of the master race, the little village
of Lidice, about fifteen miles northwest of Prague, near
the mining town of Kladno, was exterminated under the
command of Captain Max Rostock. The entire male population was executed, and any women who were not shot
were rounded up and dispatched to the Ravensbrück concentration camp. Four of the women about to give birth
were taken to the maternity hospital in Prague. Their babies
were murdered as soon as they were delivered, and the
mothers were then sent to join their neighbors in Ravensbrück. The small children went to another concentration
camp and later into Germany to be brought up as Germans
under German names. The village itself was burned to the
ground.

The only note of grim satisfaction in this dread and
somber tale is that Captain Max Rostock was hanged in
Prague in August 1951. It is unfortunate that he had but
one life to give for his iniquity.

Considering their behavior one wonders how the Germans bring themselves to return to those countries they
victimized with such peculiar barbarism but one of our
guides said with a little shrug, "It is the classic story. The
criminal returns to the scene of the crime." And ob-

viously, had sensitivity been their attribute, the Nazis would not have behaved as they did in the first place.

A church with a less harrowing history is the cathedral of Saint Nicholas. Born in the fourth century, Nicholas was the bishop of Myra in Asia Minor. The Dutch adopted his feast day, December 6, as a suitable occasion for giving presents to children, but then other countries took over. They combined his feast day with Christmas. He became Saint Nick and in New York, oddly enough, blossomed out as Santa Claus. No doubt the original Nicholas would be astonished to see all the embonpoint, red woolen suiting, and bulging sack of toys.

Nor has his church in Prague anything to do with carols, roast goose, and stuffed stockings. It is a baroque affair of great richness and complexity of design with an undulating or serpentine façade and a magnificent cupola, reminiscent of that of St. Peter but smaller in scale. There are statues and columns and carvings and exuberant frescoes. The great baroque churches, an extension of the surging Renaissance, always look as though everyone involved had had a whale of a time in their creation. As though masters of stone, plaster, paint, and carving gave a great shout: "Let's go!" as they soared off into a realm of beauty, color, and good cheer. They may have been religious; they were not pious.

Another church, that of St. Peter and St. Paul is built on a height and fronts on a beautiful park called Vysehrad. In the spring the perfume of the lilacs floats over the city like a fragrant cloud. Another height used to be dominated by a huge statue of Stalin, but after he went out of fashion the Czechs removed it.

A district we fell in love with was Mala Strana, Lesser Town. It is low-lying, and the river and a canal flow through it turning it into a baby Venice. When we asked who lived in an enchanting pale blue rococo house, we were told it belonged to Jiri Trnka, an artist whose animated cartoons are well known throughout Europe. Not

far away is the garden of Belvedere, the royal summer
palace, considered to be among the finest Renaissance
buildings outside of Italy.

Curiously enough, in one of the most beautiful capitals
of Europe the atmosphere struck us as rather sad. The city
was as I have said, badly in need of renovation and
there seemed to be something poignant about the people,
a seeking restless quality, a questioning look in their eyes.
"The individual works hard and has very little," one of
them explained. "Everything belongs to the State. Everything."

In order to make ends meet many women are obliged
to take outside jobs, so that the problem of caring for their
children is a pressing one. There are state nurseries and
they are nearly as compulsory as schools. Free compulsory
education is, in many respects, admirable, but for tiny
tykes to be kicked out into a communal world would seem
to be rushing the season. Yet what are the parents to do?
Servants, private children's nurses, baby sitters . . . they
do not exist. Small fry are dependent on grandparents,
many of whom may be working themselves, or on women
too old for state employment, who may come a couple
of times a week to take care of them and do a little
cleaning.

Looking at the people it occurred to me that even under
a strong dictatorship human emotions reveal themselves
and I said to Norton, "You know, I think I may call my
book *The Human Face*."

"I shouldn't do that," he said, "your readers are likely
to be curtailed to medical students."

Still, despite their difficulties and a comparatively meager
supply of consumer goods, we found the food in the
countries we visited to be abundant and often well prepared. The Muscova, a big bright restaurant where we
lunched one day with Mrs. Kopecka and Mr. Shbrt, the
director of the Cedok Travel Bureau served a first-rate
meal. Do not be put off by the lack of vowels in the

gentleman's name. It's pronounced like our Shubert. They just resort to shorthand, more economical.

As we were leaving I noticed a big good-looking man, a five-star general in a blue uniform with red epaulettes. A little thrill of apprehension ran up my spine. "Who's that?" I whispered to Mrs. Kopecka, "the Russian commander-in-chief?"

"There are no Russians here," she assured me. "He is a traffic policeman."

"My God," I said to Norton later, "if she was telling the truth what do you suppose a bona fide general looks like? An Inca potentate, I imagine, gold-encrusted."

Although we saw no representatives it just might be that members of the Czech army do have pretty dashing uniforms because the people are by temperament dramatic. They claim to have seventy-six professional theaters, relatively the densest network of theaters in the world.

We went to see one of their performances, *Lanterna Magica.* As at the opera we were early, for we didn't seem to grasp their theater semantics. We were told the curtain was at seven-thirty. It was at eight, but this time there was no difficulty getting into the lobby. We showed our tickets, which Cedok had helpfully obtained for us beforehand, someone pointed downstairs, and we descended in the wake of two men. Reaching a landing, we saw an arrow pointing up another staircase. We and the gentlemen exchanged glances and shrugged. But although the architecture seemed peculiar we followed the arrow upward, turned a corner, and found ourselves back in the lobby confronting the woman who had just directed us downward. We were all five surprised.

Obviously thinking foreigners were not too bright in the head she again pointed down the stairs. Back we went, the two men, ourselves, and another woman, who appeared from nowhere and who kept insisting we give up our coats on which we intended to keep a firm grip. Suddenly one of the men stopped and murmured something in French

1 The Big Bluff of the Lorelei.

2 The tower that Hatto barred with care. Theoretically.

3 Town on the river Rhine.

4 The clock tower in Prague.
Taken by Ilka and a bit out of
focus. The figures appear in the
little square windows at the top.

Ancient tower at one end of the
Charles Bridge.

6 Pietà in the Narodni Gallery in
Prague.

7 Vladislav Hall in the Castle of Prague, where meals were served on
horseback.

8   Part of the gardens of Wallenstein Palace in Prague.

9   Marble staircase in the Hotel Imperial. The Franz Josef portrait hangs above the lady.

which I did not hear. No response from the woman except gestures for the coats. The man tried German. I thought he was telling her not to importune us, but still the gestures. At that he decided on shock treatment. "Toilet," he yelled in English.

"Ah, toilet," she said, charmed to have found a point of contact, and indicated the way he should go. This time we did not follow but went on down into the theater. It was an enormous underground projection room seating between eight and nine hundred people.

Some time before a Magic Lantern performance had been given in Carnegie Hall in New York, but we had not heard about it and found ourselves enchanted with the lunacy, imagination, and art which are its features. A combination of movies, projected slides in color and black and white, music, and live actors, the show attempts to marry the best of all worlds and succeeds pretty well in its ambitious undertaking.

There was curious and ingenious color photography—stanch marionettes tossed in a stormy cardboard sea—but full of tricks and laughter the sequence that most delighted the doctor, that notorious non-moviegoer, combined early Hollywood slapstick, in which a wife hides her lover in a cupboard when her husband returns unexpectedly, with a European slapstick version of Othello. Sound idea. Jealousy was the motive in both stories, and by inspired photographic abracadabra the twentieth-century American lover found his cupboard sliding into Desdemona's early seventeenth-century Italian boudoir. It didn't make sense, maybe, but it made for a lot of hilarity.

There was another fine bit with a bearded man roller-skating through the city streets, missing cars by inches and vice versa, skidding down one of those staircase streets at breakneck speed, and, as he landed at the bottom, his real self zoomed from the film across the stage to the footlights. Resounding applause! Culture is wonderful and another reason why people should travel.

That night we were successful in our search for the Opera Grill and happy that we had tracked it down. Situated in Divadelni Street, off the river, it is as Sonia Kopecka had told us, not far from the opera but still not easy to find, looking like any other building in the dark block, the sign that says RESTAURANT no more than a narrow strip over the door. Persevere, however, because it is charming. A small room with only seven tables, the seats very comfortable banquettes and overstuffed chairs, a tiny bar, and an open fireplace. There are soft lights and candles and the atmosphere is private house. The service is leisurely but one orders a drink and relaxes. The food we thought palatable if not outstanding, but I am not a great lover of Czech cuisine. Everything is too breaded and gratiné for my taste, but that is purely personal and you are certain to enjoy the intimate cheerful room. Indeed the Opera Grill is doubly to be recommended because in most of the Communist countries we visited the *en masse* philosophy prevails. The intimate, the private, the cozy is very rare.

CHAPTER TWO

Vienna   Budapest

The flight from Prague to Vienna takes forty minutes, and
on arrival we found the city even more crowded than her
northern neighbor. A little later we learned that the second
week in September is always crowded because that is when
they hold the big trade fair. People come from far and
near. They were also holding a medical convention or congress as those get-togethers are called in eastern Europe,
and doctors came from even farther and nearer.

Since our stay in Vienna would be brief we had decided to splurge and returned to the Hotel Imperial in
the Kärntnerring, where we had stayed during our first
visit in 1959, which I wrote about in *The Carthaginian
Rose*. The Imperial is one of the grand hotels of Europe
still run in the grand manner, and it is as luxurious as all
hell and not one bit homelike. A suite will strain your
budget, but you are living!

Since readers of travel books may be divided into two
classes, those who do not travel and those who do, I will
say for the information of the latter, that our accommodations, called a junior suite, cost $36 a day without meals.
Actually, it wasn't really a suite but a large room divided
by diaphanous curtains, the smaller section furnished as a
living room, the larger containing beds and bureaus. The

bathroom was super de luxe. We were in it a couple of days, moving to more modest quarters when we were ousted by newcomers who had reserved it ahead of us.

A fairly nauseating little booklet called "A Love Letter to Vienna" is not recommended to the diabetic, but if you suck a pickle while reading it to offset the sugar you will learn about some of the sights to be seen in the city and a little of the history of the Imperial, which started life as the palace of the Duke of Württemberg. It was less lofty in the duke's day—they have added a floor or two— but the marble staircase, its low treads carpeted in crimson, its columns, cream and gold ceiling, crystal chandeliers, and full-length portrait of Franz Josef are distinctly ducal and a lot of fun. Befitting such splendor the food and service are first rate and the concierge desk very nearly omnipotent.

In Vienna the offices of the American Express Company are almost next door to the Imperial so we went there shortly after our arrival to arrange a bit of tourist work. On our return to our elegant apartment, doom struck. The doctor's dispatch case with masses of photographic material and *all* the film already exposed was missing.

The hotel was turned upside down and alarms rang out over the city. Church bells tolled as they would have done if the Germans had invaded England. High officials of the land and of the American Express Company and the airport were called in. That is where it was, at the airport. It had been left behind when we cleared customs. The head concierge at the hotel, who had been about to hang himself, cut the noose and relaxed. The day was saved! "I think, dear," I said gently, "that since there will be more and more film as the trip progresses, you will be wise *never* to let that dispatch case out of your hands. Remember James Bond, how he cherished that well equipped little arsenal of his." "Roger," said my quack.

That night we went to the opera. We were, after all, in Vienna. Our previous visit had been at the height of the season and we had been unable to obtain tickets so the remodeled house was new to us. The concierge had said that a cocktail dress and dark suit would be sufficient so that is what we wore. No one else was dressed either but in a way it seemed a pity. There are great halls for promenading that are ideal backgrounds for beautiful evening clothes.

On the whole, however, the opera house was more restrained, more chaste than I had imagined it would be. It is sternly non-rococo with the seats, the ushers' redingotes, and the curtain a staid maroon instead of lush crimson. This made me unhappy, and I grumbled. "I never saw a worse colored curtain in my whole life."

"But it comes down so nicely." My husband loves Vienna and all that is there is good.

The opera was *Bohême*, which set neither us nor the Danube on fire, but we had been told it was the Zeffirelli production and not to be missed. The settings, they assured us were extraordinary.

The first act was not. What are you going to do with that attic? It was the same for Zeffirelli as it is for every other producer. A spacious drafty dusty old barn. Then, however, we came to the street scene in the Latin Quarter, and here the master pulled himself together. It was on two levels, the brightly lighted café close down by the footlights and throngs of people milling quietly back and forth above it. When the soldiers paraded through they did so on the upper level and the flag-waving crowd watched them pass, backs to the audience. It looked very real. The barrier scene was charming too, snow-covered trees receding into the misty milky distance. Then back to the attic, tried and true, and poor dead Mimi.

In the intermission we went to the bar, where champagne seemed automatic, but they don't give it away even in *alt Wien*. Austrian money is schillings and groschen. A schilling is worth twenty-five and a half cents, but if you ignore the half and simply count them as quarters it's easy, four to the dollar, just like home. No matter how you count, though, a small glass of champagne comes to eighty cents. A more plebeian choice was the open-face sandwiches, which were very welcome after no dinner and another long stretch before the final curtain.

We paid a return visit to the opera to hear *Der Troubadour*.

This time, unfortunately, our seats were in the back of a box. The first comers were naturally in front and the one seat behind us was occupied by a fat female music lover who knew the score by heart and sang directly into our ears accompanying the artists on stage. She did not mute her tones, and I cannot believe that in the quieter moments they didn't hear her. I am perhaps not cultivated but I find *Il Trovatore* trying when performed throughout the evening in shadows so deep that it is virtually impossible to see either sets or singers. If sound is all I want I can stay home with the phonograph.

This time, during the intermission, we walked in the long and elegant gallery embellished with modern tapestries that adjoins the spacious bar. Norton had his opera glasses hanging around his neck, and two or three times we passed a small Japanese gentleman who was festooned with a similar pair. On the last go-round he stopped, bowed, and showed his teeth. "Tokyo?" he asked, pointing at Norton's glasses. "Tokyo," said the doctor. I chimed in, "We've been there, we enjoyed it so much. Are you in Vienna for the medical congress?" A bow from the waist. "Yes." "How long does it last?" Another bow. "Yes. Good-by." He leaves us. The idiot exchange remains in one's memory when the pregnant phrase has fled.

A famous and *gemütlich* place to dine after the opera is the Drei Huzarren. It is a good deal larger than the Opera Grill in Prague but has the same overstuffed, homey, early-years-of-the-century atmosphere, and although the waiters seem busy it is a long time before they are busy at your table.

When we were there in 1959 we thought the prices moderate considering the high quality of the meal. This time I made a note: Good, but expensive. Prices have crept up in Vienna and so have they in Greece, as we were to find to our sorrow. Compared to America they are still human but not the dear little things they once were.

Two other good Viennese restaurants are the Rotisserie Coq d'Or, where we had excellent medallion of venison and melting apple strudel, and, of course, the almost legendary Sacher's. When it comes to restaurants and theaters I find the old decor far more sympathetic than restrained and sterile modern. There is an opulence about it and many good smells. There's good wine at Sacher's too, a notable one being Holenwarther Herrenburg 1964.

Our one Viennese disappointment was the shops. Not that the merchandise wasn't attractive, but we had had our hearts set on a wine heber, those charming and usually ornate carafes shaped like a retort with a straight stem. They are suspended in a framework of delicately wrought iron, and instead of tipping them one places the glass under the spout and gives a little push up which releases the wine. They are decorative and useful, and having seen them when we were there before we assumed Vienna would be studded with them like raisins in a cake. Diligent search failed to reveal a single one. The old order changeth and maketh me very sad.

Since we had visited the beautiful palace of Schönbrunn and remembered it quite well this time we decided to go to Belvedere. A long long wall encloses the enormous garden, and once within there is an immense amount of walking to be done so to go to the entrance on foot, as we did, is a mistake. You're exhausted by the time you get there. Take a tram or taxi and conserve your strength for the palace and extensive grounds.

There are a good many Belvederes in Europe, the word meaning beautiful view or the place from which one sees the view, and while the exterior of Vienna's is princely

wedding cake architecture, the rooms, with one or two ex-
ceptions, are of no particular interest.

The gardens are the treat. Vast parterres of grass and
formal flowers, high clipped hedges, and a huge reflecting
pool and leaping fountains. That is what is so marvelous
about Europe; the people long ago learned that space and
beauty and quiet refuges in a great city, where children
may play and old people sit in the sun, are of far more
value to the inhabitants than real estate taxes and con-
tractors' greed.

After the long hike we betook ourselves for a bit of refreshment to the Konditorei Aida which had been highly
recommended. These coffee shops or confectioners are typi-
cal of Vienna. Demel's is another famous one, all pink and
blue and silver like a boudoir, and in his love letter, of which
I have spoken, the eager lover of the town assures you that
"the waitresses seem to date back to the days of the Emperor the way they kiss the ladies' hands and talk old-
fashioned German."

Alas for love's delusion. Not only has all the *"Küss die
Hand gnädige Frau"* atmosphere been dispelled, rudeness
is rampant. Seeing others standing about holding plates and
thinking it the thing to do I picked one up and started
prospecting for a couple of mouth-watering yummies to accompany my *Kaffee mit Schlag*. "No self-service," snapped
the girl behind the counter in her courtly old-fashioned
German, snatching the dish away and slamming it down in
front of her. Her irritation may have had something to do
with getting a commission on the number of pieces you
select, if that *is* the system, but I wasn't attempting gyppery,
merely helpfulness. Obviously from her point of view the
road to hell and I had much in common.

We went, of course, for a return visit to the Kuntshistor-
iches Museum, Vienna's great art gallery. Their Brueghels
and Rembrandts are superb, particularly one of the self-
portraits of the latter as he is getting older with a questioning deeply poignant expression in his eyes.

We went also to call on Dr. Wolfgang Hofsttater, another friend of Thomas Hoving who had kindly invited us to his own small gallery. He specializes in Gothic and medieval carvings, and we waited quite a little time while he sold one. "Congratulations," we said, "we hope the sale was *most* profitable." He replied sadly that it was, adding with a sigh, "But what a loss! One of my favorite pieces."

Those who harbor the impression that merchants are in business only to make money are very wrong. They too savor life's more subtle emotions; a lesson I learned to my sorrow in my childhood. On returning from one of her periodic trips to Europe my mother told me that traveling in Germany she had seen a doll she wanted to buy for me, but the old man who kept the toy store refused to sell it. Mother even upped the price and by a generous margin, but the man simply said, "No, I love that doll, I will never sell her." Needless to say that was the doll of my dreams and for a long time I held it against Mother that she had told me about her.

Mr. Hofsttater took us on to his apartment to show us his personal collection. He lives just down the street from the Town Hall which is spurious Gothic, having been erected in the nineteenth century, but it is very beautiful nevertheless, of extreme grace and delicacy. Our host lives in a small museum, but what we enjoyed most was seeing the apartment itself and meeting three of his children. There were two more, but they were in the country with their mother and he was joining them that afternoon. We gathered he owned a large property some hundred kilometers from Vienna and although it was only Thursday he was obviously eager to be off. Continentals are beginning to outdo British and Americans on the institution of the weekend.

Leaving the hospitable Mr. Hofsttater we walked down the two flights of stairs to the street. An early vintage elevator, which tenants unlocked with their own keys, had hauled us up, creaking and groaning in protest, but one descended on shanks' mare. We didn't mind, having gotten in training at the Zlata Husa Hotel in Prague, but I don't understand the system. The elevator has to go down anyway, why not go with it?

Having already seen a Sunday performance of the famous Lipizzaner horses of the Spanish Reitschule, the *haute école* of equestrianism, we decided this time to take in a rehearsal. Several hundred others had made the same decision, so we inched our way under the hot sun in a long sluggishly winding crocodile until we could enter the Imperial Palace, where the white and gold ring is situated. The entrance fee is ten schillings or $2.50. As they have big crowds every day eager to see the magnificent horses and their centaurian riders they make a very good thing of it. The horses live in luxury which is as it should be and the school is able to keep on buying and training new ones.

To be frank, while we had found the actual performance a unique and fascinating spectacle—the snow white horses weaving their patterns, changing from one gait to another in time to the off-stage music, the rehearsal seemed on the slow side. Also it wasn't easy to see the ring for we had been halfway down the queue and all the vantage points were occupied by the first arrivals, a dedicated crew reluctant to give an inch to the less favored. We left the beautiful creatures to their own devices and went to Demel's for *Kaffee mit Schlag*.

The next morning before starting off on the day's excursion I dropped into the café of the Hotel Imperial for a stirrup cup. When they brought the bill I gasped. Thirteen schillings or $3.25 for a cup of coffee! So it is topped with whipped cream, yes, I still consider $3.25 high flying.

Our driver for the day was a pleasant young Dutchman who was going to be an automotive engineer. His Austrian wife was studying architecture at the University of Vienna. While she was working he drove cars to implement their income and when she graduated and they went back to

Holland she would get a job while he completed *his* studies. Turn and turn about. All very fair and contemporary.

Our first stop was a small baroque church in the little town of Laxenburg, marvelously ornate with a lovely carved and gilded pulpit.

From there we went on to one of the countless castles built by Maria Theresa. Die Franzenburg, a small summer estate, was almost entirely destroyed during the war but has now been largely restored. Pleasant, if undistinguished, it is set in a delightful park on the edge of a lake. One must be hauled across the lake on a cable ferry and while we were waiting for it on the shore a strange gnomelike creature approached us. He was dumb and I think also imbecilic and there was something strangely unsettling in the way he shrugged and grimaced and rolled his big head from side to side. He pointed first at the ferry, which did seem to be tethered to the further shore for an unconscionable length of time, pointed his bony finger toward the gray cloudy sky and shook with silent laughter. We were in for it! Actually we did suffer minor sprinkles, but I should say that on a clear day the park would be a charming place for an outing and a picnic lunch. One could ride as well for there are miles of good bridal paths, but it is a by-the-way thing not, in our opinion, an end in itself. Nor had we regarded it as such, our true goal being Mayerling.

I was not expecting Charles Boyer and Danielle Darrieux from the picture of the same name but the scene of the murder and suicide that rocked Europe in 1889 still evokes curiosity.

The story of Rudolf, the thirty-one-year-old heir to the throne of Austria-Hungary and of Maria Vetsera is well known, but sometimes the stories we know still fascinate us.

Rudolf had married Stephanie, the daughter of the King of the Belgians, in 1881. Their marriage seemed happily launched, and they had one daughter, but as time slipped by it became apparent that whatever his other qualities

Rudolf was not an uxorious husband. His interest lay in womankind rather than in woman. Qualities, however, he indubitably had. He was a good linguist, he had an instinctive love of history and natural history and a vigorous reasoning mind. In his day, and in the milieu in which he lived, he was a notably progressive thinker. He was outspoken in his opinions of both the nobility and the clergy who heard him loud and clear and what they heard they did not like.

But if at court his popularity dwindled, in the boudoirs of Vienna his reputation soared. His detractors, as so often happens, were preponderantly male, and one may suppose there was a good deal of head-shaking and lip-smacking in the drawing rooms and clubs of the capital when the news was brought that the bodies of the archduke and his latest inamorata were found dead in bed in the hunting lodge of Mayerling where they had gone to spend the night.

Back and forth the rumors flew. The event was a tragedy, granted, the heir to the throne and a girl scarcely more than a child . . . it was a dreadful affair. It was also a remarkably juicy one. Accounts of it appear in various memoirs of the period and in articles and books, the latter largely romanticized and imaginative. One that seems sane and solidly documented was published in 1958; *The Road to Mayerling* by Richard Barkeley, from which we gather that a natural tendency to melancholia was aggravated in Rudolf by his sense of frustration, a conviction that his country was determinedly set on a wrong path politically and that he was powerless to change or prevent what he saw as a disastrous outcome of national policy.

He had often spoken of suicide and had, even while courting Maria Vetsera, proposed a suicide pact to a former flame, Mizzi Kasper, a down-to-earth lady who considered it a harebrained scheme and refused to take him seriously. Rudolf appears to have fallen as much in love with Maria as she had with him for he gave her an iron wedding ring on which were engraved, in German, the words UNITED IN LOVE TILL DEATH. She wore it on a slim chain around her neck.

From witnesses and reliable accounts it is known that on that last fateful night in the lodge several bottles of wine were sent into the bedroom, and Rudolf's servant, Bratfisch, sang sentimental Viennese songs for them. He had a very sweet whistle and a great talent for imitating bird calls which particularly delighted the archduke who was interested in natural history and ornithology.

When the old man was dismissed, apparently Maria and Rudolf discussed the manner of their death. Poison or revolver? Maria recorded their decision on an ash tray. Rather revolver, revolver is safer.

They wrote their last letters. In the one to her mother Maria said, "Forgive me for what I have done. I could not resist my love. . . . I am happier in death than in life. Yours, Maria." And to her sister, "We are going blissfully into the uncertain beyond . . . do not weep for my sake. I am crossing the line merrily."

Rudolf shot her and then waited in what must have been an interval of peculiar anguish until half-past six in the morning when he came out in his dressing gown and told an attendant to prepare breakfast and call him in an hour. Whistling softly he went back into the bedroom and closed and locked the door.

An hour or so later those who broke in found Maria lying peacefully, her eyes open, a flower in her hand. Rudolf had apparently poured out a glass of brandy, sat down on the bed beside her, and placed a small hand mirror on the bedside table. Looking at his reflection he found the correct spot, raised his revolver and shot himself through the temple.

In my imagination I had always had a pretty accurate impression of the hunting lodge where the deaths took place. It was a sort of Swiss chalet in a forest, simple perhaps but with every comfort and convenience and a good deal of charm. Well! If there was a forest there in 1889 it

has been razed and the house itself was minuscule: one
room upstairs, one down, and a servant's room on either
side. After the tragedy Franz Josef had the building
gutted and ironically, in view of Rudolf's sentiments toward the clergy, remodeled into a small chapel. Today's
caretaker, a tiny woman with the voice of a hoarse mouse,
gives you a capsule version of the story and shoos you on
your way.

A couple of mustard-colored stucco houses for personnel
adjoin the chapel. They are not prepossessing, but the
address of the first one is Number One, Mayerling. Somehow the name is still haunting, but be content to be
haunted and do not go there. The place itself is anti-
climactic.

On our return we passed through Grinzig, one of the
wine villages where from the wooded heights there is a
superb view of Vienna clustering on the Danube and of the
hillsides dotted with tiny one and two room summer
cottages like the toy houses one hangs on Christmas trees.
We drove through the Prater, but our Dutch driver had
to inform us we were there. The days of pretty women
tooling along in elegant carriages, of dandies, and high-
hatted footmen and spanking pairs have gone, and the
Prater today is a sort of Coney Island amusement park.

The next day was Sunday and we were leaving Vienna.
Poor Norton was the physician who failed to heal himself
and was suffering from a wretched cold, but the glorious
weather overrode my modest Florence Nightingale pretensions and I deserted him, taking a cab to Kahlenberg, a
high hill about twenty minutes outside of Vienna, from
where one gets an incomparable view of the city and of a
large slice of Austria. The morning light is wrong for
photography, but it is pleasant to have coffee on the terrace
or tea in the afternoon when the sun is obligingly behind
the camera lens and the splendor can be recorded.

Coming back I took a taxi to St. Stephen's Cathedral

and not knowing how much to tip the driver, realized from his gushing *auf Wiedersehen* and glowing smile that I had gone overboard. No matter how sophisticated or experienced I think I am, tipping tends to induce panic in me and I either hand out largesse that would cause Mr. Paul Getty to raise his eyebrows or tender a coin of a non-nutritious denomination, the sort of thing the recipient is apt to flick into the gutter with a four-letter word.

One should see St. Stephen's Cathedral because it is beautiful, but my preference would have been for the small chapel in Josefplatz. That is where the boys' choir sings and we were eager to hear it again. Unfortunately it didn't come together until school opened and there was still a week to go.

In *Second Spring and Two Potatoes* I wrote that Sunday is a mess all over the world, and by and large I stick to my guns, but I had primarily in mind Sunday for the traveler in Anglo-Saxon countries. Oddly enough Moslem or Buddhist ones too, because in those lands they shut up shop on their own holy days and then, for good measure, on the Christian days as well, especially during the tourist season.

I am obliged to backtrack, however, when it comes to certain Latin or predominantly Roman Catholic lands. They tend to feel strongly about Mass, but once assured they have saved themselves from eternal flame, they are apt to treat the rest of the day with considerable liberality.

In Vienna this is certainly true. The ethereal voices of the young choristers soar upward, but one leaves them to go next door for the unique spectacle of the Lipizzaner horses, to lunch in any one of a number of sophisticated restaurants, and to take off for the opera in the evening.

In France, after Mass is over, summer Sundays are great days for picnicking and frolic out of doors. In Spain they turn from God to gore with the greatest of ease, filling the churches in the morning and bull rings in the afternoon. That barbarism is untenable, but by and large Catholics are better off on Sunday than are Bible Belt Protestants or Jews on their holy days.

Religion is a strange conceit. Because of it, throughout history, millions of people have been willing to destroy with peculiar ferocity millions of others.

Despite the great art it has inspired, when one considers the cruelty, hypocrisy, distortion of fact, and invasion of personal privacy, the nurturing of superstition and the downright silliness religion can engender, it is understandable that there are those who feel its evils outweigh its virtues.

The ideal way to travel from Vienna to Budapest is by hydrofoil along the Danube. The trip takes about five hours, the lovely pageant of the countryside unrolling on either bank. Norton and I had planned to do it but were told that it was too late in the season, the service had closed down. It was a big fat error and an inexcusable one. Travel bureaus should have that sort of information at their fingertips. We learned that we had unnecessarily missed a very pleasant experience when we met an Englishman in our hotel in Budapest who had just arrived via hydrofoil and was chanting its glories.

Instead of the boat we took the Orient Express, that shabby ghost of former grandeur.

Sharing our compartment was an attractive young Argentine who spoke English and told us he was going to meet his father and stepmother in Budapest. "They have gone to visit her old home," he said. "It was once a great estate, but I am afraid she will be very upset and unhappy when she sees it. Those places, you know, if not used for a specific purpose by the State, they go to rack and ruin."

At the border a Hungarian official came to the door of the compartment and harangued us a long time in his native tongue. Norton and the Argentinian and I looked at each other and smiled at the conductor. Finally, with what sounded like a stinging oath, he banged his hand against the door jamb and departed enraged and frustrated.

We read the signs in German, French, and Spanish cautioning passengers not to lean out the windows. No sign in English. Presumably the English know better, or maybe the Société des Wagons Lits doesn't care if they get their heads chopped off.

That literature palled, but there was no alternative, for when it began to grow dark, we sat drowned in gloom, the one light bulb in the ceiling emitting a glimmer far too feeble to read by. Out of the window we could see nothing. We sat, until four and a half hours out of Vienna, the train pulled into the station at Budapest.

A nice young woman from Ibusz, the Hungarian travel agency, met us, and we clung to her as to a loved and able nanny. She could speak the language! In Prague people had spoken English, French, and German. In Vienna, English and German, which, after all, has some vague rapport with the mother tongue. But Hungarian! Oh, Zigeuner!

The parents of the Argentine had not showed up, so we asked him to share our car as we were all staying at the same hotel, the Royal. Like the Zlata Husa, the Royal was second or even third choice and for the same reason: the famed Gellert, overlooking the Danube, was filled to capacity.

The famed Gellert, however, as I was to discover later, was not without its shortcomings, although it does have an enormous swimming pool of thermal health-inducing water that is periodically whipped into quite large artificial waves. It is a spacious old-fashioned building with flowering window boxes, very attractive from the outside, but when I went there to have my hair washed the salon was so dirty that when they asked me to wait a few minutes, I fled, murmuring I would have a cup of coffee and return. I never did.

I had the coffee, though, on the hotel terrace overlooking the Danube and watched the people in the streets. The streets were what the hairdressing salon was not; immaculately clean. After the sidewalks of New York it was a genuine pleasure to walk along them or just to sit and look at them. Occasionally we watched the grooming taking place. It was a leisurely performance with a cast of four. One man would lift the pavement grill surrounding the tree trunks, another would pick up the bits of paper and cigarette stubs that had accumulated under it, a third would come along and rake the earth, and the fourth would watch the other three.

We had met the attractive, young-looking father of our Argentine train companion, and he said that's the way things always are when the State runs a country; inefficient. He may be right, but in this instance the results were agreeable and the city far more prepossessing than capitalistic, privately unrun New York.

He also told us that he and his wife had returned to Budapest, saddened by what they had seen of her girlhood home. The lower floors of the lovely big old house had been gutted, and the place was now used to store grain.

Nor was it only the lady's house and the Gellert hairdressing establishment that had deteriorated.

The Royal too was in bad shape; paint flaking off the window sill, paper peeling from the wall, and the curtains dirty. The bed linen was clean but dingy, and there was a general atmosphere of what we came to think of as People's State Gray.

Detergents are not yet big in the Communist bloc. Nor is the lighting system. The hallways have bulbs of such low voltage that we needed a trained mole to find the keyhole in our door. The bright spots were plentiful hot water and big European capitalist bath towels. Service too was prompt and efficient. Our first morning there we tried ringing for breakfast but when no one materialized we decided the bells were not connected and telephoned room service. The waiter came at a sprint. Not much protocol but everything hot and as ordered. Our room maid was good too, and when I tipped her as we were leaving she actually did kiss my hand as the young ladies of the Vienna coffee shops were reputed to do.

On the evening of our arrival, after we had removed a little of the Orient Express encrustation, we went down to the dining room. It was large, glaring, and noisy, but the gypsy fiddler looked so like Groucho Marx that it seemed almost homey.

Hungarian currency is forints and fillers. Twenty-three forints make a dollar, and we ordered caviar as it didn't cost many of them, and thought: "Hurray! Satellite state, favored trade relations with Russia." Great gray globules was how I envisaged it. Tiny black salty seed pearls is how it was. We shrugged and ate. The rest of the food was flavorful but cold. By that time it was nine-thirty, and I suppose they didn't care.

We watched with amusement two young sisters dining with their father at the table next to us. The smaller of the two, she couldn't have been more than five, was as precocious a tot as I have ever seen. She hung on Daddums, caressing his arm, looking up into his face, listening enraptured to every word he said. She would rest her chin in her hand, still listening, positively sighing with pleasure. She had golden curls too. We decided it was time for the Gabors to move over.

A woman with bottle-shaped legs came to the table, spoke briefly to the two children and their father, and went away. I decided she was the sister of the man's wife from whom he was divorced, and this was his Sunday with the kids. When we left, Norton waved to Zsa Zsa, who crinkled her nose, trilled a merry laugh, and waved back. Quite a girl.

Our night was, as the French have it, white. No sleep. The beds had all the give of X-ray tables, and I have a suspicion the blankets were U.S.S.R. army surplus. Also our room gave onto a broad thoroughfare and because of

the admirable tram service—every minute on the minute
—was hideously noisy.

We later asked an American friend who lived there if
such frequency was necessary. A certain amount of night-
owling is understandable, but was it possible that *that*
many Budapestians were bent on nocturnal errands? "No,"
said the friend, "of course they're not and no private
company could afford to keep the trams running that way
but they're owned by the State. The State must employ
people so they can earn a living, so they allot tramcar
conductors certain routes, and that's it. They have to take
them." It shifts, let us hope!

Since we were without car or guide for our first day's
sightseeing, we hopped a bus that was just leaving for a
tour of the city, and a very good idea it turned out to be.

To our way of thinking, Prague perhaps has a little edge
on Budapest but the latter is very beautiful too, and its
ardent devotees have every reason for their devotion and
enthusiasm.

In the old days Budapest was a great center of the
arts, theater and music especially, and a gathering place
of wits who considered it *the* city of Europe. If the natives
could be got to budge, they did so reluctantly.

When the plays of Ferenc Molnar were popular (*Liliom,
The Swan, The Guardsman*), more than one New York
producer tried to lure the great man to New York, but he
was not marine-minded. "Ferenc, that's silly," they said,
"on those great ocean liners . . . you feel virtually nothing."

"Ah," replied their quarry slyly, "but on those little
liners on the Danube, you feel even less." He was right to
stay on its bonny banks, perhaps he had a premonition,
for eventually he did go to New York and that is where he
died.

As in Prague, our impression was that a film of sadness
dimmed the city. Even when there are no longer any
surface signs, the scars of a tragedy as great as the result

of the Hungarian uprising in 1956 must take a long time
to heal. Still, the splendors of Budapest are many and real.

It became the capital in 1873, when Buda and Obuda
on the hills and Pest on the flat left bank of the Danube
merged into one entity. They were originally Roman towns
built on Celtic settlements, and throughout history they
have been harrowed by the Mongols, the Turks, the Hapsburgs, the Germans, and the Russians.

Even though, as in this instance, their behavior was not
admirable, I am glad to be able to mention the Hapsburgs,
a family with whom I do not have frequent dealings, for
I have recently learned the origin of the name. It comes
from a castle that was built in Aargau, Switzerland, by
Werner, Bishop of Strasbourg in the 1000s. The word is a
corruption, not of Werner but of Habichtsburg, and that
means Hawk's Castle.

As far as the Russians were concerned, for a while the
Hungarians must have been grateful to them because they
did drive out the Nazis, although at the desperate price of
a fourteen-week siege which all but leveled the city. The
seven bridges that had been built over the Danube in the
course of a century were blown up. As a guidebook states:
"from December 1944 till February 13th 1945, when the
town was liberated by the Soviet army, 33,000 buildings,
80,000 flats were demolished by explosion and fire. Practically no building in town was left undamaged. There
was no gas, no electricity, no railway traffic."

It was the optimists who felt the town might recover in
thirty to forty years, yet, according to the book "it was
rebuilt within five years." In a period of five days in 1956,
it is estimated that 10,000 Hungarians lost their lives and
190,000 fled the country in their efforts to free themselves
from Russian liberation. On this grim occurrence the book
is restrained, saying merely that "the counter revolution
in 1956 was another heavy blow to the capital; yet this
time the new wounds were healed within a few months'

time." It might have been written by Dr. Pangloss, that first Christian Scientist.

Before Norton and I left Rome I had been reading the dispatches of the New York *Times* correspondent in Hungary. They were interesting, and I phoned the paper to ask if I might have Mr. David Halberstam's address, we would like to meet him while we were there. The young lady was obliging. It was a long address full of difficult spelling and impossible to pronounce, and it ended up Warsaw, Poland. "Poland? But doesn't he live in Budapest? That's his dateline."

"No, he lives in Warsaw and goes to Budapest on assignment. We used to have a stringer there, a Hungarian, but the government made it too complicated and difficult for him to get any information out."

That is the kind of thing that baffles a Westerner. Once they have given one of their own citizens permission to act as correspondent why frustrate him at every turn?

As cloud shapes change, so do attitudes. The attitudes of the eastern European countries vis à vis the United States are changing, sometimes radically, sometimes subtly, and on the whole the atmosphere is more friendly; but a love of mystery, a relish of confusion, a tendency to color fact, and an ingrained instinct for roadblocks and censorship that are, I think, as much Slavic as they are Soviet, still persist.

In old Buda the ruins of a Roman amphitheater and fort still remain, and today children play around them as they probably played in A.D. 160. A small domed Turkish bath building dates from 1570. Long before then, Crusaders, returning from the Holy Land, passed that way to bathe their wounds in the therapeutic waters for which the area was famous. Today its baths are one of the city's important industries. We should probably have tried them, but we felt quite well and didn't have much time.

One of the striking physical features of Budapest is its boulevards. They are enormous; great wide thoroughfares stretching for miles. There is Rakorzi Avenue, the Avenue of the People's Republic and the huge Hero Square built to commemorate Hungary's thousandth birthday in 1896. It was about 896 that Arpád the Magyar led his ferocious hordes through the Vereczka Pass into what was then the Upper Theiss and is now called Hungary.

The country is proud to be so old and the people today are themselves Magyars, but the original inhabitants who had to cope with the original intruders were probably less pleased. They were a bloodthirsty, barbarous, merciless crew, and the days of those who opposed them were brief.

The Museum of Fine Arts fronts on Hero Square and mettlesome sculptured horses top a handsome colonnade. When we were there the museum was showing an exhibition of Spanish pictures, many on loan from Vienna and Leningrad.

Spacious ex-private houses of the ex-rich line the boulevards. Today they are offices and legations, for, as the bus guide said, "There are no rich people any more," adding with a hearty laugh obviously directed at us, "except in America." I gave her a cold sickly smile. The doctor said, "Damn fool."

We stopped at the People's Stadium, enormous also, and our jocular guide informed us it seated 100,000 people. The doctor was unimpressed. "No baseball diamond," he said. There was a star though. Many structures in the city are topped by the red star of Russia.

Like Prague, the silhouette of Budapest is a lovely conglomeration of domes and spires. The baroque forms of architecture filtering down from Vienna proved very popular with the Hungarians.

The most fascinating part of Budapest is Castle Hill, many of its buildings have arching entrances and beautiful gray stone window moldings from the fifteenth century, upon which are set pink geraniums of the twentieth. In some respects the war proved a brutal blessing. The destruction of indifferent contemporary houses occasionally brought to light magnificent architecture of an earlier day which afterward was restored. The Royal Palace is on Castle Hill, as is the modern Fisherman's Bastion built in Romanesque style. It got its name because in time of siege it was the job of the fishermen to man that particular section of the original rampart. From the rampart one has a sweeping, uninterrupted view of the city and the curving glittering river. However, the sight that charmed us most was a crocodile of fifteen tiny kids each holding onto the waistband of the chap in front of him as they followed two young teachers from the nursery school. I also warmed to the woman in the information center when I went in to ask if I might use the phone and if she would be kind enough to get me the number. She was on her hands and knees scrubbing out a spot on the floor. "I can't stand dirt," she said, and I wished with all my heart that she was the manager of the hotel. She would have been co-operative about the telephone, I am sure, but explained that it was out of order. "I don't know why, it just doesn't work." That we found was often the case in the countries of the Communists or Socialists (which is what they call themselves). They had all kinds of things and systems but usually they didn't work.

Close to the Fisherman's Bastion is the church of St. Matthias. It was built in the thirteenth century but has been partially destroyed and rebuilt many times since. Painted with brilliant frescoes in a rich abstract design it has some fine stained glass and storerooms of ecclesiastical treasures.

Another Budapest landmark that we feel should not be missed was a restaurant, the Hungaria. It is a sort of glorious mating of New York's old Murray Hill Hotel with St. Peter's in Rome, all plush and marble, gilt, and twisted columns, and the food is fine. It was also fine at the residency of the American Legation where we were invited to lunch with our chargé d'affaires, the Honorable Elim O'Shaughnessy and Mrs. O'Shaughnessy. Theirs is a roomy

10   The Vienna Opera House.

11   Belvedere Palace, Vienna.

12   The gardens of the Belvedere.

13   Dr. Wolfgang Hofsttater with two of his children.

14 Mettlesome horses atop the colonnade in Hero Square, Budapest.

15 Section of Fishermen's Bastion and equestrian statue of St. Stephen, first king of Hungary, on Castle Hill.

16   Babies crocodile on Castle Hill.

17   Liberation Monument, Gellert Hill, Budapest. Heroic Soviet man downing dragon of capitalism.

house located in a pretty garden. Mr. O'Shaughnessy is
tall and lean, Madame is pleasant and forthright, and they
are the parents of three attractive children.

Our representative struck me as being a man who is
under few illusions. When I said, "I can't explain, I can't
put my finger on it but Norton and I both feel a kind of
despondency in the atmosphere here. Of course we may
be wrong—that's only a first impression," he replied, "I
don't see any particular reason not to trust your first impressions." He also told us that the stadium seated 92,000,
not 100,000 as the guide had boasted but we did not hold
that against her. Noble capitalists are prone to toss off
round numbers too.

Mr. O'Shaughnessy said that after the war, rather than
repatriate our surplus material, we left it in Hungary, and
our government accepted real estate and undeveloped areas
in payment. We cannot build on the property and it is of
no particular value to us, but it serves as collateral for the
counterpart funds out of which we pay embassy expenses.

The system is not unique to Hungary. India pays us in
rupees for shipments of grain, but since rupees are not
the preferred currency of other countries in international
trading, we leave them there to take care of our local
housekeeping. Around the world we have more local funds
than local housekeeping, so are in the curious position of
stashing away in foreign banks delicious yet unusable
money, a situation to drive a budget-minded housewife
crazy.

After lunch Mrs. O'Shaughnessy drove us to a small
antique shop near St. Matthias Church. She had her eye
on a cake plate. The prettiest things were all china, but
that is impractical when traveling, so I refrained.

Much of the modern Hungarian glassware and china
is first rate. They come by their penchant honestly since
the first china shop in central Europe opened in Buda in
1472. The establishments we saw were doing a brisk trade
with the homebound indigenes, but for the traveler getting

anything out of any of those eastern European countries, the most trivial purchases, requires the skill of a dental surgeon and the pull of the State Department. Once you have bought something and they have the money, why do they mind sending it to you? I cannot explain.

Leaving the antiquary, we went downtown to a shop that sold hard-boiled painted eggs. They were quite pretty in color and design, but they, too, seemed impractical, and I settled instead for a little embroidered dress for a one-year-old friend. It was a considerable transaction. You say, "I'll take it." You are then given a slip and go to a cashier to pay. The cashier stamps the slip and gives it back to you. You then go to another counter and wait in line till your purchase comes into view and is wrapped. You give your slip to that woman, she stamps it and hands it back to you with your package and you can go. The system seems unnecessarily time-consuming, but they like it.

While waiting in line I noticed, not for the first time, the footwear that seemed very popular. Many women had on high laced shoes made not of leather but of cloth, black or brown with open toes and heels. Even the doctor, who is no Parisian boulevardier when it comes to noticing women's clothes, had noticed those and remarked that they looked like the devil. They do too.

And I do not think they are worn because, in the euphemistic phrase of American politicians, the people are "disadvantaged." I suspect it is a question of taste.

Perhaps we were unduly footwear-conscious because of my own experience. The night we went to see a musical comedy I noticed on leaving the theater that my black evening pumps were gray. People's State dust in the People's State carpet.

In spite of its dinginess, however, the theater itself, the Fovarosi Operettszinhaz, was pretty, the house was sold out, and we were interested to see that the pretzel man hawking his wares in a big basket before the curtain

went up did a thriving business. We ourselves did not
dare to try them; too thirst-inducing.

In a Budapest theater the counterpart of our asbestos is
quite literally an iron curtain. It creaked up to disclose
the regular curtain covered with ads like old-time vaude-
ville: nylons, tools, beads, cosmetics and luggage although
travel seems to be mostly internal or within the Communist
bloc.

The operetta itself, a salad of brashness, and elementary
comedy was rather touching.

The locale was a beach resort, and a young Jewish comic
played a visiting Turk with a harem. That established the
atmosphere straight off. The sets were garish and the beach
costumes of the young ladies deplorable, but I suspect they
supplied them themselves out of tiny salaries.

We thought it refreshing that, rid of governmental propaganda, the hands-across-the-sea spirit was in full swing.
The heroine was supposedly an American girl named Daisy
Parker and the actress who played her—although needing
the discipline of a director with a whip of iron—was by no
means untalented. The song hit of the show was "Carnival,
Oh Yes!" Norton and I thought it great. Those were the
three words we understood.

Halfway through the performance a sign was lowered
from the flies. On it sparkled the legend BROADWAY SHOW,
and an interlude ensued which, although out of context,
proved quite sprightly. The cast was dressed in would-be
Uncle Sam costumes and swung into a Cole Porter medley
with special emphasis on "Night and Day." I would be
surprised to learn that Mr. Porter's estate collected so much
as a filler in royalties, but his music made two fellow
Americans very happy.

Had there been more of him, or even more of his Hungarian colleague, we would have been content; music the
universal tongue and all that but for our needs the supply
was skimpy. We were sitting in the front row and at
intervals the orchestra simply withdrew from the pit. When

we saw them retreating through the little door under the stage we knew we were in for a long spate of dialogue and while the rest of the house laughed merrily at the passing quips, we sat like dolts, longing for the musicians to return.

At one point we had more than music and cast to interest us. We watched a lady violinist cry her heart out through an entire act. She sawed away at her fiddle, tears streaming down her cheeks. We felt very sympathetic, and I said to Norton it was quite possible she was crying because she had to witness a performance of that show every night.

Our Niobe was not the only woman in the orchestra; there were five others, and I should say that in the Communist bloc equality of the sexes has been achieved. We saw several women taxi drivers, and robust females in overalls worked on construction gangs.

Personally I feel that there *is* a man's world, their place is *in* it and I am delighted to take advantage of *la différence*. I am not at all happy when, in the country, my dear husband asks me to help him lift and tote large metal things and cold frames and pieces of lumber. They hurt your hands and snag your stockings, and I want no part of them.

After the performance we were lucky to get a taxi, for they are birds of swift passage and rare. We drove a long way out on one of those huge boulevards to Gundel's, which Mrs. O'Shaughnessy had told us served the best food in Budapest.

The restaurant proved to be a very large uninspired room with an orchestra of several men and many tables only one of which was occupied. The diners were Workers, trustworthy and noble. One could tell by their clothes: gray wool shirts and no ties. It was after ten o'clock, but that is not so very late, and we thought that had there been much dinner trade some of it would still be lingering over coffee. Perhaps the Gundel specialty is luncheon.

Our dinner was fairly good and I should say that basically there is nothing the matter with Hungarian food that a little restraint would not cure. If they would just stop sooner, not load everything with bread crumbs, sauces, and fried eggs.

In the course of the meal a gypsy fiddler detached himself from the orchestra, came over to our table and played for me alone. His costume, a sack suit, was not picturesque nor did he have melting eyes and mustache of silk, though even if he had had I would have been uncomfortable. I know violin music at table is supposed to be romantic and occasionally restaurants in the States go in for it at heavy expense to the patrons but my own reaction is one of embarrassment rather than romance. I never know where to look, and I am well aware that Norton is thinking to himself, "What the hell am I supposed to give this guy for a tip?" My husband wrestled with his Anglo-Saxon ignorance, did his best, and we were both relieved when the maestro returned to his comrades.

The next day was one of clouds and showers interspersed by bouts of dazzling sunshine. We drove up to Gellert Hill, a companion height to Castle Hill from which one has an unimpeded view of the Liberation Monument, an example of that overwhelming heroic statuary so dear to the Russians. This one they erected to themselves in self-congratulation over having defeated the Germans and occupied Hungary in 1945.

Gellert Hill takes its name from a Venetian bishop who, invited by King Stephen I, came to Hungary in the eleventh century to convert the Magyars to Christianity. They were cold to the idea so they took Gellert or Gerald, sealed him in an iron spike-studded barrel, and booted him down the hill. Surely an excess of wild gypsy spirits.

We had heard about Wiesegrad and decided to go there for lunch. There is little traffic and it is a pretty drive along the Danube, past fields of roses and sunflowers. At first I thought the latter were for the Russian market, as in Russian novels the characters are forever chewing the seeds, but although some of them may be sent there, their chief use is for sunflower oil.

Having heard a good deal about Godless Communism we were interested to see the great number of shrines dotting the countryside. The government may not be enthusiastic about them, but it does not eliminate them.

When we arrived at the restaurant in Wiesegrad we found masses of young men were shoveling food into their mouths. They all finished at the same time, rose, and departed, and a battalion of girls arrived to take their places. We decided they must be a student tour of some kind.

When our own lunch was served it was a shock of pleasure. Excellent fish soup, chicken paprika, and beef-steak.

We were fortunate in the evening too, dining that night at the Kis Royale. The gypsy music was as good as the food, and the fiddlers stuck sensibly together instead of coming to woo the foreign trade with their old European charm. The place was not luxurious, but there was something warm about it. It looked as though it might once have been a private house, and dinner was served on flowered Herend porcelain, no commonplace in the restaurants of the U.S.A.

CHAPTER THREE

Romania

Although we had requested space long before we left home seats in the plane from Budapest to Bucharest were unobtainable on the date we wanted them so we were obliged to settle for the Orient Express. The train is a miracle of inefficiency and discomfort. Our stateroom was cramped, yet it is only fair to say that the carriage we were in was new and clean, with the exception of the lavatory at the end of the corridor. That had not participated in the general uplift. It was dirty, and the paper, in the best American privy tradition, consisted of pages torn from magazines. The whole train seemed devoid of food and water, and while I was able to scrounge a cup of coffee from a passing waiter, he stood tapping his foot while I drank it, causing Norton to observe that he had me under forced draft.

We went to bed, anticipating, correctly, a night of interruptions. I was hoping for one at the border, but there were three. Three times the knock at the door by the passport control.

As we retired, the dear doctor had been the soul of chivalry; an American husband, the dream of every woman in the world. "I, of course, will take the upper berth, sweetie; you take the lower," and up he swarmed out of harm's way. Snugly tucked in, he stuck his head over the edge and beamed down at me. "Sleep well, darling." Judas!

Every time a knock came it was I who had to reach groggily for the latch, open the compartment door, and root around under my pillow for our passports. I gave the official the first one that came to hand. Mine as it turned out. He examined it with hostility and handed it back with a grunt. He then rolled a suspicious eye up at my loved one, a large inert hulk under the covers. "And what about his?" he said coldly. "Your associate?" More fishing and rooting about. Associate's passport emerges.

To the official's annoyance we seem to be in order.

"Any cameras?"

"Yes, masses of them, there they are." I wave in the gloom toward the cameras stacked in a neat little mountain on the floor.

"Any transistor radios?"

"No."

This is a lie. We have one but what of it? Europe pullulates with transistor radios. They make life hideous wherever you go, and people love them. Why shouldn't we have one, too, on which to try, by way of blessed change, for a little good music from time to time? At 2 A.M. the last nuisance looked over our passports, handed me assorted papers, and departed.

With the dawn Romania emerged as a great expanse of fertile farmland, and indeed it is a rich country, with huge reserves of wheat and oil. We started the long long trek to the dining car, walking through crowded second- and third-class carriages full of people with the exhausted, blunted look of those who have passed sleepless hours and who know that more must be endured before release. Some were making their breakfast from a piece of fruit, others unfolded greasy paper to disclose a sandwich or a baloney roll.

The carriages made me think of American trains in war

time, grimy and filled with tired humanity: soldiers in crumpled uniforms, weary young wives with babies in their arms, traveling from one part of the enormous continent to the other to see, perhaps for the last time, the men they loved before they were shipped overseas.

The diner was People's State Gray and the linen soiled. Not many passengers seemed to be bothering with breakfast, although behind us there was a table of four giggling girls. We passed a line of soldiers standing at ease in a field, their rifles on the ground in front of them. The girls waved merrily. The soldiers smiled but refrained from waving back, as beneath the dignity of military men. There was very little spit and polish about them, and Norton thought they were perhaps a kind of Civilian Conservation Corps.

The few other people in the diner appeared to be laborers rather than the white-collar or professional class. Not that we were expecting representatives of what, in the old days, would have been considered the aristocracy or "landlords." We knew that they had been swept away. Not always killed but deprived and displaced. Still, it was interesting to see that those whom one might think had the least money were the ones who were traveling. On reflection, however, why not? The ferris wheel has brought them to the top, now it's their turn. The dictatorship of the proletariat was the goal of the Communist Revolution, and it achieved what it was after.

In a booklet written in 1965 called "Report Concerning The Draft Constitution of the Socialist Republic of Rumania" the author, Nicolae Ceausescu explains that "the Constitution proclaims our Republic a State of the working people in towns and villages, sovereign, independent and unitary, whose territory is inalienable and indivisible.

"The working class, oppressed and exploited in the past, lacking political rights, has become master of the means of production, of the fruit of its labor, successfully fulfills the

role of leading class in the entire society. . . . it's high revolutionary consciousness place(s) the working class in the
most advanced positions of the people's struggle for socialism . . . The continuous strengthening of the leading role
of the working class is an objective necessity for the successful implementation of the historical tasks in the entire period
of building socialism and communism."

An apathetic member of the new nobility, a waiter, finally
shuffled up to us, and before I could stop my husband,
before my unbelieving eyes, he pulled a fistful of forints
from his pocket and asked if they would be acceptable
as payment for breakfast. The predictable at once took
place. The waiter shook his head. "Lei," he said.

"But you see," explained Norton, "we got on at Budapest last night. We've had no opportunity to get any Romanian money."

"Lei," said the waiter. It was his little refrain.

"All right, I'll buy some," said Norton. The waiter shook
his head. I tried French, spoken by many Romanians as
though it were their mother tongue. It was not spoken by
our man, and his interest in our empty stomachs was
obviously not that of an anatomist. My temper, I fear,
was a bit short. I had had a bad night, I was hungry, and
Norton's tendering of the forints seemed to me pure idiocy.

"For God's sake, why did you have to do that? You
could have waited till we'd eaten."

"I thought," said my spouse stiffly, "it was the honest
thing to do."

"Oh, honey, come off it. I believe in honesty too but I
also believe in survival. Eat first and hammer out the payment afterward."

At this point the waiter surprisingly enough turned
human. "I bring," he said. What he brought was coffee for
Norton, slices of ham, bread and butter, and apricot jam
cloyingly sweet. We were going to have trouble with the
preserves for the rest of the journey. The Ottoman Empire
occupied the Balkan peninsula for some five hundred

years and the Turkish love of sugar and syrups sank deep.
I had asked for tea and was served some tepid, nauseat-
ingly sweet lemonade. The Romanians simply do not understand tea, and if you want it, take your own supply with
you. I had done so and fared better thereafter, but when
I was in the diner the tea was in my suitcase and no
rapport was possible.

After breakfast Dr. Brown's honor was assuaged when
he was able to do business with another waiter in charge
of the cash box. Although the man seemed absolutely
astounded to discover that Hungarian money was forints,
he did hand over a few lei in exchange. That this should
be mysterious to him was mysterious to me. The Orient
Express traverses Europe from Paris to Constantinople and
one would think the train personnel might have developed
a certain sophistication in currency but Norton said he
thought the individual waiter's beat was probably circum-
scribed. They got on at the borders of their own countries
and got off when the train passed beyond.

We rolled on through pine-clad mountains and across
plains and lavender glinting fields of autumn crocus, and
at last we arrived in Bucuresti. Bucharest. Many Romanian proper names end in *i*, but the letter is never
pronounced. The site of the city is ancient but unlike its
neighbors to the northwest there are comparatively few
buildings of historic importance and it is the systemized
city planning for the future that commands the traveler's
interest. There are big parks in Bucharest and several lakes
adjacent to and within the city limits. It is spacious and
a good many of the buildings are handsome, so I am hard
put to it to say why the town lacks charm.

One reason may be that it is very flat, and the other is
that it is very open; we saw no tantalizing alleyways or
small courtyards or streets so steep that they are really
staircases. Candor is admirable but reticence, restraint,
the feeling that there is more to know and investigate than

appears on the surface is intriguing in both people and places.

In Bucharest however we did get into the number one hotel, The Athenée Palace, but not without a tussle. Although I had telephoned to Carpati (pronounced Carpat), the International Travel Bureau, to tell them of our inability to fly down from Budapest, there was no guide to meet us at the station. Fortunately, we were capable of getting ourselves to the hotel but when Norton asked for our reservations the man at the desk glanced down at the open book before him, shrugged, and said, "Your name is not here. There are no rooms."

"May I see the book, please," said the doctor. The man spun it toward him with some irritation. Norton looked at the page. There, in large printed capitals, were our two names with the correct date of arrival. The clerk was amazed, and we learned later that if you telephone someone in Bucharest and want them to call you back, it is wiser to leave your room number than your name, which is completely foreign to them and hard for them to pronounce so that the desk will usually say you are out.

The Athenée Palace is the number one hotel, but do not let that give you delusions of grandeur. It is old, and while it is not uncomfortable, it is something of a rattletrap affair with dirty bathroom floors, although that was true of all the Communist bloc countries. You either put up with it or wash them yourselves, for the personnel ignores them.

We were getting settled in when our guide arrived, and we sensed at once we were in luck. She was a sturdy young woman with vigorous dark red hair, misty blue eyes, and a ready smile. Her name was Edith Ilovici, pronounced Ilovitch. She spoke excellent English and French, she was a professor at the university, and we were to become good friends and learn a great deal from her.

Her subject she told us, was English. She taught it to advanced students who wanted to read the most authoritative English or American textbooks dealing with their special interests. Communists mean what they say about education. They *do* want it for everyone. They will lie to their people and their students about intentions and politics and living conditions in the West, although there are times when the West is fairly imaginative about the East too. But while party indoctrination may be part of the curriculum they are not fanciful when it comes to accurate knowledge and information. They want facts.

Lunching at the hotel, we thought the food was adequate, and afterward we set off with Edith for a tour of the city.

On entering the Orthodox Church, I glanced down at what I took to be a pile of old black rags on the floor. They moved and I became aware that they clothed a woman on her hands and knees, her face pressed to the ground praying. Such self-abnegation struck me as excessive, besides being unhygienic.

There is a large circular building in Bucharest which is a permanent circus with performers and animals quartered nearby but I do not like what they do to animals in circuses so declined Edith's invitation to visit it. Instead, we went to an area that used to be the city dump and is now a large park surrounded by low-cost housing units. Unfortunately, the units are frequently jerry built as are our own, and we were told by some Americans who live in Bucharest that a young embassy family unable to find a house, rented one of the apartments and was having a pretty cramped time of it. There were three small bedrooms and no sitting room, and the vital appliance in the bathroom was so placed one could not close the door.

We stopped for tea on the terrace of a large restaurant on Lake Herastrau, the Pescarus or Seagull. Unhappily, rock-and-roll music from a transistor radio imbued the air. It would have been pleasant to sit quietly looking out over the water as we speculated on how much freedom of thought went on in the enormous printing center that rose on the opposite shore. It is there apparently that most of the government brochures, books, and propaganda pamphlets are turned out.

Their high moral tone is apt both to amuse and exasperate, when it does not outright stun, the venal Westerner accustomed to viewing his own government as a cross between a pack of thieves and a place of refuge for the feeble-minded. An opinion he has no hesitancy whatever in voicing.

In Communist countries the government tells the citizens how great it is, and since it is true that in many circumstances where people are infinitely better off than they used to be they tend to swallow the self-commendation with docility, gagging only slightly when the doses of saccharine and nobility become too concentrated. To a dispassionate eye some of the presentations and claims may seem questionable but they are provocative.

In the two brochures we read we found statements ranging from imprecise—"The decisive role in obtaining victory over Fascism was played by the Soviet Union that bore the brunt of the Second World War" to fanciful "Man's exploitation by man has been done away with forever." Fanfare of trumpets, ruffle of drums, quick curtain! They're enthusiastic if nothing else.

As Mr. Ceausescu's "Report" goes on to tell us, "The boundless love and confidence with which our people follow and implement the policy of the Party of the Communists— whose lofty mission is the devoted service of the interests of those who work—is the historical consequence of the victorious unfolding of the socialist revolution." And God help those who would dispute it.

An even more lyrical style may be found in another government booklet with the succinct and inspiring title of "Draft Directives of the Fourth Congress of the Roumanian Workers Party on the Turning to Account of Power Resources and the Country's Electrification in the 1966–1975 Period." Catchy, isn't it? Among other paeans of praise in the Draft Directives we find the following, "In the past an

afflicted corner of Europe distressed by poverty. . . .
Rumania now steps up on a . . . safe road, becoming an
advanced socialist country with an ever higher level of
civilization. This is the fruit of the enthusiastic selfless labor
of our wonderful people, free and masters of their own
destinies, aware of the fact that all their achievements and
endeavors serve the country's progress, the building of a
better life for all the working people."

Such wholesome, co-operative patriotism may prove a little wearing to skeptical old meanies—I know one who
literally burped on reading it—yet those people are trying.
Things *are* getting better for them.

If the Balkan countries are plotting a world take-over
they naturally are not going to publicize that fact in government brochures available to foreigners, but at the risk of
sounding naïve, I should be greatly surprised if they are.
To achieve their aims the people must have peace. War
would mean devastation to all their hopes and plans and
progress.

They yearn to progress, and their idea of progress is the
material wealth of the U.S.A. In consumer goods they do
not begin to match our standards of manufacture, our vast
quantity nor our bewildering variety, but their desire for
them is cogent.

There is a great deal of talk about ideology, but there
is much more about industry: pig iron and steel and oil
and the extraction of methane gas—an American business-
man would feel right at home. Romania has a five-year plan
that tells you how much of everything they will have in
1970, and I am keeping the brochure to see how accurately
they will have called the shots.

People who live there are not yet permitted to travel
outside the Communist bloc, but non-Communist travelers
are encouraged and welcomed in those countries and inevitably they bring with them news of the outside world
and the cars and clothes and cosmetics produced in that
world. As a rule the foreign products are of good quality

and the hosts are aware of it, and it must be a little confusing to those schooled in the evil ways of capitalism to reconcile the good products, the money, and their visitor's obvious preference for it with so distorted a way of life.

However, regardless of the confusion, doubts or even any envy they might feel, the Romanians we met were extremely courteous. They did not needle us for some of our more questionable folkways such as a high percentage of alcoholism, drug addiction, crime, highway accidents, the trash on our television programs, our southern courts of justice, the dreadful destruction of our wildlife both fauna and flora . . . they did not even question us about Vietnam for which the doctor and I were grateful, not being people who have on the tip of our tongues a convincing explanation of our country's actions in Southeast Asia.

It is of course possible that they do not know about these things but if as much anti-U.S. propaganda as we have been led to believe exists over there, they had tempting material at hand. We were pleasantly surprised when they let it lie dormant.

We were not surprised to discover that they knew virtually nothing of Boris Pasternak, the distinguished Russian author who had been forced by the Soviet government to refuse the Nobel prize for *Doctor Zhivago*.

I cannot say whether the more recent case of Andrei Sinyavsky and Yuli Daniel, who were sentenced to seven and five years hard labor respectively, for smuggling manuscripts, hostile to the Russian government, out of the country was publicized or not. It might have been presented as an example of what rightly happens to those who criticize the State or possibly concealed as an unfortunate slip of a splendid ally. I can say that a writer in Romania, and probably in the rest of the bloc too, works pretty much for the love of his art. Especially is this true of the authors of textbooks.

The government is the publisher and it is the only one. To be published at all a book must be accepted by a committee dealing with that special subject. If they do not like it, that ends it. If they do, it will be printed at government expense, the author will be paid a stipulated amount and regardless of the number of copies sold, he doesn't get a penny more. Prestige is considered by the government to be reward enough.

When we learned about this, Norton said later that on the *whole* he thought my reaction had been quite restrained. Another thing we learned was more encouraging.

The term iron curtain is outmoded. To some extent a barrier still exists between east and west but it is more fretwork than iron. There are many, many peepholes, and one of them is the press.

Our second morning in Bucharest we went to confer with the travel bureau on the motor trip we were to make through Romania with Edith as our guide and a chauffeur the bureau would provide.

We met two or three members of the personnel who were most helpful in their suggestions of places to go and things to see and we met also one of the directors, Mr. Prager. Mr. Prager was, or had been, a lawyer with a supple and cultivated mind. In the course of our pleasant conversation and over one of the innumerable tiny cups of sweet black Turkish coffee, I made some quip about the iron curtain.

"No," said Mr. Prager, "no, that is not true. We do not have an iron curtain, we are not shut off from the rest of the world. I, for instance, see the New York *Times* every day. To be sure, it is the European edition, but I see it."

My silent reaction to that was, "I bet you do, Mac, or possibly you and the rest of the top brass, but the People . . . not likely!"

Several days later we were at Mamaia, a beach resort on the Black Sea, and one morning as we stood buying stamps at the hotel desk a great pile of newspapers was delivered, most of them, naturally, printed in Romanian; but there was also *L'Humanité*, the French Communist paper, and *Les Nouvelles de Moscou*, whether printed in Romania,

France, or Russia, I do not know, *Le Figaro, France Soir,*
and, in perfectly recognizable English, the New York *Times,*
the *Herald Tribune, Time* and *Newsweek.* Mr. Prager, so
it developed, was quite right and Miss Chase quite wrong.
Edith bought the *Times,* and we bought the two magazines and gave them to her. The only restraint involved
was that of money. Foreign magazines are not exorbitant,
but Romanian salaries are not large, the foreign press is a
luxury, and Edith was contributing to the support of her
family. It is true that we did not see English language
papers on the street kiosks, but how many American news-
stands carry foreign papers and magazines as a matter of
course?

The reason, by the way, that so much French is spoken
in Romania is not only because it was for many years the
language of diplomacy but also because modern Romania
as such did not come into being until 1859. In 1877, with
the help of the French armies, she expelled the Turks and
has had a solid trade relation with her ally ever since, ex-
porting grain and importing heavy machinery.

Opening the *Times* that morning at breakfast I read
aloud an entertaining and reasonably scathing comment
on President Johnson in James Reston's column. Edith's
blue eyes widened. "But does the President *see* that?" she
asked. "You're damn right he does," said the doctor. "It
behooves him to know what's going on. Any President's
dream is re-election which means finger on the public pulse
and all that." Edith obviously considered this food for
thought. In a modest way we were doing a little brainwashing too. Foreign visitors inevitably do it even if not
deliberately. People talk about their way of life, their am-
bitions, their hopes, they show pictures . . . windows are
opened.

Mr. Prager had made his point. The iron in that curtain
is being melted down. One must hope the desirable process
will continue.

In our morning conference at the travel bureau I had

tried to be as honest as I could. The Romanians knew I had written books about trips Norton and I had taken—far-ranging, ever helpful Mr. Policano of New York had told them so—and since their job is to promote tourism they hoped I would write favorably about them. I said I would try to. "I am," I said, "temperamentally disposed to like countries we visit; I long to see the whole world. But as I see my job, it is to report as honestly as I can my personal reactions. They may not be those of other people, my conclusions may be wrong, but I can only do the best I know how."

That, Mr. Prager conceded, was understandable. "Maybe you and the doctor will see things you don't like," he said. "All we ask is that you treat us fairly. For instance this kind of thing . . . it's upsetting," and he laid on the table a clipping from an American newspaper in the Middle West whose correspondent had visited Romania. "We did everything we could to make his trip agreeable. Whatever he wanted to see, wherever he wanted to go, we arranged it for him, and then look." He pointed to a passage in the article. The reporter's approach, to put it kindly, was negative, but the dig that hurt was a supercilious remark about the streets in a small village being muddy. "Are there no muddy streets in American villages?" Mr. Prager asked, and his distress and puzzlement were obvious.

Norton laughed. "Mr. Prager, you must come to see us in New York sometime, our great metropolis . . . you should see our streets. They're normally pretty dirty and after a snowstorm . . . the filth and slush—the slippery mud where they're putting up new buildings. You'll feel very cheerful about Romanian thoroughfares."

Norton was right. In Bucharest the streets were as clean and well kept as they had been in Budapest. We might have wished the system for achieving such desirable results had been different when we saw work in progress that night but it is their system.

Our ambassador, William Crawford, was away when we

were in Bucharest but his chargé d'affaires, Joseph Neubert, and his wife invited us to dine. They have an attractive house, and we were six for dinner: the Neuberts, an American named Hunt, Shirley Froelich and ourselves. Mrs. Froelich's husband was out of town and we were sorry not to meet him but she was an enterprising woman who two years previously had started a school for diplomats' children. When she first opened it she had five pupils. When we were there she had thirty. The population explosion among American diplomats isn't *that* violent, but representatives of other countries stationed in Bucharest sent their children there as well and were deeply grateful to the able Mrs. Froelich.

We also met a Mr. and Mrs. Braun who came in after dinner. He is our cultural attaché, and Norton and I were impressed by the caliber of the four men present that evening, as well as our other chiefs of mission whom we met in that part of the world. They have had early training in Moscow and have a practical understanding of the Communist mind and Communist goals, and almost to a man they speak the language of the country in which they are posted, a far cry from the days when the commercial attaché at the American embassy in Stockholm, having been there for seven years, had not bothered to learn a word of Swedish.

Mr. Hunt was in Bucharest in the service of NBC and, more specifically, of Huntley and Brinkley, trying to set up a working frame for Chet Huntley, who was coming over to do a documentary. He said the Romanians were amiable and willing to co-operate, but their comprehension of the mysteries of American television was limited to the point of invisibility—not too many Americans understand it either—and the situation was further complicated by bureaucratic inefficiency and lethargy.

We ourselves were victims of the inefficiency part particularly when it came to cashing traveler's checks. Trying to get fifty dollars transformed into lei took fifty minutes.

It's the passports and the carbon paper. Every page of
the passport would be examined microscopically because
they could never learn where the information they required
was printed and then, once they'd fastened on that they
had to get the sheets of carbon organized in their little
pads. The idea of a repeating block had not occurred to
them. There were many sheets of carbon paper, and they
curled up on themselves and blew away. By the time you
had helped the cashier gather them up and get them in-
serted, the spontaneous impulse to buy the local merchandise had evaporated. We estimated that they lost several
million lei in sales because of the poky system.

One thing we learned at the Neuberts' dinner was that
the Romanians have decided that they now want the English version of their homeland spelled with an O. *Romania*,
not *Ru* as it has been for so many years. The reason is that
they wish to be associated with the Romans, the Latin
world, and they feel that psychologically Ru has a Russian
connotation. As we have seen they are loud in their praises
of their own Communist Party but as they strengthen their
ties with the West, the role of satellite begins to pall.
Furthermore, Romanians consider themselves a Latin civilization unaccountably surrounded by Slavs. Slavs have
many virtues; stanch, splendid people and all that, but
sophisticated, witty, urbane—hardly. Romania prides herself on having been the bridge between the exotic barbaric
Byzantine world and the modern West.

In accordance with this expressed desire, the United
States Department of State has issued orders to all our
missions that they are to use the preferred spelling, Romania.

The only hitch is that the Ro or Rumanians themselves
frequently forget it, and, as we saw on their own travel
folders, it may be Ro on the outside, Ru within, and Rou
down the back.

It was in returning to our hotel around midnight that
we saw how the streets are kept so clean. They are swept

with old-fashioned besom brooms, the kind used by witches
on Halloween, by women old and not so old. They sweep
up leaves and rubbish and dump it into big canvas sacks
on wheels, and then men come and roll them away and a
water wagon follows and washes down the gutters. It must
be a sad task, sweeping in the darkness in the dead of
night, but apparently many women apply for the job and
are grateful to get it. The results are enviable.

In planning our Romanian tour Norton and I had said
we would like to go to the churches of Moldavia, renowned
for their frescoes and also to the Danube Delta.

The river rises in the Black Forest and flows 1750 miles
into the Black Sea. Its three branches, Chilia, Sulina, and
Sfintu Gheorghe form the Danube Delta, an area of approximately 2700 square miles of extraordinary beauty. We
had read of its network of streams and channels, its weeping willows, white and yellow water lilies, of the great
oaks and shifting islands of reeds that stretch for miles
and that are the home of millions of birds including fla-
mingos and pelicans, cormorants and swans, and the great
aigrettes. Fish and game are there in their multitudes and
it is one of the magic places of the world. Unfortunately
we did not see it.

We also missed out on the churches of Moldavia, a
group of chapels in northern Romania dating back to the
fifteenth and sixteenth centuries. Their great interest lies
in their exterior frescoes. Scenes crowded with figures and
movement, many of them detailing battles with the Turks
showing the Romanians triumphant—wishful thinking, alas,
for once again God was on the side of the strongest bat-
talions. Considering the relatively rugged climate of the
area scholars and artists are still baffled as to how the
original brilliant colors have survived. They must have been
composed of a pigment lost to the world when the last of
the Moldavian craftsmen disappeared.

The delta and the churches were there long before Communism and the travel bureau people, naturally enough, were concerned with having us see their own achievements; the new hotels, for example, that have recently been built and of which they are justifiably proud. Yet it is only fair to say that our limited time was the deciding factor. Had we been able to stay in the country longer they would willingly have sped us to the goals we wanted to see and to which, I hope, we may someday journey.

Our tour was to start in the late afternoon and we spent the morning visiting the city, passing the Council of Ministers building—clean, good modern design, beautifully illuminated at night. We stopped at the National Art Gallery, a handsome structure erected in 1954. The exhibits are artfully hung and admirably lighted and the gallery boasts an exquisite pair of seventeenth-century wooden doors carved in linenfold and floral pattern.

They have a Rembrandt, three lesser El Grecos, and a marvelous Japanese Kano scroll of a hunting scene that is both delicate and spirited. Having recently seen Brueghel's *Massacre of the Innocents* in Vienna we were surprised to see it in Bucharest but were told it was a copy by Brueghel the younger. The sculpture I thought poor, especially a gargantuan statue of noble proletarian man with muscles of stevedore, brow of ape. What struck us as excellent was an exhibit of modern posters daring and imaginative in design. The rest of the work was largely nineteenth-century Romanian. There were many canvases by their famous Nicolae Grigorescu, a gentleman devoted to battle scenes and oxen. I preferred the latter but my real favorite, by another artist, was a charming conversation piece of ladies and gentlemen of the eighties sitting on a terrace at luncheon, servants in attendance. They were obviously well-to-do, and Edith said a little coldly that they were landlords. I suppose they were, in the sense that they owned property, but the jargon of Communism with its superior moral tone, is trying.

We had a little conversation one day on the subject of

the servant problem in America, and Edith answered that
Communists did not believe in servants because they did
not believe in exploitation. I'm afraid I let fly with a few
terse comments to the effect that if there was any exploitation in America it was the employers who were exploited,
and besides, Communists have waiters and chambermaids
and a kitchen staff in their hotels just like the rest of the
world. Probably, in theory, they are the ruling class, and
who would quibble so long as there is service?

On our first day, as we had started out to see something
of the city Edith had said that Mr. Prager would meet
us for luncheon at three o'clock. Our stomachs sank. To
fortify ourselves we sneaked a snack when our guide wasn't
looking. Beer and bread fair, salami delicious.

We were to lunch in a restaurant at Benesa, a suburb
adjacent to Bucharest, where they have established a folk
museum. It is a tiny village composed of authentic peasant
houses from different parts of the country and from different
periods. There was one from the north, built below grade;
the lower part sunk into the ground, the windows at ground
level. It had a big fireplace and in wintertime must have
been dark, snug, and highly aromatic. Nearby was a church
with amusing murals of specific punishments meted out to
transgressors. The innkeeper who watered the wine was
obliged to lug great heavy casks through eternity—one can
sense the satisfaction the defrauded artist took in painting
it—and there were gay naked ladies condemned to con-
sort with hideous demons for ever and ever.

At the restaurant we discovered that three o'clock luncheon was late even for Romania. There was nobody there
but ourselves and the time had been chosen only because
Mr. Prager was tied up in business meetings. The restaurant
has an enormous terrace, very pleasant, I imagine, in sum-
mertime. We were there in autumn so we ate inside downstairs in a kind of grillroom. Somewhat to my surprise vodka
is not common in Romania, but they do have a fine and

18 Edith Ilovici, our
Romanian guide.

19 Hotel Alpine, Romania.

20 Lunching at Predeal, where I received the little bouquet.

21   On the banks of the Danube. V for victory.

22   Beach and hotels at Mamaia on the Black Sea, Romania.

23   Shopping and restaurant complex, Mamaia.

24   Outdoor theater, Mamaia.

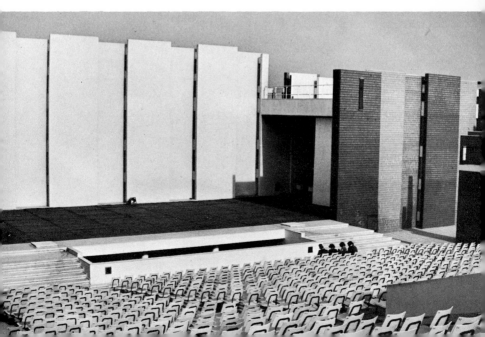

25   Adriana, our incandescent partisan.

26   The generous dispensers of hazelnuts.

potent plum brandy called Tuica. It is perhaps a little sweet as an apéritif, but one can become acclimated.

In the course of luncheon we fell to talking about education and Mr. Prager said that as a young man he had had to clean streets to pay his college tuition. Understandably he preferred the present system, whereby, if you pass the examinations, the State pays your way. He started no argument with that one.

We were sorry to leave him, but it was time to get under way as we had a reasonably long drive before nightfall. It was then, as we got into the car, that we had our first meeting with our lunatic driver, whom I will call Horia.

Although he spoke virtually no English and our Romanian was non-existent, we had the impression that he was rather an agreeable fellow. But as a driver he was a menace to life.

Heading north we passed the great Ploesti oil fields that were so fiercely bombed by the Allies and so savagely defended by the Axis powers during the war. The losses of planes and pilots on both sides were staggering.

Edith pointed to a monument we were driving past and said it marked the spot where one of the earliest Romanian pilots crashed his plane and died. "He went to France to learn to fly." There was something sweet in the proud way she said it. "He didn't learn well enough," said the doctor.

Our first stop was the Casino in the village of Sinaia. In the days when the village harbored royalty it was perhaps very gay, but its day has passed. In the large dining room the tablecloths looked to be freshly laid as though awaiting customers, but the atmosphere was glum and the only people around were two or three beatnik couples who looked as though they didn't have the price of a meal and didn't care. Foreigners are permitted to gamble, indeed, encouraged, for the State wants their money. The Romanians themselves are not allowed to do it. Edith did not seem to feel the situation unequitable. "We work hard for our money, it is better not to lose it. *We* don't *want* to gamble."

"Now listen, Edith," I said, "if that's the law, it's the law. I myself hate gambling, it bores me to death, but all over the world people love it, and Romanians must too. I should think they'd feel resentful, being deprived."

Edith smiled. Perhaps they *don't* mind. If you're conditioned to believe that the government knows best I suppose it saves you thought and inconvenience. In this instance it indubitably saves you money.

From the Casino the road starts to climb, winding up and up the mountain side. As it was dark by now and the drop fairly precipitous, I did not care to look. However we arrived safely at our destination, the Alpine, an enormous shabby hotel built in 1931. In the winter it is crowded, patronized by diplomats and tourists who come for the mountain scenery and the skiing.

The modernization and building of new hotels stand high on the country's priority list, and later on we were to see some that were truly impressive, but the Alpine—it has since been considerably spruced up—was that night a little bleak. However, one does not have very solid grounds for complaint. The rate for two without board comes to about $5.12 a day. Romanians themselves get twelve lei for the dollar, but the visitor is allowed eighteen.

Yet, despite economy and the fact that our room was large and reasonably comfortable, the doctor was feeling homesick. We changed for dinner. I teased my hair a bit, applied perfume, and put on my controversial mink jacket. "You look and smell like a capitalist," he said.

"How is it?"

"Very nice."

You couldn't call that garrulous, perhaps, but I was delighted he had noticed me at all. That man can diagnose coarctation of the aorta in a stranger at forty paces. His is the original X-ray eye, but if, after a much-needed, long, and costly seance at the hairdresser's, I say to him, "How do you like my hair? At least it's an improvement over yesterday, don't you think?" He says, "It looked all right yesterday." Let us hope it has nothing to do with their affection, but I believe men really do not see their wives much of the time. Form of self-preservation, I expect.

Edith, of course, noticed at once that I was gussied up from earlier in the day. "How very American," she said.

We teased her a little about her own wardrobe. She seemed to have an infinite number of changes, and one day I said to her, "Hey, I'm supposed to be the decadent capitalist, but you have all the clothes." She laughed. "Well, you see, I don't get much chance to rest, so I bathe and change my dress, and I feel refreshed." It was a reasonable explanation.

The atmosphere of the Alpine lounge we thought dreary. The lighting was meager, and a couple of proletarian beat-niks, unshaven and unwashed, were dictating to the juke-box. There was no other public room to flee to so we could not escape the blaring rock-and-roll and decided that a proletarian dictatorship is as unattractive as any other kind and worse-looking. Dinner was unfortunate, and the waiters, exceptionally young and wearing soiled jackets, were, we were told, students learning the trade before going back to school.

We had now been in three Communist countries, Czecho-slovakia, Hungary, and Romania. Our curiosity deepened. Why were they down at heel?

True, they had endured the convulsion of World War II with its attendant anguish and loss of life and property, but so had virtually the entire planet. Yet the West and Japan were booming. A further drawback that many of those lands had had to contend with however was the fact that for them the conflict did not cease in 1945. Thereafter they were grappling with Communism, either to embrace or re-ject it.

Perhaps another element in their slow convalescence was that, unlike a great part of the world, they had no tradition of unity and parliamentary government to revert to once the crisis has passed. Much of eastern Europe and the Balkan peninsula had been living for nearly five hundred years in feudal conditions under Turkish domination. It was not until 1912 that the last Turks were driven from Greek soil, and many still remain on Cyprus, which they consider home.

Such a historical experience requires a long period of recuperation, yet, interestingly enough, it is the two non-Communist lands of the area, Austria and Greece, which have advanced the furthest from the point of individual freedom and enterprise.

When we asked what had happened to the erstwhile "landlords," the aristocracy, we were assured they were in splendid shape. "Working, you know, and happy." From what we could learn, the working part was true. The intelligentsia and the moneyed class who had been antagonistic to Communism were working as laborers, usually at a distance from their old homes. Friends from other countries who send them packages report that sometimes they receive them, sometimes not. Those who are old enough and quiet enough survive on tiny state pensions and are forbidden to travel. Even if one should be able to manage financially, passports may be withheld indefinitely at the whim of the State, with no explanation offered.

In the course of our journey we met three or four elderly people, and they all said the same thing. "For ourselves we do not care, we have not long to live in any event, but we would like our children to get out. To get to countries where they would have opportunities and freedom." We did not hear that said in Yugoslavia, and those who said it elsewhere were sophisticates of another day, experienced in other governments and the ways of the West, and the children they referred to were for the most part middle-aged. It is possible that their grandchildren do not feel the same way.

By daylight the Alpine Hotel looked a great deal better. It is magnificently located on a mountain side overlooking other mountains and valleys and pine forests, and the weather was glorious. We went walking and admired the up-to-date ski tow and could well imagine that it was an ideal spot for winter sports. In that realm Romania will surely attract tourists and winter-sports enthusiasts, for the equipment is good, the whole Prahova Valley is very beautiful, and the prices are extremely reasonable.

These are not luxury resorts, they are no match for Klosters and Gstaad and Garmisch-Partenkirchen, or Vail in the United States, but they are exhilarating places and now that tourists are welcome in eastern Europe they are bound to draw people who will have enjoyable and affordable holidays. They will also be cozy when indoors. Methane gas brought from Transylvania is used for heating and is amazingly cheap. A small apartment may be kept warm the entire winter for about $2.77.

Romanians themselves obviously take advantage of their natural resources, and the Saturday we were there several busloads of trippers arrived, even though no snow had yet fallen, and amused themselves by riding up the ski lift and walking down the mountain side.

Edith had said something about a sporting club she and her family belonged to, and Norton and I had unthinkingly assumed it to be like a private club at home, which of course was not the case.

Clubs are extensions of the factory or office or store where one works. The big printing plant we had seen in Bucharest, for example, has its own gymnasium in town and hotels or rest houses for outdoor sports in the country.

This kind of recreation involves more togetherness and supervision than many people care for, and indeed, much of the value of recreation lies precisely in getting away from those with whom one passes one's daily life. But within their limits the clubs are admirably equipped. All the paraphernalia needed, canoes or skis or tennis rackets, whatever it may be, is provided free of charge. In the winter resorts there is even warm clothing for the children. No child, or grownup either, for that matter, misses out on the fun because of lack of funds.

Perhaps it is because under the old systems the general public had little opportunity for play and athletics that the Communist-Socialist regimes produce such dedicated sports enthusiasts.

So too did Hitler Germany with all its Strength through Joy. To me there is something ludicrous in brawny health groups rushing about in their undershirts tossing soccer balls, hiking en masse over the mountain passes, or thrashing the waves in an Olympic pool, but I am not athletically inclined and it may be that much genuine pleasure is passing me by.

To accommodate some of their athletic activity the Romanians in four months' time built a sports stadium seating 30,000 people. They did it through what they call voluntary, and we would call forced, labor. The difference between Communism and capitalism is largely one of semantics. Of the same action they say liberate, we say enslave; they say voluntary, we say forced . . . so it goes.

In any event the stadium got built so quickly because all the schools sent groups of students including girls to work on it after classes. It was voluntary except you couldn't refuse. We were to find that the same custom prevails in Bulgaria and there they send them into the fields at harvest time as well. The harvesting assignment is considered a plum as it keeps the scholars from the classroom, a fate devoutly to be wished for. Actually it probably does the young people more good than harm . . . all that fresh air while they are learning something about agriculture as well. Norton and I chuckled when we thought of the reaction of American parents—of American labor unions too—if they heard children were being pressed, and for free, into the service of the State.

Our next stop was a visit to Peles Castle in Sinaia. This

is a curiosity a visitor should not miss. I believe nothing quite like it exists anywhere else which some people may consider very fortunate. Still it is instructive to see how the other half lives or lived.

In 1866 a German prince, Karl of Hohenzollern, came to the Romanian throne, assuming the name of Carol. In 1873 the castle was begun by a Viennese architect, Wilhelm Doderer, but it was added to and tinkered with by assorted builders up until 1914. The First World War was an appalling holocaust, but one good thing it did do: it brought to a halt the building of Peles. A local guidebook gives a description of its style, which is perhaps best summarized as Turn of the Century Hideous but Non-Monotonous. It doesn't have *time* to be. The castle, and I quote from a brochure, "built of stone, timber, brick and marble has 160 rooms. The predominant style is that of the German Renaissance, but there are also elements of the Italian Renaissance, the German Baroque, the French Rococo and the Spanish-Moorish style. The building has terraces in the Italian Renaissance style, arranged like an amphitheatre, with statues and fountains." The architects were global in outlook if not discriminating in taste. The magnificent mountain scenery is all but obliterated by the heavy stained-glass windows through which the sunlight filters weakly onto sets of massive beer steins and a pretty comprehensive collection of armor from all over the world.

The central hall is three stories high, carpeted, with balconies running around it, all open to the sky. There *is* a roof that pulls over it in case of rain. The whole palace writhes with carving; a Moorish Hall with arabesques of colored stucco, a Turkish cozy corner, Indian furniture so intensively carved it seems to be nothing but holes held together by morsels of dark wood inlaid with mother of pearl. There is a Florentine Hall with heavy ebony cabinets set in mosaics, a French salon, and one redeeming feature, a pretty, small rococo theater seating sixty. But the general impression is of suffocation, of thick glutinous Teutonic taste, a sort of womb of Nazism.

The guidebook observes coldly: "It is interesting to note that none of the many rooms of this castle and none of the items to be found in them represent Romanian art or any element of Romania's extremely rich folklore. This is yet another expression of the former royal family's disdain for the Romanian people whom they exploited so cruelly and whose interests they betrayed."

The comment is understandable, and you don't have to be Romanian or Communist to feel that given such rulers as Carol and Michael and Marie and Madame Lupescu, the time was ripe for a change.

Peles is a great tourist attraction, and the day we were there enormous crowds were shuffling through it, their heads turning docilely as guides pointed out items they should appreciate.

I couldn't help wishing that all those people had the money, the freedom and, obviously, the inclination to travel to other parts of the world to see some of the truly beautiful castles and museums that delight the eye and refresh the mind. Peles gives royalty *too* bad a name.

The place to go for luncheon is Predeal, where Norton thought I behaved rudely because I complained about the ubiquitous transistor blaring. Edith kindly got it quieted down, and a slightly tipsy gent of great charm came over to our table to apologize—it was his radio—and presented me with a little bouquet of autumn crocus.

Driving from Predeal to Brashov we passed more of those buildings called Casa de Cultura. Edith tried to explain them to us but we never did grasp exactly what transpires within. They are, we think, small town halls for amateur theatricals and meetings and probably indoctrination centers where young people gather to listen to long, stupefyingly dull lectures on the virtues of Communism. However, that is only a guess.

From Predeal we drove to Brashov, a place we fell in

love with. To begin with the hotel was the cleanest we had been in, and our room was quiet and pretty, overlooking a park and a hillside. The clientele was far superior to that of the Alpine. At dinner the men wore ties and jackets, and many of the women were in cocktail frocks. Not Dior and Givenchy, but the trend was sprightly. There was a band and a man who sang with it. He was a middle-aged party wearing steel-rimmed spectacles, who crooned "O Sole Mio" into a mike gripped close to his chest and then, ripping off the specs, swung into "The Merry Widow Waltz." In Romania the old ones are the best although the selection may be capricious, depending on the mood of the government. Sometimes the Communist bloc is allowed current American successes, sometimes not. Theirs is the kind of unpredictable reasoning that, in Russia, led to the banning of *Hello, Dolly!*

After dinner we strolled up the street and across the square to the Carpathian Deer, an extraordinary building. From the outside it doesn't look particularly large, but upstairs there is an enormous dining room, seating, I should think, easily a thousand, and downstairs another room of equal dimensions where a wine festival was going on. There was a tremendous crowd, the tables were loaded with bottles, and the room was crisscrossed with strings and wires from which hung tiny pennants and confetti. We listened to the music and watched the folk dancing for a while and then went down another flight to explore the wine cellar lined with gigantic casks. For our taste the wine was too sweet, but the atmosphere was festive, and Brashov, we decided, appreciated the good life.

Returning to the hotel to reach our elevator, we were obliged to pass through the dining room where a large wedding dinner was in progress. It was late, and, still sitting at table, the bride looked tired and bored. I should think so. She undoubtedly had something else in mind. That crowd of guests eating and drinking until all hours . . . what kind of wedding night was that?

We gathered that for big parties such as the wedding banquet everyone chips in. Average salaries in the Communist countries are not large, and with taxes and expenses it is difficult to save anything. Theoretically, of course, you don't have to, the State takes care of you in your old age. The State is promising to take more and more care of us here in the United States, too, but a private nest egg would still seem a prudent precaution.

Explored by daylight Brashov turned out to be a pretty town with a lighthearted spirit; much more appealing, we thought, than Bucharest. Like Sinaia, it too is a ski resort with excellent runs in the surrounding mountains.

As it was Sunday morning, I said to Edith I would like to go to church, so we went down the street to Black Church, an ancient edifice much restored. The organ music and singing were very good. Excepting the weddings and funerals of my friends I rarely attend church services at home but in the countries of Godless Communism I went every Sunday to see what the atheists were up to. All I can say is that capitalist and right-wing propaganda to the contrary every church in every country we visited was wide open: Orthodox, Catholic, Jewish, and Protestant. They were not very full, and the congregation was, for the most part, elderly. By and large the governments incline to the theory that "religion is the opiate of the people." It is not taught in schools, but you can attend the service of your choice or tradition if you want to and woe does not betide you.

We wondered aloud how, without some religious background, you are to comprehend three quarters of the world's art or the allusions of literature. Edith assured us, however that people are familiar with Christian beliefs, or those of any other religion, as their history of art classes are comprehensive and well attended. The life of Christ and other comparable figures is taught as history, not liturgics, and as long as the older generation lives, they will continue to pass on to their descendants their own convictions.

Norton and I were interested in the Communist attitude toward religion, but we did get rather a jolt on learning that they do not celebrate Christmas.

If you are not interested in the birth of Christ, that is understandable; neither are millions of other people; Mohammedans, Buddists, Confucians . . . any number of religions; but it is a charming and heart-warming story, and it seems too bad to deprive children of so much mystery and delight.

In the countries of the West, especially the Anglo-Saxon countries, Christmas has degenerated into a commercial debauch, and whoever imagined the three kings and their gifts would probably today be aghast at the floodtide of hysteria, debts, exhaustion, and satiety that his moving and generous conceit has fathered.

Yet while the idea of presents is delicious those brought by the Kings, and which presumably originated the avalanche, always seemed to me curiously ill advised. The Magi were, after all, going to call upon a baby and what did they take? Gold, frankincense and myrrh. No rattles, no strings of bright beads, no soft cuddly stuffed animals. He did have live ones around but one can only conclude that though the Kings may have been wise men they didn't have much common sense. The baby must have thought them balmy.

As far as Christmas observance in Romania is concerned, I believe I am right in saying that one may stay home if one wants to and not be docked a day's pay, but that covers Yule. They do have two big holidays early in the year, and those who can manage it usually bridge the day in between just as those of us who can get away with it sneak the Friday after Thanksgiving, making a very respectable weekend.

Yet I do not think that the devout should be downcast over the turn of religious affairs in Communist countries. Religion has been heavy industry since we emerged from the ooze and swung down from the trees. The wealth of the temples and priests since the dawn of antiquity has been incalculable (one reason Communists are against them) and their power and influence awesome. And since we are willing slaves to our prejudices and superstitions it is unlikely that a political system constantly shifting and changing and much derided will prevail against deep-rooted beliefs to any impressive extent.

Your true believer is even reluctant to follow a change of heart in his own high command as witness what happened with the Vatican's switch of policy on fish. Despite its about-face on the subject, there are still Catholics who are as fearful of eating meat on Friday as is a timid swimmer of stepping into the surf. And on that score it may be said that it is hard to fathom which was the more peculiar, the edict itself or the suspension of reason that caused millions of people to adhere to it through the centuries.

And all those who gave things up for Lent! Was it truly kind to deprive them of the sense of virtue that was theirs because they had gone without for forty days? It's enough to make the older generations, who did all the sacrificing, very much annoyed with the younger, who can now have their souls saved and their characters strengthened by abstaining from their cherished victuals for only two days, Ash Wednesday and Good Friday.

In Communist countries with predominantly Catholic populations the divided loyalty imposed on people must be the source of much soul-searching. It is understandable that those creeds should be the two great antagonists. They are battling for the same prize; control of the human mind.

When Edith and I returned from Black Church, we went to visit the new wing of the Carpathi Hotel. Seven stories high, 200 rooms, it made up for the shortcomings of all the other hotels we had stayed in.

It was not yet open for business, so I cannot report on the service; but they obviously intended it to be good. Serving kitchens and pantries on every floor, the most modern kind of linen rooms and laundry chutes, outlets for electric appliances galore. The rooms were fresh, comfortable, attractively furnished and the baths super-American. The view from every window was delightful, overlooking either a pretty park and wooded hillside or the velvety roofs of old Brashov. The prices were tender. Double rooms $5.00 a day, suites $10.00, and a truly magnificent suite on the top floor with balconies and a charming little Japanese garden approximately $13.00. That one, the lady manager told us, was available to anyone when empty, but it was planned with an eye to visiting diplomats.

It did occur to us that there might be hidden microphones, but who wouldn't put up with a little bugging in exchange for so much comfort and charm? One could start right out by saying in heartfelt tones, "What an entrancing spot!" and hope that, satisfied, the government agents in their hideout in the cellar would turn off the tape.

From the Carpathi we went to lunch in the country at the Poiana, which means meadow. It is an enormous hotel, and the surrounding meadow is enormous too, the People's quite beautiful playground reached, for the most part, by the People's buses and ruined by the People's transistor radios.

The Poiana boasts several restaurants, and we drank an apéritif on the terrace of one of the outside ones and then went upstairs to lunch. The wings of the hotel stretch forever, and hundreds of rooms open off the long corridors.

In the large dining room we had a small table to ourselves bedecked with a little American flag in a cellophane envelope.

In all the Balkan countries they break out these little flags for their visitors and it is interesting to see how many people from the Western world are burrowing for both business and pleasure through lands which many Western governments still regard with uneasiness.

We lunched on sarmale, a delicate and delicious dish of stuffed cabbage and watched an enormously long table down the center of the room fill up with members of a medical congress that was in progress in the hotel. These congresses or conventions are well attended, as the delegates' expenses are paid in addition to their regular salaries, which go to their families.

Norton and I were amused when Edith called out to one of the doctors whom she knew, addressing him as Tovarich. To us it seemed theatrical but apparently the term is still quite common and it is only recently that the old-fashioned Monsieur and Madame and their equivalents have been permitted to creep back into usage. They were considered bourgeois. I thought of the days of the French Revolution, when, through fear that courtesy might survive, everyone was addressed as Citizen, including that prominent couple hapless Citizen and Citizeness Louis and Marie Antoinette Capet.

Returning to Bucharest Sunday afternoon in our car, a Russian Volga, was a pleasure, if you don't count the nervous tension induced by our driver. There was virtually no traffic: some horse-drawn vehicles, a few motorcycles, a few bicycles, *very* few cars. Most of them are government-owned, and one can tell them by their license plates. High numbers . . . the Feds.

I appreciate that a lack of automobiles indicates a comparatively weak industrial economy, and I can only say that it is delightful, provided of course that one possesses the luxury oneself.

A few people do, since in Communist countries there are just as many classes as there are in the rest of the world. This was borne in upon us that night. Edith was returning to her family, and Norton and I were dining alone. We asked her about the Beer Cart, an old restaurant with dark wood, marble columns, and stained-glass windows that we had seen on our first day's sightseeing, but she shook her head. "Not on Sunday night." That, we gathered, was proletarian night, and we might be contaminated. At her suggestion we went instead to the Lido and found it extremely pleasant. We dined in the garden beside a big pool, and the linen, silver, food, and service were exemplary, in the tradition of any topflight restaurant anywhere. Norton says that as he recalls the bill it was relatively expensive, although nothing like what the same food and service would have cost in the United States.

The next morning, Horia pointed the nose of the Volga toward the east and we set off for Constanta and Mamaia, the resorts on the Black Sea. Much of the road lay through farmland, and it was interesting to speculate on the gradual evolution that is taking place in Communist agriculture.

Ten years ago a Romanian farmer was obliged to give everything he raised to the government. Produce, livestock, everything.

Happily the system is changing. A farmer may now own chickens and a cow of his own. Any surplus raised over the established quota he is allowed to keep. Damn gracious of the government! Still, step by infinitesimal step, an egg at a time, Communism is inching toward the ways of capitalism.

I am not one to think our system sacrosanct and apparently neither is our own government if the growing tendency of cradle to grave insurance may be considered inching leftward, but I do think our way—possessing something of one's very own—is more solidly based on human behavior and yearning than that of the other team. If we are to believe the anthropologists, and in this instance their observations would appear sound, the territorial instinct of living creatures is stronger than that of sex or self-preservation. What is cruelly ironic is that millions of people have been persecuted and in the Ukraine, deliberately starved to death, while waiting for the wheel to come full circle.

One individual whom Communism has not yet curbed is Horia. Through the rich Romanian farmland he was at his most dynamic. He speeded up to seventy miles an hour, passing on turns and missing oncoming cars by inches. In order to stop short of a barrier at a grade crossing, lowered while a train was passing, he jammed on the brakes with such force that we were thrown to the floor, and he sat, shoulders hunched, hands gripping the steering wheel, gasping from his exertions. Norton and I thought that maybe he was unhappy at home and wished to commit suicide, but we didn't feel it fair for him to endanger his compatriots, not to mention us, en route to his own oblivion.

He was indignant at our lack of trust and had Edith translate his credentials for us. In Romania a chauffeur has four tickets on his license. Accident by accident they are removed. If he loses all four he loses his license. After twenty years behind the wheel Horia claimed to be still intact. If he was telling the truth they must allow considerable latitude on the Romanian roads. Perhaps a certain amount of slaughter is permissible before the authorities frown.

That bright morning, aiming for a goose he missed it but did exterminate two chickens. Their owner saw him do it, too, and came running from his house, waving his fists and shouting. If he saw our license number and recognized it as one of the State-owned cars I would be surprised if he entered any complaint. Horia almost nailed a horse, and we felt that surely on the next spurt, with any luck, he would wing a child.

If a visitor has traveled in Portugal, Italy, and Japan, where horrendous drivers are the norm, he may be relatively unflappable. If he has not had this grim apprenticeship, he is apt to be shaken by Horia.

At Hirsova, where we crossed the Danube on a barge and lunched at a little restaurant on the river bank, we discovered we had a flat tire. It had evidently deflated on the ferry, and it was a pure fluke that it had not blown on our wild drive.

The food was not good, but the wine, a local Riesling called Odobesti, was very pleasant. Leaving Norton to take the pictures of a group of farmers at the next table, who were holding up their fingers in Sir Winston Churchill's V for victory sign, Edith and I retired for a few minutes. The amenities were primitive in the extreme—the good old rudimentary hole in the ground, and dirty. Edith, I could see, felt apologetic about it. "Never mind," I said comfortingly, "I've seen it often, it's the same in Africa."

"But we are not in Africa," she cried. Tovarichism can go just so far.

Sensing I had been tactless, I added hastily, "But in Asia, in Asia too. And in Japan, in the best hotels." That is true, but there one has a choice of Western or Oriental style, and everything is clean.

Once arrived at the Black Sea ports we found that cleanliness was a basic virtue. We drove through Eforie, a health spa known for its mud baths but more memorable for its fragrance. Great beds of petunias stretched along the wide seaside boulevard, and the air was sweet with perfume. There are those who claim that petunias have no odor. When there are that many of them, they have. Constanta or Constanza, thirteen kilometers to the north, is an ancient community dating from 600 B.C Here Ovid came in 8 A.D., when driven into exile by the Emperor Augustus, a moral man who had grudgingly tolerated *Ars amattoria* but balked when the poet became involved—if apparently only as a bystander—in some scandal involving the royal house. In 8 A.D. the town was known as Tomis, and Ovid was not happy there. A brilliantly cultivated man, moving in the highest social and intellectual circles of Rome, he suddenly found himself in the Scratch Gravel, Indiana, of the day, and it palled. Today it does not strike one as a particularly sophisticated center either but it is only supposed to be a resort town and its archaeological museum, although it houses many reproductions, is interesting. We gnashed our teeth in frustration when we could not see an avenue of exquisite mosaics recently unearthed, but as work was still in progress, it was hidden behind a long wooden wall. Should you go there, however, let us hope that the walls, like those of Jericho, will have come tumbling down.

There is also a mosque built originally in 1389, but it has been so restored and renovated that it has little appeal. The Christian church is only one hundred years old, but the exterior frescoes are copied after those of Moldavia, so that at least one gets an idea of what the ancient monasteries were like.

Mamaia, our final destination is, in its field, a triumphant achievement. It is a splendid stretch of beach, a spit of land over three miles long with the sea on one side and a freshwater lake, Lake Siutghiol, on the other. The great virtue of the community that has been built there is its sense of spaciousness.

In Florida and I believe also in South America, most of the great sweeping beaches are lined with hotels and apartment houses cheek by jowl. In Mamaia they have erected only seven hotels. They are very large but each one is surrounded by an enormous open area and although that is where they have placed the restaurants and shops the units are low, the view, the light and the air unimpeded.

We stopped at the oldest hotel, the International. It was built in 1937, and our room and bath were spacious. The restaurant was unusually inviting. Distinctly *not* People's State Gray. The white tablecloths positively glistened, and the chairs, all with arms and very comfortable, were upholstered in a soft, pretty shade of blue.

Our last luncheon there was memorable. "Not well balanced," said Edith, but she wanted to make sure we tried certain Romanian specialties and had arranged with the chef to serve us eggs in pastry shells, eggplant and cheese patties in a flaky crust, and a mysterious and wonderful concoction of cream and mushrooms. Dinner seemed unnecessary.

We gathered that the International was grander than the other hotels which had been built more recently to accommodate more people at less expense. Their rooms had

showers but no private baths. They all had balconies, however, boundless light and air, and a view over the water,
either sea or lake.

With the exception of the International, these pleasures
are available only four months a year. The rest of the time
it is too cold to make beach life enjoyable, and probably
even the government cannot afford the luxury of accom-
modating a few rare snowbirds.

One afternoon, as we were strolling back from a brief
promenade, I said to Edith, "What's the name of our hotel?
I know it begins with *i*, but I forget what it is. The Imperial?" She stared at me wide-eyed. "The Imperial? Here
in Romania? What have you said?" We both burst out
laughing. Yet in Budapest, even more Communistic, they
have a Royal.

Actually it's a wonder the Romanians *don't* use royal or
imperial; they embrace everything except monarchy. The
government refers to itself as The Communist Party of The
Socialist Republic of Romania, and they consider that theirs
is a democratic system. What could they lose with a dash
of royalty?

The Mamaia beach is very wide, scrupulously clean, and
has a good deal of bush planting, forming alcoves where
two might obtain a modicum of privacy. We were happy
to see young people at their games, because we could not
overcome a slight sense of regimentation. It was reassuring
to see nature still on the march. When the State doles out
the jobs and the money and the holidays and the permission to take them *if* you have behaved yourself—the feeling
of Big Brotherism is pervasive despite the sand and sea,
sun and air.

Still, whether it seems desirable to us or not, the Communist bloc may have the key to the recreation of the
future. Certainly if the population is not curbed the only
way people will be able to get fresh air, sports, exercise,
and a general change of pace in their daily lives will be to
get them en masse: vast groups replacing one another at

mountain and seaside resorts and in the stadiums. Who knows? They may even enjoy it.

In the course of my springtime flit to France and Spain I met a young Swedish girl who was telling me about a place that seemed to be a kind of camping hotel. Tennis courts, a great central swimming pool, lots of gay people . . . "Super!" was her comment. "It sounds a lot of fun," I said, "although I shouldn't imagine there's much privacy."

"But you don't need it," she cried. "Everything is there!" Everything and everybody.

One particularly nice thing at Mamaia was the outdoor theater. Painted in pastel colors, seating surprisingly few people, it was very attractive, and I was sorry there were no performances going on while we were there. Although it was the latter part of September the bathing was still good, but the actors were out of season. Probably back in Bucharest, rehearsing for fall openings.

In other quarters entertainment was rampant. The Melody night club was wide open, and whatever the restrictions may be in other Communist communities, they were frugging in Mamaia. Edith spoke of other dances, too, that Dr. Brown and I, in our quiet backwater New York, had never heard of. The Shake, The "Medicine" . . . possibly they are well known to habitués of discothèques but not to us. Not that my curiosity wouldn't lead me to visit one, but when I mention it the doctor looks at me as if he were about to call one of the city's leading psychiatrists into consultation.

From what I understand of these haunts from those who have ventured into them, the noise is deafening, so I guess the Melody was In. The *de rigueur* brain-paralyzing din roared relentlessly on into the small hours. Norton had ordered champagne to act as a kind of anesthetic, and the acts, while not good, were at least an interlude of relative quiet. The most successful was performed by a small totally boneless young woman who, costumed as a cobra, wrapped herself around the torso of her male partner. There were a couple of tap dancers too, but we decided the Messrs. Draper and Astaire had nothing to worry about. Eastern Europe is a rich field for some of our more enterprising entertainment agencies to mine.

The world of hairdressing is another vacuum in dire need of expert attention. I had a shampoo in Mamaia, and there was only one tap with running water in the establishment. The girls poured water over your head from little tin mugs which they were obliged constantly to replenish, and setting was not their forte.

My suggestion to the omnipotent rulers of the Free Democratic Socialist Republic People's States is to send their hairdressers scampering right back into the arms of decadent old capitalism to learn their trade if they don't want to face counter-revolution from frustrated, outraged women when they discover what *can* be done in that line of business. Since the Communist leaders give our society only about twenty years before they bury us, what can they lose? Our toes and the ends of the hair of Soviet women will be turning up together.

As I was walking back to our hotel along the waterfront after my hairdressing disaster, a woman crossed the road to ask me in French where I had bought my black handbag. It was not for herself, she said, but for her companion, who was sitting on a coping across the way watching us. I told her it came from New York, and she asked if I would sell it. When I replied that I couldn't do that as I needed it for traveling she asked if I had anything else I wanted to sell. I was sorry I said but traveling by air I had very little. She seemed even sorrier than I but thanked me politely and returned to her friend. It was a curious little episode but it is true I think that consumer goods are still comparatively scarce and not of first-rate quality, so that even if a woman has a little money there is nothing particularly tempting on which she can spend it. Certainly not on iron curtain shoes, they are frights.

As far as the bag was concerned, the lady had a sharp eye. It was the best I have ever found for traveling. Of fabric rather than of leather, it had an infinity of pockets and compartments and was so constructed that when folded it was a rather shallow normal-sized handbag. Unsnapped and dropped to its full length it formed a capacious carry-all for books, souvenirs, packages, sandwiches, what have you. I bought mine at Bonwit Teller in New York.

An excellent buy in Romania would be one of the small rugs that are woven in charming colors and designs. The price varies with the size; a small one costs about $50. But there again, you are faced with the problem of transportation. They are too heavy to carry if traveling by air and the red tape involved in getting anything out of the country is an instant deterrent to having them sent. With great thoughtfulness and generosity Edith insisted that I accept from her a small, very pretty woven square that could serve many decorative purposes. The colorful native embroidery is done with skill, but from the tourist point of view those blouses with the drawstring neckline and full sleeves once popular in the Western world are no longer worn. If they could be restyled by someone with a sound fashion sense they would be a popular item for export.

Some unexpected imports were cosmetics. In one of the shops in Mamaia I walked through a large cosmetics department where the products of the Mesdames Arden, Rubinstein, and other American manufacturers were on sale. An American lipstick cost in lei the equivalent of $5.00. The ladies would appreciate a reduction, and the Romanian commercial gentlemen should see that they get it, since, in the long run, it is they who profit from looking at prettily made up women.

A fashion that was amusing and indigenous was the children's hats shaped like little jockey caps in a fabric so soft I took it to be suede. Edith said they were made from the bark of a tree that grows in Transylvania. We bought four for small fry of our acquaintance.

It was our last day in Romania and we left Mamaia driving back to Bucharest behind our suicidal Horia. We were flying that evening to Sofia and looked forward with relief to the safety of a stable plane.

Edith's husband, a civil engineer and an attractive man, came to the hotel to meet her and take her home. We parted from her with genuine regret. She was our first friend in a strange world. She had been informative, receptive, warmhearted, and fun, and we felt that our brief encounter was proof that left to themselves, unharassed by propaganda, basically sympathetic people will always draw together.

CHAPTER FOUR

Bulgaria

Our mood of benignity was dissipated at the airport when we found that although there were only six passengers on the plane we would have to pay an excess luggage charge of five dollars. Not much perhaps but for what? Muttering, we handed over our lei. When the man says "Pay" at an airport, you're powerless.

I had already been a little put off by the sight of pilot hurrying by in his shirt sleeves. There are times when informal clothes are the only possible thing—astronauts are apparently far better off orbiting in their underwear—but on a cool evening a commercial pilot, hatless and in his shirt sleeves, creates unease. Are the skies turbulent? Is he stripped for action? Or, if he is all that dégagé maybe the maintenance of the plane is too?

As matters turned out, it was not. We were borne aloft, and successfully despite our man's costume, in a Russian Tupelev II. The Tupelev II is utilitarian. It grinds through the air with a steady reassuring burr, but the seats do not recline. One is obliged to sit bolt upright. The safety belts are dubious, and you feel that one good bump and they'll fly apart. Finally, there are no announcements. Absolutely none. I have often felt that at home in the United States we tend to overdo the graciousness—the crew can't be *that*

ecstatic to have us aboard—and we might tone down the
welcome and farewell a trifle and still not be boorish. But
not to have a *word* addressed to you . . . no little informative snippet as to altitude and estimated time of arrival and when they will be breaking out the goodies . . .
seems downright surly.

We rose from the ground into Romanian air, flew about
forty-five minutes and descended through Bulgarian air to
the Sofia terminal, where we were met by a gentleman
who presented me with three stalks of gladioli and by our
Bulgarian guide, Adriana.

Adriana was on the short side. She had long black hair,
full melting eyes with the kind of lids I think of as Turkish,
and a silhouette not reminiscent of a greyhound. But she
had an overflowing heart and a brisk way with officials if
she considered we weren't receiving from them the last full
measure not only of devotion but of co-operation and service.

As our acquaintanceship progressed I was glad to have
said nothing about sloe Turkish eyes. A Turk to a Bulgarian
as we quickly learned is standard opposition; cat to dog,
red rag to bull, damn Yankee to professional Southerner.
They hate 'em. Considering the Turkish behavior during
the five hundred years in which they dominated the Balkan
peninsula, the sentiment is understandable. Adriana was
positively incandescent with partisanship. The barricades
were her spiritual home, guerrilla warfare her element.

Obviously we did not learn all this at the airport. There
our attention centered on our vaccination certificates—the
Bulgarians place considerable stress on them—and getting
ourselves through customs.

Driving to the hotel we passed two or three attractive
restaurants all doing business at 11:30 P.M., and when we
commented on how gay the city looked, Adriana explained
that their national holiday had occurred two weeks before,
adding "Tomorrow comes Tito." The decorations were doing
double duty.

In Sofia *the* hotel is the Balkan. It is of vast proportions, shabby and seemingly very ancient. The bottom of the bathtub was in such condition that our bathing was perforce confined to cat washes. The shaft which housed the elevator had big holes in the plaster and we concluded the hotel must have been erected by the Turks in the early days of their occupation, around 1400. We asked Adriana how old it was but realized she did not understand what we meant, for she said it had been built in 1958. A couple of days later I asked the doorman, an elderly party who I felt would have some historical knowledge of the native architecture, "When was the hotel put up?" "Nineteen-fifty-eight" he said. It seemed inconceivable that any building could have got that run-down in seven years, but the Balkan did it. It has to be constructed of papier mâché, flour, and water.

In keeping with the exterior proportions, our room too was enormous and overlooked a huge, quiet courtyard, really a walled square, with a small and authentically ancient church in the middle. "It is romantic," said Adriana. We agreed. "It dates from the Roman period," she explained. That too.

We asked if we could have a couple of bottles of beer and the room waiter shook his head, which didn't surprise us, as it was getting late. "He'll bring it right away," Adriana assured us. "But he said no." She laughed. "Oh I forgot, you do not know. In Bulgaria we shake our heads when we mean yes and nod when we mean no." To each his own.

The beer arrived shortly, borne by the most cheerful of gnomes. "Hello there, how are you?" he cried gaily. We said we were fine. "That's good. I'm glad!" In Bulgaria they care. The cloth covering the tray was filthy, but we rose above it and beamed at our new-found friend.

In the morning, driving out of the city en route to Rila Monastery, we passed groups of young women who looked as though they might be secretaries and salesgirls all hurrying in one direction, all carrying small flags for waving purposes. They were en route to their spontaneous demonstration of affection and of loyalty to Tito, who would soon be passing by.

They made me think, in reverse, of a time President Kennedy was in New York. Coming out of a Park Avenue office building at lunchtime, I said to the man I was with, "He'll be along any minute, let's wait and see him." Sure enough in five or ten minutes the motorcycle cops heading the cavalcade came roaring toward us, and moments later the President's car appeared, the top down, the President himself sitting up on the back of the seat. He whizzed past, and we got a brief but reasonably satisfactory glimpse of glory. I was content enough, but my cynical companion shrugged. "Big deal," he said. "Let's eat." Whatever the Bulgarian young ladies' personal reactions to Tito, they probably kept them to themselves and waved with a will.

We were interested in the Bulgarian-Yugoslav *pas de deux* largely because of the difference in shadings in our own dealings with the two countries. With National Communist Yugoslavia we have a warm, well, comparatively warm, relationship, but through the years Bulgaria has been mean to us. From 1950 until 1959 we weren't even speaking. Then, when we did reopen our legation, it was one of those that patriotic students "spontaneously" stoned and vandalized with gusto. Our representative, the Honorable Nathaniel Davis is a minister plenipotentiary, the only one we possess, and it means that he has unlimited power to negotiate and act on behalf of the United States.

Unlike Romania, which is a good deal more flexible and independent in her relations with Russia, Bulgaria willingly snuggles into the great bear's embrace and gets lots of aid for doing it. The doctor approved of the arrangement. "High time the Russians did a little dishing out," he observed. "Lets *us* off the hook for a change."

Now, however, the Bulgarians are beginning to woo us. They have tobacco, of which we import only about a million dollars' worth a year, whereas our trade with Greece, Turkey, and Yugoslavia nets those countries somewhere in the desirable neighborhood of $100,000,000. Bulgaria is now busy explaining that she doesn't care either how many Americans develop lung cancer just so long as she rakes in the leva. There are two leva to the dollar and their subdivision is a comical little thing called stotinki or, inevitably, stinkies, by Americans. The Bulgars would like to exchange them in a rich tide of Yankee dollars.

Apparently our government is nodding in avuncular fashion but saying things like, "Stop falsely implicating our ministers in phony, fabricated international deals, stop throwing stones at our embassy, and stop jamming the Voice of America. *Then* maybe we'll do business with you."

We were interested to see the actual tobacco growing in the fields, drying on racks, and hanging in bundles, along with bunches of red peppers, against the sunny whitewashed walls of the farmhouses.

As far as we could gather, the peasants of Bulgaria have more independence than their Romanian counterparts. They sometimes own the land immediately adjacent to their houses and when they want to build they put up one third of the cost, the state two thirds, which, in time, is paid off on a mortgage basis and the house then belongs to them.

This is not to say that they do not have co-operative farms. They do, and the state takes and disposes of the produce. The co-operative stores and service units on those farms are staffed, for the most part, by formerly independent craftsmen and professional people who may or may not like the system but have to abide by it.

Women too work in the fields, and although the children come home in the evening, daytime separation from their parents is pretty much obligatory. The trained teachers and nurses are firmly convinced that they know a great deal more about caring for children and, in the centers, are better equipped to do it, than their mothers. This may be true, but the philosophy is not likely to be a maternal one. On the other hand youngsters themselves probably have more fun playing together and being fed at regular times than they would have wandering about the fields or left to their own devices all day long in an empty house.

Americans are apt to ask, "But why don't the mothers stay home?" They can't afford to.

Wages, on both farms and in city employment average about 100 leva—$50.00 a month. A suit costs between $30.00 and $50.00, shoes between $5.00 and $12.00 a pair. On the other hand apartments rent for about $3.00 a month. Food is cheap, and Bulgarians are under the impression they pay nothing for schools and medical care. They do, of course, which is why their salaries are so small. The money that they might be earning as individuals is being disbursed directly by the state to meet health and education costs.

As far as co-operative farming is concerned, broad boundaryless fields scientifically cultivated seem to produce more for everybody than did the tiny, laboriously tended individual plots of former times. According to their own published statistics, before 1945 Bulgarian rural economy was one of the most backward in Europe. They now trade with 110 countries, and their volume of export is ten times higher than it was before World War II.

Perhaps, however, they should read Robert Ardrey's fascinating and brilliant book, *The Territorial Imperative*. He contends, and I believe correctly, that the American farmer on his comparatively limited acreage—one in ten of our two and a half million commercial farms contains over 500 acres —raises enough to support himself and twelve other people while on the 15,000- to 70,000-acre state farms of the Soviet Union one worker supplies himself and one other person.

China, newer at the game and even more communal and communized, requires six men in the field to support one in industry.

Apropos of Russia, Mr. Ardrey goes on to say that

"Private plots occupy about 3 percent of all Russian cultivated land, yet they produce almost half of all the vegetables consumed, almost half of all the milk and meat, three quarters of all eggs, and two thirds of that staff of Russian life, potatoes."

There is probably no doubt that Bulgarian agriculture needed modernizing, but even more than the ukases of an all-powerful state the urge to own one's own piece of earth stimulates the adrenal glands.

It seemed to us that the need for housing in Bulgaria is reasonably acute, for we saw families already living in houses where the rough brick still showed, the hardened surplus cement still had not been chipped away, and the plastering was only partially finished or not even begun. From our point of view the houses appeared primitive, but from the point of view of the Bulgarian peasant, who for so long had nothing, it is an immense improvement.

Compared to Romania, Bulgaria is poor, with a somewhat scruffy air, yet we felt less of a sense of regimentation there than we had in the former country.

"You are not the first people who have said that," we were told. "Oddly enough, although there is considerable latitude in Romania's dealings with the West she seems to keep a tighter grip on people at home. Of course," our American informant added with a laugh, "it's hard to say whether that's political or Bulgarian. They're a pretty relaxed bunch."

Relaxed but not lethargic. Not Adriana at any rate. Adriana was an *exaltée,* her enthusiasm ranging from the Cyrillic alphabet through Bulgarian history to the brotherhood of man and raspberry wine.

She was devoted to St. Cyril and St. Methodius, two Greek brothers who lived and died in the ninth century. They traveled as missionaries through the Slavic lands, were accused of heresy by the German rulers of Moravia and recalled to Rome, but were exonerated by the Pope. The Slavic alphabet was named after Cyril, who, as I later learned, to my surprise, did not invent it. Adriana was convinced he did.

Her rapturous account of his life story was interrupted only when we passed a peasant family on the road and stopped to take their picture. They were a good cohesive group—father, mother, and a plump, red-checked two-year-old astride a donkey. They posed willingly and pressed upon us a big bag of hazelnuts which they had just been gathering. We promised to send them copies of the pictures via Adriana and in due course received a letter from her saying she had forwarded them and was sure they would be received with pleasure.

Another of her enthusiasms, the raspberry wine, we were introduced to when we stopped to lunch at an inn in the Rila River Gorge. The drive through the gorge had been beautiful, the gold-tipped autumn trees on the mountain side glittering in the sunlight. The inn was attractively situated overlooking the river, which in that season was dry, and needless to say, the jukebox blared. Our hearty luncheon, however, was good: vegetable soup, an excellent tomato and cheese salad, broiled pork chops, and nourishing, flavorful bread plus the raspberry wine. For our taste it was overly sweet, but for a Sweet Things contest it would be a fine entry, and Adriana sipped it with relish.

By way of a digestive we visited the monastery. It is about seventy-five miles from Sofia. The roads are excellent and one may either go by car, as we did, or there is a twice-a-day bus service. It is a fascinating spot, a rich, elaborate complex, its architecture special and strange. It was supposedly founded in the tenth century by a nobleman named Ivan, who, disgusted with the corrupt life of the court, moved into the valley of the Rila River and became a hermit.

In the fourteenth century the original monastery was destroyed by an avalanche, and it was the feudal ruler Hrelyu who began the edifice one sees today. The Turks burned it down with monotonous regularity, but it was always rebuilt and restored and was brought to its present state in the middle of the nineteenth century.

Set among oak and beach trees it is an enormous affair built around an irregular courtyard, some of the sections two stories high, some three and four, with carved staircases, a rabbit warren of covered balconies and brick colonnades outlined in black and white and dull red. The buildings are monks' quarters: cells, rooms, and a refectory.

In the center of the courtyard stands a three-domed church and the original tower which survived the Turkish onslaught. There are fabulous icons of carved and guilded walnut, but more than any other feature it is the frescoes that draw the traveler and delight the eye. The frescoes are marvels of color, design, and storytelling . . . religious comic strips with quantities of wings and halos, cotton-blossom clouds, cherubs, and dancing prancing devils. In all the primitive and medieval art we saw, it was the devils who were having the high old times.

We climbed some of the wooden staircases and saw a few of the apartments with charming ceilings of carved, painted wood and low divans around the walls. They told us that the best rooms were used for visiting bishops, and certainly their accommodations were picturesque and colorful, but even after opening several closed doors and peeping into unorthodox corners, I could discover nary a smidgen nor a sliver of a bathroom. But then, as we know, monks are very, very spiritual.

If ever there was a subject for postcards it is the Rila Monastery, and we would gladly have bought several, but the stand in the fourteenth-century tower was closed, the attendant absent.

Why be on your toes if the money you take in must be turned over to the government?

The more one encounters this system, the more thought-provoking it is and the more confusing. I have always considered Socialism to be a step up and away from Communism. Theoretically it appears more moderate, indepen-

dent, and civilized, but the Balkan peoples do not feel that
way. To them Socialism is a steppingstone to the pure Communist state, which they see as The Top and desirable. They
spark to the Marxist battle cry: "From each according to
his ability, to each according to his needs."

To the cold-fish eye of a capitalist the philosophy would
seem inescapably to imply total dictatorship, yet in practice
would not such an arrangement result in a spongers' paradise?

"I'm doing the very best I can, Statsie, but I need a
lot. You take care of me and I'll relax." Theoretically the
state would say sternly, "You do not work, you do not
get." Yet to keep itself in power it could not afford to
curtail handouts.

When we advanced this argument to Adriana she replied
that human nature might be a *little* that way now, but
she explained that in twenty years the conscience of man-
kind will be so developed that honesty and integrity will
be the order of the day. Adriana is twenty-three. Norton
and I are older and more battle-scarred, and we doubt that
twenty years will be quite enough to revolutionize the
human animal but it's a dear thought and blessings on
those who hold it.

In the late afternoon we arrived at Borovetz, a small
community in the mountains and stopped for tea at a hotel
on a pine-clad slope. On the balcony a party of men were
seated around a table, singing, drinking wine and beer—
and playing the accordion. They were joined presently by a
group of women piling out of a country bus. With the
harvest over and the crops stored, the peasants have time to
go junketing around the countryside, enjoying themselves.
They were sturdy vigorous extroverts, they looked happy,
and they posed readily when Norton asked if he might
take their pictures.

That night we arrived in Plovdiv and stayed at another
large, shabby hotel. I really don't know why the staffs of
those old behemoths have to be so ill-clad. The boy who

took our bags was wearing a dirty, faded khaki suit, an open shirt, and no tie. It is gratifying to think that man's exploitation of man has now ended, as the Romanian Communist brochure assured us is the case, but it's hard to see why the non-exploited can't be clean. They're like those priests in old monasteries. Holy and filthy.

On reaching our room it once again became apparent that the interior decorator's touch is a refinement that has not yet reached the Socialist Communist People's States. There are those who may consider that the S.C.P.S. are rollicking in clover, a point of view to which I am not altogether blind. More than one of us, I imagine, has had the experience of waiting months for the curtains to be made, for the furniture to be returned from the upholsterer, has blanched at the bills, only to gaze upon what the expert hath wrought and moan, "God in Heaven, what goes *on* here!" Tangling with decorators takes experience and a stout heart. I mean, you don't think to say, "Oh, by the way, while I'm in Europe don't take my lovely old chairs and paint them slaughterhouse red," because it doesn't occur to you that it will occur to them to do it. It will though, it will indeed.

Edith Ilovici had never heard of interior decorators, and when I had tried to explain their function she gazed at me unbelievingly. "You mean a strange man or woman comes into my house and tells me how to furnish it and takes my things and redoes them?"

"Well, yes. I suppose it does sound odd, but it's quite a business in America." She shook her head, and I could tell she found the idea unnerving. Even so, a *little* guidance in assembling hotel rooms in the Communist bloc might dispel an air of bleakness that, with the exception of the new Carpathi in Brashov, they all seemed to share.

On going to dine in the garden of the Plovdiv Hotel, however, we decided that Communism had redeemed itself. That garden is a glamorous, beautiful spot. The hotel is built around a courtyard, and the French windows of the upper story open on to an arcade that overlooks it. Below the arcade a wide balcony, on which are set tables and chairs, runs the length of the building. It is lighted by softly glowing moons, and the air is fragrant with the perfume of thousands of petunias spilling from bordering window boxes. Broad steps lead down to ground level, and under the trees people were dancing on the flagstones. As we watched, the couples broke and joined into a long crocodile, the conga line of old but the rhythm was a lilting polka. Influenced by such charming surroundings, many of the guests were nicely dressed, and the shirt-sleeve-and-no-tie brigade, looked by contrast not democratic but slatternly.

Later that night, going up to our room, I stepped into the elevator with three men, one of whom I thought for a moment to be Richard Nixon. The resemblance was startling. The other two were Chinese. In the tiny car relationship was intimate. Having seen the numbers on their keys I pointed to mine, smiled and pointed to theirs meaning we were all on the same floor. This winsome ploy failed to elicit so much as a crack in the veneer, and I thought to myself, inscrutable Oriental is right.

The next day I was telling Adriana about them and she said "Oh, but they were not Chinese; they are Mongols, and Mongols are suspicious of everyone. We Bulgarians are so open and friendly. We laugh and sing the whole time."

She was right about the singing part, she nearly drove us crazy. Her specialty was folk songs, which she sang in a wheezing, breathless little voice or else she recited long, turgid sagas of Bulgarian heroism against fearful odds, which she insisted on translating for us. She would recite them to Nasco too. He was our driver, a sane, reasonable chap, a refreshing change from our Romanian madman—and he would keep shaking his head, meaning, Yes, yes I know them.

In the course of her performance she would work herself into an ecstasy, exploding at the end, throwing her arms out and crying, "Oh, it is so wonderful to be Bulgarian!" There was a mutter from the doctor in the back seat beside me. "That one's brain has been washed and *pressed,* for God's sake." But I don't think it was only indoctrination. Adriana was romantic, and the mountainous country through which we were driving evoked memories of ancient battles, desperate last stands, and life well lost for the motherland.

It was fair enough that she should be enthusiastic about Plovdiv, for it is a charming town on the Maritsa River, being built on six hills that rise from the Thracian Plain. It is an ancient town, too, that has been overrun by Thracians, Macedonians, Romans, Byzantines, and the Turks who for 514 long years held it under harsh and unrelenting rule. It has had many names, the present one being a corruption of Philippopolis after Philip II of Macedonia, the father of Alexander the Great. Philip established a military post there in 341 B.C. Understandably the name of his community was a tongue twister for the local inhabitants, who shortened it to Plovdiv. One of the most striking houses, overhanging a sheer rock wall, sheltered the French poet Lamartine, who on his way to the Orient in 1833 stayed in Plovdiv and wrote of it with admiration.

The ethnographical museum is an enchanting pale blue house with white gingerbread ornamentation and an undulating yoke-shaped roof. It was built by a wealthy Greek merchant in 1877. The gentleman's name was even more of a challenge than Philippopolis, his thoughtful parents having christened him Argyr Kouyumdjioglou. Mr. Kouyumdjioglou was a man of taste, and the most striking feature of his house are two enormous rooms, one upstairs, one down, with exquisitely carved and painted ceilings.

The exhibits are tools and pottery and costumes; there is a string of cowbells ranging from very large to very small, and if you brush your hand along them you create a sweet melodic musical scale. It must be lovely to hear the soft tones as the cows and sheep move quietly about the meadows.

The town also boasts a richly painted church with sixteenth-century icons, a spacious terrace planted with old trees from which one has a sweeping view of the city, and a Turkish mosque. There are walled gardens, winding picturesque streets, and ancient archways, and in my ears I still hear the click, click of Adriana's spike-heeled golden mules as she picked her way over the cobbles. This inappropriate footwear was the delight of her heart, and no matter what she wore, tweeds or wools or knits, they were accessorized with "oh, them golden slippers."

The mosque only opens at noon, so we did not wait to see it. However, one could pass a charming morning in Plovdiv. Sleep late, have a leisurely breakfast, wander about the town, taking pictures on the terrace, visiting the museum and the mosque, and be on one's way.

It is often the second cities of a country that are the most attractive. I would not say this holds for Chicago but when we were in Japan, Norton and I preferred Kyoto to Tokyo; in Romania, Brashov was more appealing than Bucharest; and we thought it true of Plovdiv compared with Sofia.

A great sight near Plovdiv, but one, alas, that was out of season, is the Valley of the Roses. The plants, from which attar is extracted, were originally brought from Persia in the seventeenth century. Apparently the millions of pink and white blossoms and their intoxicating fragrance are unforgettable, but that glory is for late May and early June.

Not that our autumnal journey lacked color. Along the way we passed peasant women walking the road wearing long bright dresses and aprons, their heads swathed in white kerchiefs. They walked with the easy swing of healthy country women and could have been of any era; the mid-twentieth century, the mid-fifteenth.

Bulgaria is an agricultural country growing big crops of fruit, grain, and the money-producing tobacco. She also has a small amount of heavy industry. I don't know what it is, but I suspect bauxite. That seems to be very popular. They export it wild to Russia and import it tamed into pots and pans. Light industry, and I am sorry about the pun but it can't be helped, appears to be matches. On our way we passed the only factory in Bulgaria that manufactures them. Bulgarian economy as constituted at present makes do and sometimes in ingenious fashion. If a dirt road drops away abruptly, instead of using rails or posts to shore it up they pack the sides with old whitewashed automobile tires. They aren't bad at all, making a rather decorative design and seeming to do the trick.

Gold however glitters in the Bulgarian sky. From afar we saw the domes of Shipka Cathedral blazing in the sunlight and they are truly of gold. Proof that man should look ever upward is the lower part of the cathedral, an architectural indiscretion committed by the Russians at the turn of the century, to commemorate the Russian soldiers who died in the war against the Turks in 1877. The interior is better than the exterior, exciting frescoes of thronging saints in crimson and gold. Adriana told us that if we wished to visit the vaults below we would see the tombs of the killed persons. We thought the phrase genteel but contained our enthusiasm, continuing on to Shipka Peak for luncheon.

Romania is grander and richer and cleaner than Bulgaria, but with the exception of their coffee, which is dreary, we thought Bulgarian food was better. A *tiny* bit greasy, perhaps, but good peasant fare, substantial, nourishing, and flavorful. It is never served as hot as we like it, but neither is it in Greece. The viewpoint seems to be: if it tastes good why mind if the temperature is tepid? The East German beer of which we drank a good deal is, I regret to say, to be recommended.

Waiting for luncheon we examined a spirited mural on the restaurant wall depicting a brave and brawny Bulgarian about to hurl his rifle at a Turk who seemed already to have lost his balance and to be tumbling backward over a precipice. Adriana's version of the battle was terrific. Out of 23,000 Russians and Bulgarians only 43 survived. As she described the bitter cold, we decided that for courage and stamina the encounter must have been a cross between the winter at Valley Forge and the scaling of Everest. While she related the tale, dark liquid eyes glowing, small hands waving, we, her listeners, switched latitudes and thought of Thermopylae and Corregidor, Dien Bien Phu, the Alamo, and Dorks Rift . . . desperate last stands in the blood-drenched history of the human race.

"The heroes were freezing for eight months!" she cried. (Winters were long in 1877.) "When their ammunition gave out they hurled their guns at the enemy. When they had no more guns they hurled the corpses of their dead!" It was magnificent!

The truth was a distinct letdown. There were actually two battles of Shipka, one in July 1877—no snow—and a second in January 1878—maybe snow—but the triumph of the Russians and the Bulgarians was complete, and the Turks, routed, turned tail and fled. The victory was the more noteworthy because the allies were vastly outnumbered—7500 men against 30,000.

Adriana's version was colorful, though, and I have always suspected that here and there the most objective historians, being but human, may have twisted the facts a little.

On the mellow September day that we were at Shipka—no snow even at 4300 feet, the stone shaft marking the site of the battle rose in clean silhouette against a hazy sky, and our girl with a nice choice of words, remarked that "it commemorates the kill."

Tirnovo, our next stop was another romantic old town clambering amphitheatrically, as the doctor pointed out, up the northern slope of the Balkan Mountains, the tawny façades and flat Pompeian red-tile roofs of the houses reflected in the Yantra River flowing through the gorge be-

low. It used to be the capital of the second Bulgarian kingdom, which endured from 1185 to 1396.

The hotel was crowded, but thanks to the eloquence of
Adriana, battling for us, her charges, and backed up by
Nasco, our driver, we were able to get a room. It was
small but the cleanest we had had in Bulgaria, and the
view out over the valley and the mountains was superb.
It was a treat we appreciated the more as Tirnovo was
suffering from a combination of drought and inefficiency.
The water was only turned on between six and nine. The
liquid trickle in the shower, unmotivated by human
hands, would turn from scalding hot to icy cold. The toilet
didn't work at any time, and there were no phones in the
room, but we liked it. That view!

Leaving our bags, we drove on to the Preobrazhenski
Monastery, a bit of old-world charm if ever there was
any. We followed a winding dirt road to where in an
acacia grove a little church covered with faded rose and
blue frescoes and shadowed with grapevines nestled
against steep cliffs. Although the present building is comparatively modern as these things go, dating from the late
seventeenth century, the whole atmosphere is that of
antiquity and tininess. In the minute chapel a service was
in progress, and we stood for a few minutes among the
gleaming candles, inhaling the sensuous fragrance of in-
cense, listening to a few bearded old men wearing the
black chef's hats and long black robes of the Greek Orthodox Church, chanting prayers in old Bulgarian. They
have withdrawn into their sheltered asylum and dream
their lives away seemingly untouched by the twentieth
century and a restless world.

To our surprise, among the ancients, we did see one lean
bony dark young man who was studying there and who
would in his turn embrace holy orders.

When not immersed in piety the monks are agriculturists
raising grape and grain and they support themselves on
their produce without state interference. As far as the

government is concerned the revenue, like the community itself, must be tiny, and the religious freedom implied and indeed practiced, is good propaganda.

High up in the sheer face of the cliffs are caves with crucifixes in them, and in the old days, when they were persecuted, the monks would retreat there to hide from their tormentors. How they ever scaled the heights is a mystery. Recently a part of a passageway has been unearthed and further work was then in progress. It is thought that they tunneled upward to reach the high chambers, but it must have been a dark and perilous journey and the transporting of provisions incredibly difficult.

Back at the hotel at dinnertime we discovered why accommodations were so tight. A congress was in session. There were men and women from various countries, but by far the largest group was Russian, ostentatiously proletarian in both dress and behavior. One man wore his shirt open to the navel and shorts up around his buttocks while another was attired in dangling plus fours, short socks, and sandals.

At the table next to us an enormous Russian, all muscle and with a low-altitude skull, a prototype of those ridiculous heroic statues of Soviet Man, sat with a male companion and two women, but despite a bottle of wine and what appeared to be amiable sallies from his chums, he did not crack a smile throughout the meal. It was an off-night, and the food—eel and boiled potatoes—was not conducive to expansiveness but the white wine, Misket, was dry and good. Oddly enough in Socialist Communist Bulgaria the waitresses all wear little white bows or caps on their heads which our demoiselles now consider demeaning.

At the table on our other side sat a group of English people and one of the men introduced himself as a member of parliament. Labor, we did not doubt, and we were glad to see that the haberdashery of the Western team of workers far outshone the Russian.

The news that a few members of the group were doctors

and engineers did not cheer us. Willy-nilly, adults today
are faced by the weird, dirty, unattractive clothes and the
unappetizing, deliberately cultivated lack of grooming cur-
rently so popular with the young, but when such personal
presentation is adopted by mature, educated people, it in-
duces melancholy in the beholder.

Our melancholy dissipated the next morning as we drove
in bright sunshine and clear air through peach orchards and
vineyards and fields of tomatoes. We passed a group of
women harvesting walnuts and they were a charming sight,
the sunlight through the leaves dappling their gay dresses
and the white kerchiefs around their heads.

In the Balkan foothills the population is still heavily
Turkish and the women dressed in the old style, long Turkish trousers showing under long skirts. Some of them even
wore yashmaks, their eyes glowing above them.

Like Romania, Bulgaria is a grand country for touring by
car, since for long periods yours is the only one in sight. The
roads are excellent, and the scenery is beautiful. We passed
a few motor bikes, and pass is the correct word, as most of
them were broken down, their owners hopefully tinkering
away beside the road.

Our destination was Varna on the Black Sea and we
arrived in time for lunch which we ate in a bucolic restaurant called Kosharata, or Shepherd's Hut. It was rather like
an enormous, wide-mouthed, whitewashed cave with a
central fireplace, benches, tables and chairs covered in
colorful homespun and dishes and glasses of native pottery.
Lights were set in recesses in the wall with animal hides
stretched across them to form lampshades. The picturesqueness was a bit deliberate, but it was fun and gay for all
that, the wine and food very good, especially the *canitza*,
a delicious dish of cheese in air-light pastry.

We tried to turn our backs on a group of beefy German
women who were there at the same time and concentrated
on a virile Bulgar, handsome in a white shirt rich with
scarlet peasant embroidery. Back in Sofia, Dr. Brown

bought one, and it harmonizes surprisingly well with his pale blue denim sulu—a kilt he acquired when we were on Fiji. The locales in which he wears this outfit are limited, but on a beach he is a cynosure!

Wishing us to see all the tourist attractions, Adriana and Nasco led us after lunch to another restaurant in the district, a sort of American Indian complex with wigwams and sawed-off tree trunks used as seats. It was a piquant conceit that didn't quite come off. The copy of an ancient mill down the road was better, but having taken a good many gastronomical beatings in places redolent of local color the doctor and I tend more to the simple and conventional in restaurant decor and never mind the violins, peasant embroidery, and dripping candles in wine bottles. Our idea of a marvelous restaurant is La Grille in Paris, and from the outside it looks so prosaic that if you didn't know about it, you wouldn't go in.

From the restaurants we drove on to Bulgaria's delight, the beach of Varna. The city may fairly be considered historic, having been founded as Oddessus by the Greeks in the sixth century B.C., and under the Thracians commerce flourished. It was also a famous battleground, for it was there that in 679 A.D. the Bulgarians routed the Byzantines under Constantine IV. In 1444 the Crusaders, led by Ladislaus of Poland and Hungary, went down to defeat before the Turks, and the Crescent rode above the Cross for five hundred years.

Having, in the mists of antiquity, changed from Oddessus to Varna, the town again tried switching names in 1949. In an upsurge of God knows what, the Bulgarians rechristened Varna, Stalin. When he went under a cloud they scampered back to the tried and true, and today their travel bureau and brochures are loud in the praises of the Golden Sands of Varna.

Varna is the most important of the Bulgarian ports on the Black Sea, and in the seventeenth century 1150 ships a year used to cast anchor there. Today they are fewer in number, but they are bigger and heavier, and huge amounts of tonnage are annually shipped in and out.

The wooded hills of the countryside slope to the bread beach which, the day we were there was gaily dotted with umbrellas and with umbilicae above the bright bikinis.

The atmosphere was relaxed and casual, the air blessedly free of transistor radios, and a good many private cars were parked around the public gardens and under the trees.

Every effort is made to attract the tourist. Even the doorman of the Ridina Hotel is done up like a rather frowsy Graustarkian general in a uniform of cream-colored serge looped and festooned with gold braid and a hat with plumes. The East German tourists squealed with pleasure at the sight of him.

All of Varna was attractive except the airport, which was quite horrible—a nightmare of noise and filth. Static blared from the loudspeaker at a deafening pitch, and the hole-in-the-floor toilet was nauseating. We could only hope the plane was better maintained than the airport, or our chances of reaching Sofia were slender. It had taken us three days to drive from the capital to Varna. We returned in an hour and twenty minutes, on another of the uncompromising Soviet planes. No reclining seats, no food, no lights.

At the Sofia airport the car that was supposed to meet us had not arrived, and it quickly became evident why. Tito was about to leave after his two-day visit and the city was at a standstill until his departure.

After some little time we were able to get a taxi and drove back to the Balkan Hotel, where traffic and crowds in an insoluble knot waited in the street for the great man to emerge. We waited too as the police would allow no one to approach the front door and in the end had quite a rewarding view of him framed between two tramcars. The trams would have been allowed to proceed on schedule, but riders and conductors were having none of that. It was known that the big official cocktail party was breaking up, that Tito would appear momentarily, and from the tram windows the passengers had an unimpeded view. Presently he came out surrounded by a group of diplomats and secret service agents. For a moment the big virile figure with the tightly curling gray hair was silhouetted in the doorway, then he was maneuvered into one of the waiting limousines and the cavalcade swept off toward the airport.

We swept into the hotel but could not go at once to our room because of the passport rigmarole. That is one really exasperating aspect of travel in Communist countries. No matter how many times you may leave and return to the same hotel, even when you have only been touring internally and have not crossed the border, you are obliged to turn in your passport at the desk.

Our Balkan bedroom this time was even vaster than the first one had been. Norton and I had to send up flares to find each other. But after we had scrubbed up a bit—the bathtub was as unusable as its predecessor—we went down to dine. The food was good and there was a very nice red wine . . . Gamza. Service was slow, but that was understandable, for the waiters were still rushing about bearing great vases of red and white gladioli that had graced the recent reception. A pretty young waitress all aglow from her contact with History placed her flowery burden on our table with a conspiratorial wink.

The hotel was still full of officials and diplomats, and for some reason the evening reminded me of the scene in *The Counterfeit Traitor*, that tense and terrifying spy movie, where William Holden and Lilli Palmer meet at a garden party in Germany in the early days of the war when the Third Reich was going to last ten thousand years.

When on The Other Side I think one is always a little surprised to find that opposite numbers behave much the same and that festivities are festivities regardless of the cast of characters. We had not been at the reception, but Norton and I were willing to bet that the loaded tray of

cardboard hors d'oeuvres were politely ignored by the diplomatic corps just as they are at home. "Of course," he
added a little wistfully—we were hungry and dinner was
a *long* time coming—"they probably had authentic caviar."

I have mentioned that our minister in Bulgaria at that
time was the Honorable Nathaniel Davis, and he did a
most gracious thing. Because of Tito's visit and our brief
sojourn in Sofia, we had not been able to get together, but
we had spoken on the telephone and he had said that if it
was our only opportunity to meet he would come to the
airport to see us off. When we urged that he not trouble himself, he said, "Nonsense, I'll be there."

At the airport Norton and I felt that the three of us were
going to have to scramble to find one another. The terminal
was crowded and noisy, and getting leva changed into
dinars for Yugoslavia was a harried, hurried, devious business.

They always tell you that they will change any surplus
local currency you may have back into dollars, but about
$12.00 is the extent of the largesse and at eight forty-five
in the morning the airport had already run out of both
dinars and dollars. We settled for West German marks.
That is one of the things I like about Europe . . . the
mixed-up salad atmosphere, the knowledge that within
two to four hours, sometimes much less as in the Balkans,
you reach any country on the continent from any other.

Since my loved one is not stimulated as I am by churn-
ing chaos he was relieved when our money was changed,
our passports stamped, and we were free to pass into the
departure lounge. There it was quiet and there we met with
Mr. Davis who good as his word had turned out to bid us
Godspeed.

We had a pleasant chat, and he said that he liked Tito.
"He has a twinkle in his eye, and he's a remarkably
vigorous man, you never think of him as being seventy-
three." Mr. Davis laughed. "Last night he wound up his

toast in English. The Western people were delighted, but the East looked a bit taken aback and suspicious." It seems that Tito is proud of his English, and although he and Mr. Davis both speak fluent Bulgarian, when Mr. Davis addressed him in that tongue the Marshal replied in English and with obvious relish.

We complimented the minister on his accomplishment, saying that taking the trouble to learn the language of the country in which he was posted seemed both wise and courteous. He replied that he liked the Bulgarians and that they were pleased that the United States representative should speak the language of only eight million people. His own feeling was that they were solidly aligned with the Soviet against the Chinese. "They're polite to the Chinese ambassador, but that's about it."

He was also an ardent advocate of tourism, being convinced that it is a great opportunity for rapprochement between nations. At the height of the season the government travel bureau frequently has to accommodate tourists in private houses, as there are not enough hotels. Even if they and their hosts only speak a few words of each other's language, a bond is created. He and his wife, he said, love to hike, and they go on camping trips in the Balkan Mountains. "Magnificent country, lots of camp sites. From one peak we can overlook seven lakes."

It is true that the whole Balkan peninsula is blessed with superb scenery. The Carpathians, the Rhodope, and the Balkan ranges are a lofty and impressive chain and much of the countryside is reminiscent of splendor of Colorado.

Mr. Davis struck us as being an intelligent and able man—we were enjoying our little visit, but the Belgrade flight was being called and we bade him a reluctant good-by. The plane was a Caravelle of Austrian Airlines; reclining seats, newspapers from the west, orange juice, good coffee, pretty stewardesses . . . civilization is charming.

We fell upon the papers hungrily. I do not know that

27 Frescoes of the Rila Monastery.

28 Painting in the Rila Museum.

29   Zagreb. Bright rugs displayed between showers.

30   An elderly peasant couple along the road in Yugoslavia.

Their vigorous young descendants.   32   Peasant woman at Jajce, Yugoslavia.

33   Whitewashed peasant's house
with black split-shingle roof.

34　Double vision. Waterside village, Yugoslavia.

35　Adorable Dubrovnik.

there is any deliberate intention on the part of the Bulgarian government to bar foreign newspapers. I rather think not. I suspect that not enough of their people can read them to make importing them worthwhile. By this time we were persuaded that Mr. Prager of Carpathi was right and that the concept of the iron curtain is an outmoded one even though Bulgaria had been, for us, a soundproof chamber. Nary a peep from the rest of Europe or the U.S.A. had penetrated our isolation. Yet, I do not, in fairness, feel that one can lay the blame on Communism. Norton and I have spent newsless holidays on islands in the Caribbean and in Africa, and it is remarkable how we have managed to get along without contact with the outside world and how it has limped along without us.

CHAPTER FIVE

Yugoslavia

Arriving in Belgrade, the thing we missed immediately was the Bulgarian currency. Two leva to the dollar, how handy. Twelve hundred and fifty dinars to the dollar, how cumbersome. Still, foreign currencies are one way to acquire agility in arithmetic which, thanks largely to travel, I am now a little better at than I used to be in my school days. This does not mean that the bank and I always see eye to eye on my balance but I am at least amenable to their suggestions.

We were to find Yugoslavia a country of extraordinary beauty, but driving about Belgrade or Beograd (White City) we decided that of the three great geographical Bs (Budapest, Bucharest, and Belgrade), only Budapest is a truly beautiful capital.

This did not hold true of the environs of the city, as we discovered when we drove through the charming wooded suburb of Didinje to lunch with the American ambassador, the Honorable C. Burke Elbrick.

Mr. Elbrick received us beside the swimming pool of the residency which he had built for himself and the embassy staff and which had been opened with modest fanfare on the Fourth of July. We were a small group; the American ambassador, the Honorable Mr. Vigeveno, the

Netherlands ambassador to Yugoslavia, and his wife and
Mrs. Campbell, the wife of the Canadian minister, who
was away. Mrs. Elbrick was away too. She had flown home
to the bedside of an old family retainer who was supposedly dying but the sight of the beloved mistress had
so cheered her that she had sat right up in bed and was
happily embarked on the road to recovery.

We had a friendly luncheon on the terrace accompanied
by two good Yugoslav wines, a red Plavac and a white
Zilavka. In the course of the meal I asked if they could
recommend a restaurant where Norton and I might dine
that evening. "Why don't you go to the Writers' Club?"
said Mr. Vigeveno. "It's rather fun, I think you'd enjoy
it."

"Does one have to belong?" I asked.

"Say you're a friend of mine, and anyway, you are a
writer." And then he added, "Come to think of it, why
don't we all dine there? Are you doing anything tonight,
Burke?" Burke was not and said he would join us. It was
agreed that we would meet at the Vigevenos' for cocktails and go on to dinner.

Norton and I returned to the Metropole Hotel. Our room
would have fitted three or four times into the stadium we
had occupied at the Balkan in Sofia, but the bathroom was
CLEAN, it was USABLE. As in many European hotels,
however, we were puzzled as to why they had bothered to
install electricity. They do not seem to understand that
one of its primary functions is to illuminate. Our room
would have been no more shadowy had it been lighted by
a couple of candles.

Immediately upon our arrival in the morning we had
gone hand-in-hand to the hotel hairdresser and barber—
the two shops were practically one—and had found them
by far the best of the trip. Having laundered our heads
we now caught up on our clothes and took a nap.

In the evening we made our way to the Dutch residency
and found the others already gathered, listening to Ameri-

can records. We had expert American cocktails and a little later set out for the Writers' Club. It was a downstairs room, a little shabby but homelike and cheerful, and the food was excellent.

Not being of the diplomatic world, Norton and I were amused to see how seriously our companions adhered to protocol on even the most informal of occasions. Here we were, the same six people who had lunched together only a few hours before and had just been having drinks together. Yet when the Netherlands ambassador wanted me to sit facing the room so he could point out any well-known figures, Mrs. Vigeveno quickly indicated that it was unthinkable, as it would place me on his right. Mrs. Campbell, as the wife of another ambassador, naturally had to take precedence, and she herself, as hostess, *had* to have the American ambassador on her right. As guests, Norton and I realized we must be serious too, but I noticed he went to elaborate lengths not to catch my eye.

We were indebted to our hosts, however, for a most agreeable evening. Mr. Vigeveno indicated two or three well-known Yugoslav writers and gave me their names, suggesting I get in touch with them. Apparently they spoke a little French and English, but I felt shy about approaching them, although I would have liked it had we been able to meet casually.

Unfortunately, in Communist bloc countries there isn't much contact between visitors and native residents although Yugoslavia is by all odds the most liberal.

The next day, Sunday, was bright and hot, and our guide, whom I will call Irena and who had come to meet us at the airport the day before, arrived with car and chauffeur to take us sightseeing. She was young, tall, and slim with a pretty, discontented face and bright red hair. As we got to know her better our first impression was borne out. She was spoiled, peevish, and ineffectual. Her English was inadequate and her experience nil. As we did a good deal of reading and inquiring about what we were looking at, we like to think she learned something from associating with us. If she has stayed in the guide business she may be of more use to others than she was to us. In one department, of course, she was invaluable. She could speak Serbian and we could not.

While the buildings of Belgrade are not impressive—they have not the beauty of those of Prague and Budapest— that city too is admirably located at the confluence of two rivers, the Sava and the Danube, which here is called the Danau.

Originally settled by the Celts and Romans, Belgrade was for centuries another Turkish fortress, and the ruins of the great walls still stand in the grounds of what is now a public park, Kalemegdan. The Turkish domination, occasionally interrupted by the Austrian invaders, lasted until 1867. The Serbians may have drawn a sigh of relief when the conquerors departed, but their surcease was not permanent. From 1915 to 1918 the Austrians were there again. In the Second World War, from 1941 to 1944 the Germans gave them a rough time.

Speaking of the Ottoman oppressors Irena said, "Things very bad when the Turkies came," and Norton and I could see them in their formidable flocks, wings flapping, red combs trembling, their dreadful gobbling filling the air.

The history of Yugoslavia is not easy to assimilate, but the thing to bear in mind—although it will not simplify matters—is that it is a federation of six states that used to be separate countries: Bosnia and Herzegovina (they count as one) with Sarajevo their capital; Montenegro, capital Titograd; Croatia with Zagreb; Macedonia with Skopje, Slovenia with Ljubljana; and Serbia with the national capital, Belgrade.

When one realizes the stew over which chef Tito officiates, one gains considerable respect for his ability.

Wandering around the park we came to a broad terrace and looking across the river at the new developments thought them very attractive, infinitely preferable to those

numbingly ugly Long Island barracks, Lefrak City and
Rego Park. The apartment houses were well spaced and
faced with colorful Mondrian squares, but we understood
that the interiors, like those in Bucharest, were cramped
and tiny.

Irena, speaking of the parks and open areas of the city,
remarked, "We have much parking." "Not as much as we
have," replied the doctor grimly.

We visited the zoo, and I was in my usual state of
misery over caged animals, although the elephants were
reasonably well off in a big open compound. From there,
embracing the spectrum, we went to the cathedral to find
the atheists hard at it. The congregation was Orthodox and
not large, but the singing was beautiful and the doors were
wide open so that anyone might enter.

We did not find our next stop, the Serbian Museum, of
great interest, although we were sufficiently harrowed by
the terrible iron balls with spikes and chains with which
people were lashed and tortured by the Turks.

Trying to find something good about them we stopped
for Turkish coffee at the Golf Restaurant. It stands on a
rise of land, and although we could see no golf course the
outdoor terrace was bright with umbrellas. The tablecloths
were dirty, but people seemed to be having a pleasant, relaxed time, enjoying the sunshine. By and large they were
nice-looking people, but we had noticed that many Balkan
women had very furry legs. Norton kept muttering about
the need for lawn mowers, but I said to him, "How do
you know? Maybe male Balks like furry legs." On this
score my man was categoric: *"That* is impossible."

The men on the whole were stocky of build and in their
square cardboard suits they looked like characters in a spy
movie. But that is the way they tailor clothes in central
Europe and the Balkan peninsula.

Leaving the Golf Restaurant, we drove out of the city
to Smederevo, about fifty kilometers from Belgrade. What
one sees today are the ruins of a fortress built in 1430 by

the Serbian Prince Djuradj Brankovic as a defense against the Turks.

Smederevo was bombarded in World War I, and in World War II the Germans used the fortress as an ammunition dump. The picturesqueness of the ruins was intensified when Serbian partisans, led by Tito, blew them up. Smederevo has always been famous for its wine, and when Prince Djuradj (George to us) became a lord of Tokay in Hungary he imported vines from the old homestead. These were the ancestors of today's Tokay grapes from which comes the famous, if for many palates too sweet, Tokay wine that Hungarians consider to be as indigenous as goulash.

Perhaps our *bon vivant* prince liked it that way. He may have felt it offset the more acid side of his character, exemplified by an endearing little habit of immuring people alive from time to time while his fortress was abuilding. Apparently such sacrifice was customary, as we today break out a case of beer when the rooftree goes up on a new country house.

The fortress had nineteen square towers and enclosed approximately twenty-five acres. The area is bordered by the Danube on one side and railroad tracks on the other, and it could be a charming park. Perhaps such is their intention when they can afford to plant and cultivate, but at present it is run-down and shabby. However that did not prevent a good many people from wandering about or lying on the ground basking in the warm September sunshine.

The flawed jewel of the day was Vinogradi in the little village of Grocka. This is a restaurant on a hillside with a lovely terrace and a beautiful view of the Danube. The flaws were the poor service and our old enemy, a screeching, inescapable transistor radio. It belonged to two Italians and was destroying the pleasure of some twenty or thirty people.

I said to Norton, "This is a divine spot, but I think we

should tell travelers that they're likely to have a long wait and it might be a good idea to bring along books, needlepoint, and a pack of cards to while away the time." Norton said, "Tell them to bring a box lunch too."

He was right. But the food, when it did arrive, was delicious, as was the wine.

We went to the post office the next day before starting our Yugoslav tour. We wanted to mail some pamphlets and travel brochures back to the States.

Irena led me to a counter where a man weighed them and scribbled down two columns of figures but did not tote them up. She explained that that was what the stamps would cost, but that chap did not give them to us. We crossed over to another window where we stood in line, and when our turn came we paid in the money and received the stamps, which we then had to take back to the first man. By that time other people were ahead of us, so we stood in line again. When we reached the window we handed over the stamps and I was about to turn away, but our guide said, "No, no. You must wait and see him do it." I waited while he licked and stuck. "I'm satisfied," I said. "Can we go now?" Irena nodded. We departed. There are occasions when the American way of life is definitely better, and if that be chauvinism, make the most of it.

The first stop on our tour was Zagreb. Having driven there, I should say the better way of reaching it, if you feel you must go, is by a short plane trip. It is only about two hundred miles from Belgrade, and the roads are excellent, but that particular part of Yugoslavia is flat and not very interesting. Mile after mile of corn and sunflowers.

Our destination in Zagreb was the Esplanade, which is an A hotel but directly on the railroad tracks. The trains shunt and snort under your windows and, in your dreams, come pounding through the room.

The furniture included a television set that didn't work,

but there was a radio vibrant with short-wave programs including a broadcast from the Vatican in English.

We were puzzled as to why our itinerary included Zagreb, for although it is of ancient origin, today it is an industrial city of little interest to the casual tourist. It is a useful jumping-off place if one is touring the northwestern part of the country, but a night there is ample. Arrive late, sleep (trains permitting), get up early, and leave. We spent the entire next day and the next night there, and that, frankly, is too much.

We did, however, telephone the American consul general, Mr. Karl Sommerlatte, who knew we were coming and kindly invited us for cocktails the following afternoon.

We dined at the hotel, an error redeemed by the dancing. They had a group of folk dancers, and although neither Norton nor I are folkomanes we thought them colorful and entertaining. They wore peasant costumes some of which were beautiful. Velvet vests over full-sleeved blouses and long, heavy, magnificently embroidered aprons. In one dance the men were in short white tunics with broad sashes and white trousers wrapped with red puttees. To fast, pounding music they did another dance garbed in full black trousers, broad yellow belts, and Cossack hats. Sometimes the women's heads were bound with white kerchiefs, but I thought the prettiest and most elegant millinery were the little red turbans with bows at the back.

The figures of the dances were charming, particularly in one that was a sort of paseo, men and girls strolling past each other, choosing partners, and dancing hand in hand and with hands on shoulders. They were accompanied by drums, fiddles, a cello, mandolins, guitars, and flutes.

The whole performance was fresh and gay and lively, and we were glad to have struck dance night. Entertainments are better on native soil, and that is indisputably the way to see them if one can: the Lipizzaner of the Spanish Reitschule in the Imperial Palace in Vienna, the Scottish pipers against the gray ancient background of Edinburgh

Castle rather than at Madison Square Garden. Tahitian dancers are better presented in the South Seas than in New York's Hotel Lexington, where many of them used to appear and the Yugoslavs would be more harmonious in a village square than in the dining room of the Esplanade but it is better to see these people doing what they do expertly in an alien milieu than not to see them at all.

Before the performance started we had noticed a large group at another table, among them a few Americans, and presently one of them got up and came over to us. He was Mr. Sommerlatte, with whom we had spoken earlier in the day on the telephone. He sat with us for a few minutes, and we said how much we had enjoyed the dancing. "Yes," he said, "they do it well, but, my God, there comes a time . . ." The poor man had had a surfeit of Yugoslav dancing no matter how good. He was obliged to accompany every visiting American fireman who wanted to see the show. Were any male dancer to fall ill, Mr. Sommerlatte could have leapt right in, heels clicking, elbows akimbo, twirling with the girls.

Being novices in the Balkans, we naturally had to detail to him, a professional, our adventures, impressions, and solutions for all their problems. Mr. Sommerlatte had been in Zagreb for fifteen months and had previously served in Moscow and Warsaw, yet he listened with courtesy and patience. Then we got onto the resorts. "Have you ever gone skiing at Brashov? Have you been to Mamaia or Varna? Lovely. You really should." "No," he said quietly. "No I haven't been there. When I get a holiday I get out of these countries."

The next day it rained, the second and last rainy day of the trip. The showers of Hungary didn't count. It had rained the first time on the Rhine, when sunshine is almost obligatory, and it happened again in Zagreb, a city that under gray skies has all the lyrical gaiety of Belfast or Glasgow on a wet Sunday. We have experienced the Irish and Scottish metropolises and know whereof we speak. The weather soured the doctor's mood, and my own spirits were low, for to make matters more depressing, Slavko had vanished from our lives. We were saddled with The Case of the Missing Chauffeur, not to mention the missing car. All we had was Irena, she of the turned down mouth, the shrug and hands outflung in a What-can-I-do-about-it? gesture.

Still, she was the link to which I could attach myself, so, leaving the despondent doctor, who assured me he preferred it that way, I took her along for a little sightseeing. When she asked directions and was not satisfied with the reply she explained that they were misinforming her deliberately because she was a Serbian and Croats hate Serbs. I didn't know how a casual passerby could tell. I *believe* Serbs and Croats speak the same language, but perhaps as American Northerners and Southerners can spot one another by accent, so can the peoples of Yugoslavia.

The old part of the city, the Kaptol, is nice with ancient walls, a Catholic cathedral, parts of which date from the eleventh century, and a lively market place where merchants risked bringing out bright rugs between showers.

On our way back to the hotel a small dirty child came up to us, begging for dinars. Irena pushed her away in disgust. "Ugh, gypsies." Our guide had the airs of a spoiled grand duchess smelling drains, but she also had an unmistakable flair for fashion, and I felt that given a little money and the access to well-made clothes she could be very elegant. I hope that the clothes of the Communist bloc are substantial and durable, for only the passionately partisan could call them attractive. The women's suits have the same square cardboard tailoring as the men's, as though cut from cloth made of ground acorns. Since Irena was not a Mind, and had few examples to follow, her fashion sense must have been innate.

She made me think of my mother, who, through the long professional lifetime she spent at *Vogue,* the magazine she edited for thirty-eight years, always contended that a sense of style was inborn. "I don't know what it is," she would admit, "I have had girls on my staff who haven't had the brains of a button, but send them out in the market and they will come back with the best hat or shoe or dress of the season. They *smell* what's good, and it has nothing whatever to do with intelligence."

When we returned to the hotel there was still no word of Slavko. Earlier on we had applied to Putnik, one of the Yugoslav State travel agencies, but they were as much in the dark as to his whereabouts as we were.

Norton and I went out to lunch at Gradski Podrum, a large café in Republic Square in the heart of town. It was depressing upstairs but pleasant down, and the food and wine were very good. By now we had got used to the Balkan custom of a little local brandy by way of an apéritif, and, although brought up in the orthodox tradition of cognac after dinner in the balloon glass warmed between the palms of the hands, we found we could adapt to the native way without balking like mules.

On the way back to the hotel we again stopped at Putnik. No Slavko. From our room we phoned Belgrade, and they promised to telephone their Zagreb branch and try to unravel the mystery.

In the end, just as we were thinking he might have been tied to the railroad tracks under our window and demolished by a train roaring out of the darkness, he turned up. "Slavko! In heaven's *name* where have you been?"

It wasn't all that mysterious. On our arrival the night before he had asked Putnik for a new tire to replace one that had blown on the road, but they had only two and refused to part with either. He had then telephoned Belgrade. The powers, in the course of the night, had sent along a new one, but it didn't fit, and he had spent the entire day scouring Zagreb, trying to find one that would. It had not occurred to him that we might want him or be wondering where he was, so he had not telephoned.

Norton listened to this tale of frustration and complication with interest. "This is the second city in the country," he said to me. "If they can get this fouled up in a town this size, and furthermore a *commercial* town, what do you suppose will happen if we get a flat in the mountains?" And he started whistling a cheery little tune. Since, with him, whistling is extremely rare and I saw no reason for merriment in a hypothetical breakdown, my curiosity was piqued. "What are you so giddy about?" "I was just thinking . . . looks as though capitalism still has a chance."

In the early evening, the car washed, polished, and retired, Slavko drove us to the Sommerlattes for cocktails. The French and German consuls were there with their wives, and it was interesting to meet Frau Von Kleibert, the daughter of Pastor Martin Niemoeller, virtually the only German churchman to stand up against Hitler. There were also two or three very nice Americans who worked in the consulate, and they all seemed to take an interest in our itinerary and immediately set about changing it.

We had been going to Ljubljana and Opatija, and there were murmurs from the wife of the French consul when they were ruled out. Everybody in the room had a favorite place that should *not* be missed. But Norton and I felt that Mr. MacVickers, an American who owned property on an island off the Adriatic coast and who *knew,* was guiding us wisely. With one exception, which I shall mention later, we did not regret the changes. Our final destination was Dubrovnik, and once arrived we were delighted to find that, thanks to our new itinerary, we would have a week in that enchanting spot instead of only a couple of days.

The morning after the cocktail party we went to Putnik to ask them please to cancel our reservations in the hotels we would not be going to and to make new ones starting with Sarajevo. The attitude of the young ladies at the desk was insolent, indolent, and inefficient, and although one of them finally conceded that she would send a telex to the hotel in Sarajevo, my feminine intuition warned me that out the door, out of mind.

"You see," said Irena, "it is as I say. They think they are superior because they are Croats and we come from Belgrade in Serbia, and they do not like us."

Norton and I thought it rather unfair that their prejudice should extend to non-partisan American tourists, and by and large we did not sense animosity in any other people we met, but that particular organization I cannot recommend. The name of the Travel Bureau is Putnik, but put not your faith in it. By now, of course, it is possible that their attitude has changed. I certainly hope that the staff of the Zagreb office has been replaced, for I doubt that they would be useful even to their fellow Croats.

Our road led through Bosnia—one of the six countries composing Yugoslavia—and in such an old land we were surprised to see so many new houses. Whole villages were being rebuilt because of the destruction wrought by the Germans during the war.

Sometimes on a lonely stretch of road small children would be walking by themselves, and when we asked why, both Irena and Slavko said they were on their way to school or returning home. They often walk many miles twice a day, in sharp contrast to small Americans who early lose the use of their legs, being transferred from baby carriage to school bus with scarcely a step between. We also learned that while the State pays for all education, a pupil who flunks exams at the end of the year and has to repeat the course must pay for the second time around.

In the town of Banja Luka the scenery began and was to extend all the way to Dubrovnik. Yugoslavia is a country of great scenic beauty, and whether one drives down the Adriatic coast from Trieste or takes the north-south inland route as we did, a panorama of extraordinary loveliness unrolls along the way.

There are woodlands; red-roofed villages nestled in the softly rolling fields; and deep gorges split the high mountains. We drove for many miles between high, craggy walls, a jade green river flowing on our left. At one point it disappeared under the mountains only to reappear later in a lake behind a dam. With the exception of thirty-five kilometers under repair the roads throughout the entire trip were admirable: wide, well paved, and well graded.

At Jajce we discovered we had arrived on market day, and many of the peasants were clad in the national dress of Bosnia: the women in long knickerbocker trousers under skirts that came to a little above the ankle, wearing long heavy aprons and white headgear. The men wore dhotis, the baggy loincloth-pants of India, sashes, and shaggy caps.

Jajce lies in a narrow valley surrounded by mountains of medium height, and a dramatic waterfall plunges from the Pliva River into the Vrbas. There are several other rivers and lakes in the vicinity, and the fishing, trout and grayling chiefly, is good. It is a picturesque, pretty town, the thickly wooded hillsides interspersed with whitewashed houses, their roofs of split shingles weathered and stained black.

The site was settled originally by the Romans—it would come as no surprise to me if one day it is discovered that the United States was settled by the Romans. It was to Jajce that Tito came when evading the Nazis during the last war and from there he commanded his forces.

The state of the country was chaotic, for it was involved in a civil war at the same time it was fighting the Germans. One faction was lead by Mikhailovitch, who had been appointed by King Peter's government in exile, and the other by Josip Broz (Tito).

In 1943 the Allies sent a commission to try to determine who was doing what, and it concluded that the Tito forces were doing most of the fighting against the Nazis, despite being Communist-dominated. That, however, was a gnat the Allies were in no position to strain at, any more than they could look down their noses at the strongest resistance movement in France just because *it* was Communist-dominated. Germany was the enemy, Tito was a formidable fighter, and the bedfellows of war are no stranger than those of politics. With Allied support Tito was proclaimed Marshal of Yugoslavia at a meeting in Jajce on the thirtieth of November, at five o'clock in the morning in the presence of 142 deputies of the Second Session of the Anti-Fascist Council of the National Liberation. Ah, those Communist titles.

Either he pleased the constituents or they knew what was good for them. In 1945 his National Front Coalition won eighty-five out of every hundred votes and the Republic was proclaimed.

We lunched at Jajce on delicious freshly caught trout from the Vrbas River and afterward went around to the catacombs, hoping to see a fourth-century stone carving of the god Mitra. Mitra was an Indo-Persian deity of the sun, who was worshiped throughout Asia Minor, but to our regret he did not cast his light upon us, since the catacombs did not open until four o'clock. It was then two-thirty and Sarajevo lay many kilometers distant.

Driving along the road we passed herds of curly, long-horned sheep and women carding wool on hand spindles, an ageless classic occupation. In today's world it is balm to lift up one's eyes to the non-political hills and quietly watch the long level afternoon sunlight flooding the fields. We stopped from time to time to savor the bucolic scene but also to succor Irena who was developing into a real liability. She couldn't help it, poor child, but she got carsick. Her head bobbed from side to side, and she held her nose as any natural country smell wafted through the open windows.

To everyone's relief we came into Sarajevo at six o'clock, having left Zagreb at half-past nine. As I had anticipated, the Hotel Europa had not received a telex from the Zagreb Putnik office. We had a disquieting moment, for accommodations were scarce because of a large veterans' congress that was crowding the town. Irena referred to them as heroes, the Communist term for veterans, and they convene as our survivors do. There may be brave men among them, but by and large veterans are pressure groups, and their vulgarity is wearing. Most politicians know it, but in need of their backing, they kowtow to them.

We eventually got a room, two, in fact, which was more than we needed, but a suite was all that was left. The rooms were large, the bath was large, and we rattled around like peas in a barrel but we were sheltered. Leaning on the window sill, looking out, we found the town very attractive, and over the old Turkish quarter the crescent moon gleamed appropriately.

Early the following morning we went to visit the quarter, and although the doctor was able to control his enthusiasm, I was happy.

Narrow winding alleys, velvety tiled roofs, tiny shops bursting with brass and copper, slippers and carpets hanging in the streets, a crowded, noisy vegetable market, and the sun striking through the wings of a flock of pigeons wheeling over an old man who threw corn for them. Why wasn't the Turkish quarter all right? Some of the copperware was handsome but much was not, and it was the old story, not only how could we transport it—but what could we do with it once we got it home? Like the embroidered blouses of Romania it was out of the stream of current fashion. However, watching them make a plate was instructive. They take a copper disk and slam it down to the ground to flatten it. Shaping and etching come later.

Apart from the bazaar there are two or three modern shops, and the merchandise in the windows looked tempting, but on closer inspection it too was mostly embroidery and dolls.

The Miljacka, a shallow river, winds through Sarajevo, and in the corner of a building near one of the bridges a stone plaque in the wall marks the place where the shots that killed the Archduke Francis Ferdinand of Austria Hungary were fired by Gravrila Princip and where the First World War began.

With rusty memories of the details Norton and I looked at the inscription and asked Irena to translate it for us. "It says," she explained, "that this is where the hero killed the tyrant." She was about to continue, when an explosion from the doctor interrupted her.

"That's enough of that, Irena," he said curtly. "The hell with the brainwashing. Princip was a bloody murderer who did more than his share to start one of the worst wars of history, and you'd better know it. And if you're being taught anything different you're being lied to. Come on, let's get going."

Irena nearly jumped out of her neat little cardboard suit. But then her mouth turned down and she gave her habitual shrug. "It is what it say." I thought my husband was rather unfair. Brainwashing implies a brain, and that was a commodity the poor girl did not have.

It was time to be leaving Sarajevo, but Irena had forgotten her luggage, so we had to return to the hotel to collect it and to wait while she rustled up some bicarbonate of soda, since she was feeling squeamish.

Finally we got under way, and about ten kilometers out of town Slavko turned off the main road and we presently arrived at a place well worth the small detour. Vrelo Bosna is an enchanting water garden with small lakes, rushing streams, shallow waterfalls, and miniature rapids. It is the source of the Bosna River and a lyrical spot with grassy banks and weeping willows. We wandered about for a long time taking pictures and listening to the gurgling chuckling liquid sounds of running water.

It was when we saw this smaller edition of it that we regretted that our change of itinerary would prevent us from seeing Plitvice, a national park famous for its sixteen lakes, multitudinous cascades and waterfalls. Judging from photographs Plitvice is of quite unusual beauty, and there is a hotel as well as camping sites and fine trout fishing.

Along our own road, however, we found much to recompense us: a tiny terrace restaurant where a whole lamb was roasting on a spit turned by a water wheel. Also Mostar, overlooking the Neretva River, where we lunched, and very well too. There are two hotels there that face each other across the river and although they are both state owned the rivalry between them is keen.

En route we learned one important Serbian phrase: *benzinski pumpa* which means, as you might guess, gas station. There are not all that many of them and those traveling on their own will do well to carry an extra can of gasoline. We passed ancient hill towns and, when the road dropped to sea level, the picturesque village of Opuzen, where small boats drawn up along the quai sat low in the water, weighed down by baskets overflowing with red and purple and pale green grapes.

I had a run-in with Slavko who, while not the demon our Romanian Horia had been, still drove so fast that we had whipped past one photogenic location after another before we could snap a picture. Also, although the coast road is wide and admirably engineered, there is not much in the line of a railing, and taking the curves at eighty is not recommended. I cannot, however, agree with a friend of mine who said, "Oh those roads of Yugoslavia! Terrifying. Fly! Fly everyplace!" I myself do not relish the hairpin bend and the precipitous drop, but they were not common. The roads are notably good and the country magnificent.

In the late afternoon we came to a sign saying Ston. "Ston," Mr. MacVickers had told us at the Sommerlattes' cocktail party, "is a divine spot. Take a boat and row over to the little island off shore. Extraordinary architecture." I couldn't wait. "Here we are, here we are," I crowed. "Let's go."

"It's five o'clock," said the doctor. "Don't you think . . ."

"Supposing it *is* five o'clock, what of it? According to MacVickers it's marvelous, and I know you. Once we get down to Dubrovnik you won't want to come back up here again."

We turn off the excellently paved main road. We start

to drive. We drive and we drive, or, more accurately, we bump and we grind and we slither over a gravel and dirt goat track for twelve long kilometers. It is getting dark. We arrive at the shore and no rowboat is in view. We are, in fact, not at all sure that a darkish lump far out in the water is actually the island referred to with such enthusiasm by Mr. MacVickers. "That's what we saw further up the road, and it's a group of fish traps," Norton said. That is all he said. That is all anybody said throughout the twelve long dark kilometers back to the main road. I was the mistress of the expedition; it was not the province of the chauffeur and the guide to chastise the mistress, but she was in Coventry and she knew it. The chauffeur and the guide and the master, united in a horrid little cabal, knew it too. My feelings about helpful Mr. MacVickers were unmixed. There may be a bona fide island off Ston, even a bona fide rowboat, but I do not want to hear about them.

At about six o'clock we pulled into Dubrovnik. That is to say we rolled down the ramp that is the entrance of the Excelsior Hotel. The Excelsior rises out of the Adriatic as the Gritti Palace in Venice rises out of the Grand Canal but from there on the resemblance is not remarkable. The Excelsior however does have a virtue the Gritti lacks; the waters lapping its foundations are emminently swimmable, buoyant and caressing, scarcely less pelucid than those of the Caribbean.

The rooms overlooking the water all have balconies and the rates are pleasant: $14 a day with full pension (three meals) per person and at the end of the tourist season they drop 50 per cent in one night. This magic time occurs between the thirtieth of September and the first of October. We were there for the drop and although it is supposed to signal the close of the season the weather was paradisiac and the swimming still perfect. Indeed, flights of people were arriving from Venice as though the pigeons of the

Piazza San Marco had taken wing, driven eastward by the torrential rains that were plaguing Italy.

The other all-encompassing advantage of the Excelsior, besides the bathing, is its proximity to Dubrovnik. It lies five hundred yards or less from the tiny magical walled city, one of the most beautiful of Europe. Venice probably surpasses it, although there are travelers, who, having seen Dubrovnik, relegate Venice to second place. Dubrovnik does not have canals, but its location and the perfection of its buildings are unsurpassed. It was dark when we arrived, and we had had a long day. We decided to wait until morning before beginning any sightseeing, but we hung over our balcony gazing to our right at the crenelated battlements against the fading sky, the twinkling lights and the minute harbor where small boats lay at anchor. Dubrovnik is romantic.

When we came to concentrate on our room we decided it was just as well the hotel had a peerless location, since there were a good many shortcomings to counterbalance it.

The dressing table was a French *poudreuse* with a mirror in the lid. The mirror was not large to begin with, and one corner appeared to have been bitten off. Also the hinge was loose so that when you opened the top it fell back so far that you couldn't see your reflection and were obliged to stuff towels or papers behind it to hold it in position.

The lamp had no switch. To turn it off you had to pull the plug out of the wall. When you slipped your lightest dress over a hanger it fell apart, like breakaway prop furniture in a farce, leaving the hook dangling on the pole.

There were towel racks in the bathroom, but the toggle bolt has not reached Yugoslavia and the slightest pressure pulled the racks half out of the wall and the towels slipped off the little arms that were supposed to hold them and crumpled to the unwashed floor. There were no hooks on which to hang anything, and although the water gushed into the tub quite merrily it took about three hours to run out, so that one's roommate had to fritter away a good deal of time waiting his turn for a bath. Our toilet flushed by itself at intervals during the night, and when Norton went to close the closet door it came off in his hand nearly knocking him over. The light in the dining room was blindingly bright and the food not overly inviting. Otherwise it was a darlin' hotel entirely.

Actually I felt rather mean making the above list, but if trifles make perfection so do they make imperfection, and enough of them piled one upon another can lead to disaster. We supposed the management had lost interest because it was the end of the season and low rate time had come.

We had met the manager when we arrived and registered at the desk, and his attitude had struck us as something short of southern hospitality but we thought no more about it. A day or two later he received a letter from Mr. Sommerlatte saying we were friends of his and would the manager do what he could to make our stay pleasant. We did not know Mr. Sommerlatte was writing, but a Yugoslav woman we met on the beach told us about the letter. "Oh, he is in a stew about it," she said, referring to the manager, "in a stew. Recently a Yugoslav journalist was here and he wrote a most *uncalled*-for article saying the hotel was not well *run*, and now the manager is afraid that if you complain his head will roll."

Although agreeing with the unknown journalist we did not complain; we were having too good a time; and I am sure that if by now the same man still holds the job it is because he is measuring up to it.

The next day we didn't care if we were lodged in a wigwam. The weather was glorious, and in the early morning light, with her gray stone walls and ochre and terra cotta tiled roofs, Dubrovnik was, if anything, more entrancing than at night.

We breakfasted on the terrace under a long awning and I could barely down the last swallow, so eager was I to get into the town, but Norton wanted sun and swimming, so

I went with him onto the plage. The Excelsior has no beach. There is no sand, nor are there rocks as at Antibes and other Mediterranean ports, but there is a long, broad well-built deck of stone and concrete running the length of the hotel, where everybody gathers and where there are lounging chairs and striped umbrellas. One either dives straight into the water—Dr. Brown's way—or lowers oneself gingerly—Mrs. Brown's way—down the rungs of any one of several ladders.

Seeing him happily ensconced—sun glasses, sun oil, African safari hat, and camera, Irena and I took off for town, four or five minutes away.

The origins of Dubrovnik go back to the seventh century. As a guidebook states: "small, isolated, threatened on all sides (she) continually strengthened her fortifications. She fought, settled down, concluded treaties and agreements, paid tribute, bestowed gifts, managed to extricate herself from difficult situations, and somehow kept alive in hard dangerous times." She was spunky!

Because of her geographical situation at the base of a range of steep hills but open to the sea, she was vulnerable to raids by the fast-striking Arab pirate ships, so that for six hundred years she maintained reasonably close relations with Byzantium, calculating that so powerful a neighbor would afford protection against both pirates and Slavic infiltration. For Dubrovnik started as a Roman settlement, Ragusium. The present name is a corruption of the Slav name for wood, *dubrava,* from the woods of Dalmatian oak, *dub.*

As Byzantium weakened, Venice, across the sea, anticipating Botticelli's *Birth of Venus* by a couple of hundred years, was rising from the waves in increasing splendor. She became the first power of the Adriatic, but spunky little Dubrovnik ran her a close second.

The exposure to the sea that had been Dubrovnik's weakness became her strength. Her mercantile fleet sailed the

36   Close-up of the harbor, Dubrovnik.

Monday morning. Looking down
from the walls. Dubrovnik.

38   Street in Dubrovnik.

39 Dubrovnik street.
Not for those with heart ailments.

40 Rector's Palace. Dubrovnik.

41 Cloister of the Franciscan monastery. Dubrovnik.

42 Pietà over a church door. Dubrovnik.

43 Sveti Stevan, island hotel on the Dalmatian coast.

44 Corinth Canal.

45   The most famous ruin in the world, the Parthenon.

46   Temple of Poseidon, Sounion.

47   Mando, Ilka, Peter, at Sounion.

Mediterranean and her ships were famous in distant seas as well.

When Charles V campaigned against Algiers, his troops traveled in Dubrovnik ships. In 1500 Dubrovnik's oak ventured toward the newly discovered continent of America, and in 1588 her caravels sailed in the Armada, but that was a miscalculation. Counting on an English defeat she lost thirty-three of her largest vessels, a blow that permanently crippled her sea power.

Actually, every few hundred years, if it wasn't one thing it was another. In 1292 the little city-state had undergone a terrific fire. She recovered from that, and the early years of the fifteenth century saw her at the height of her beauty and glamour. Cathedrals were built, the Rector's Palace, the Bell Tower, Onofrio's Well, and the aristrocracy and the rich merchants constructed exquisite palaces in which they gave magnificent parties with dancing troupes and theater companies performing nightly. This high, wide, and handsome life continued for about 150 years, and then, in 1667, catastrophe struck in the form of an appalling earthquake. A contemporary description creates a lurid picture.

"Easter Sunday arrived. A session of the Grand Council had been fixed for April 6, 1667. At precisely 9 o'clock a terrible underground rumble was heard, then immediately afterward came a powerful tremor of short duration, which rocked the whole city and with cracking and crashing literally demolished it. While palaces and church bell towers cracked and fell, above the city a thunderous rumble broke out, as rocks from the peak of the neighboring Mount Srdj crashed down, destroying everything in their path. Above the city a suffocating dust arose, darkening the sky and preventing the blood-red sun from breaking through the darkness. The earth cracked; and men and buildings tumbled into the craters that were formed. To make the apocalyptic terror complete, terrific claps of thunder were heard out at sea; and several times the coastal waters receded from the shore and returned in gigantic waves, smashing and carrying away all the ships anchored there. To make the tragedy more complete, fire broke out immediately after the first tremor had struck the city, and within an instant it was spread by a sudden gale which followed the fury of the underground forces. Many wounded people buried in the ruins died in the fire, which transformed the devastated city into a heap of scorching hot stone."

It is estimated that two thirds of the population of over 6000 people perished. The person who did most to reorganize the demoralized population that remained, who had looters and bands of hooligans shot on sight and who brought about some semblance of order in the devastated city was Maroje Kaboga Kabozic. He was a young nobleman who had been notorious for his dissolute way of life and who, at the moment the earthquake struck, had been chained to a prison wall in a death cell, accused of secretly co-operating with the Turks and of the murder of a senator.

In a marvelously operatic stroke of justice the earthquake severed his chains, and he escaped the toppling walls, assumed leadership in the midst of the holocaust, and became known as the Savior of Dubrovnik.

The city eventually regained her equilibrium, and much that is there today dates from the period of rebuilding after the earthquake.

Coming from the hotel, one crosses a bridge, passes under an archway, and arrives at an enchanting baby Piazza San Marco. The Placa or Stradun—the main street—divides the town in two, and one meanders with ease for within the walls no cars are allowed. Narrow streets, no more than steep stone stairways, climb the hillside. Flowers spill from the window sills of stone houses, and laundry flutters on clothes lines, crisscrossing overhead.

To the left, still facing *down* the Placa, the ground at first is flat in the quarter of shops, restaurants, and the market place. The street then mounts gradually to an upper level, the sunny square of the cathedral and the fortifications fronting on the sea.

The other incomparable enchantment of the town is the walls. For a modest admittance fee the visitor mounts and descends the inner staircases and while on top of the walls makes a tour around the city encompassed below him— an endearing patchwork of huddling terra cotta roofs, belfries, streets, tiny blossoming terraces, and the blue Adriatic stretching to the shores of Italy. Walking at leisure, photographing as one goes the circuit takes about forty-five minutes. I did it three or four times and the perfection of the scene wooed me afresh every trip I made.

There was only one flaw in my happiness.

Off and on I have spent perhaps four to five years of my life in Europe, and I have never been convinced that on any part of the continent the month of October would be warm enough for swimming. This merely goes to show that convictions should not necessarily be trusted. In early October bathing conditions in the Adriatic are ideal but since I am a sophisticated type the intelligence had escaped me.

In these travel books I occasionally give Travelers Tips, among them the appropriate clothes for the place and the season. I *help* my readers. I should have referred to my own authority or, having failed to do so, I should have heeded the wisdom of the ages and stood in bed. On a hot October day in a tiny walled city on the shores of the Adriatic I was equipped with a couple of chic woolen suits and little else. A cool cotton dress was obviously a must. But there was a hitch.

Although her winters are not severe, Dubrovnik too buttons up for the equinox, and the stock of cotton or linen or silk frocks was low. Thanks to my own eyes and the fashion nose of Irena, we sniffed out a little shop where many dresses hung from a rack. One caught my eye, a cool simple cotton, a pretty shade of red. I slipped it on. In New York my size is ten. Though aware that European sizes differ greatly, forty-eight still seemed abundant but that was the smallest they had and who was I to bicker? I liked the color, and the price was right, the equivalent of

$4.50. I said to Irena, "Tell them I'll take it." A few doors down the street I found a gay belt that spruced it up considerably. I was also able to snaffle a black bathing suit, the chief feature of which was a pair of falsies that would have put Jane Russell to shame, and a pair of beach shoes. The right one fit, the left did not. The shoe people are not sticklers for accuracy, but I returned to the hotel feeling reasonably well equipped and almost in love with my Dubrovnik Dior.

It is true that my head and arms stuck out from it as from a tent but through the mid-section, thanks to the co-operative belt, the material and I adhered. One day looking at my reflection in the elevator mirror—our room did not boast such full-length luxury—I said to Norton, "It doesn't really look so bad, does it?"

"Yes, dear, it does," said my loved one. There are times when a woman has really got to concentrate on all the advantages there are to being married.

Since he had been swimming and sunning in the morning on our first afternoon in Dubrovnik, I took Norton on the guided tour when the town opened up again around 5 P.M.

On the Placa, in the warm Mediterranean evening, girls on one side boys on the other, stroll arm and arm along the ancient street in flirting promenading courtship.

Before the earthquake of 1667, the way was bordered by magnificent Gothic and Renaissance palaces, but today, although from an American viewpoint they are very old, the buildings are restrained, unpretentious, and of modest height.

While Irena and I had been sightseeing I spotted a poster announcing a concert to be given the following evening in the Rector's Palace. I asked her to get tickets for us or to tell Slavko to do so. That night shortly before dinner she arrived in our room wide-eyed. "Concert not tonight. Tomorrow night." I took a firm grip on myself and said as gently as I could, "Yes, Irena, that's what it said on the poster, remember? Tomorrow night, it said. Did you get the tickets as I asked you to, you or Slavko?"

The moue of discontent, the turned-down mouth, the helpless shrug. "I was having my hair washed. I go tomorrow."

After a glance at me the doctor said to her, "I think, Irena, you should be very sure that you *do get* the tickets." She left and I poured a shot of vodka with shaking hand.

Going down in the elevator one evening we found ourselves in the company of an African whom I had noticed in the dining room. The night before he had dined alone and that day at luncheon he had sat by himself.

I had some letters in my hand I wanted to mail and Norton said to me, "Have you any money for stamps?"

"No. Haven't you?"

"No. I left mine upstairs."

The African reached in his pocket. "May I lend you some?"

"Thank you," I said. "You're very kind, but it doesn't matter. I'll mail them later."

We got out together on the lower level where the dining room was, and as we were walking to our separate tables I felt so sorry for him, having all his meals alone just because he was black, that I murmured to Norton, "Let's ask him to dine with us."

"No," said my spouse brusquely.

"Why ever not?" I asked as we were sitting down. "He may be very interesting. Just because he's African doesn't . . ."

"Oh, him," said Norton, "I thought you meant Slavko."

"Slavko! I didn't even see him. Is he here?"

"Yes, sitting over there behind the pillar, and if you don't mind, I don't want to have dinner with him."

"Well, no more do I, but what about the other fellow?"

Norton grunted. "O.K. If you insist." He got up and went over to the African's table and asked if he wouldn't join us. The man said that he would be delighted, and we were glad he had accepted. He was interesting. His name was Ahmed, and he was in the Sudanese foreign service. He seemed a bit guarded but told us that he had been traveling in western Europe. Though his English was good it was all he spoke, and in many places he had had difficulty with the language. We gathered he had been lonely, not being able to speak with people and being black as well. Always to eat by oneself is a sad business. Table manners are important and no one wants to associate with bores, but to be ostracized because you are black or plaid or have green hair is idiotic.

We fell to talking of wild life, and he said that the Sudan has game reserves in the South, but I got the impression that the whole idea of conservation of wild life and of its habitats was new to him.

That is true, unfortunately, in many newly independent African countries. The problems facing the politicians and rulers are manifold, complex, and acute, and besides, animals don't vote. Gradually, however, especially in Kenya and Tanzania the governments are coming to appreciate the enormous source of tourist revenue inherent in the animals themselves and in the game reserves. I like to think that perhaps our Mr. Ahmed will look through the window we opened just a crack into the wonderful *and* remunerative world of wild creatures living free.

On our next visit into Dubrovnik we found we were sharing the antique splendors with Mr. Krishna, the Vice-Premier of India. He was a small, frail, gray-haired man, and in his long tightly buttoned black redingote must have been very hot, but he looked distinguished and acknowledged the sporadic applause with grace. For such an exalted personage the ruling against automobiles within the walls was suspended, and Mr. Krishna, his companions, and Dubrovnik officials drove down the Stradun or Placa in a cavalcade of cars. Since that is the only street in town that could accommodate them there were only two ways they could go: down and back.

When they had departed we visited the Franciscan monastery. The fourteenth-century cloister designed by Mihajlo Brajkov is preserved intact with its exquisite double colonnade, each capital carved with a different, delicate, and fanciful design of leaves or medieval bestiary or small human heads. It is delightful to stroll around the rectangular arcade, looking through the slender columns into the courtyard. The courtyard is tattered and run to seed, but it is an adorable spot just the same, and opening off it is the apothecary shop, the original fourteenth-century porcelain jars still on the shelves. Piquantly enough the church is also the location for a modern, functioning apothecary shop or drugstore.

In the afternoon, after an unaccustomedly good lunch at the hotel, we set off for Trebinje. It is twenty-six kilometers away, and while apart from the public square with its magnificent old plane trees, there is nothing much to see, it is a pleasant drive with some fine views and a truly superb panorama of Dubrovnik glimpsed from the mountain on the way back.

In the evening we dined in town at the Riblji or Fish Restaurant in Ulica Siroka. Ulica means street and as you stand in the piazza it is the fourth or fifth one on your left opposite the blue awning of the Trafika shop where they sell cigarettes and tobacco. Be sure to ask for a table on the roof where you will dine under a leafy arbor. The food is good if not extraordinary, the Pivo beer excellent, and the atmosphere charming—one of those few rare cozy spots in the Communist world. The Riblji's quality is appealing probably because it is privately run, although we had a very good luncheon one day at Jadran (Adriatic), a restaurant just behind the beautiful Great Well of Onofrio.

In the restaurant or catering business in Yugoslavia a man may have five employees before he becomes a menace to the People's State. In other businesses three is the limit. The state sets these arbitrary numbers, and I believe the temptation to squeeze in one more is not often yielded to because the system of wages and pensions, insurances and benefits to be filled out in quadruplicate are so harassing that if an employer must cope with them all he has neither time nor energy left to run his business.

After dinner we walked around to the Rector's Palace for the concert. The palace is a rich brew of Gothic, Renaissance, and baroque and the carvings of the capitals are florid and fun. Used today as a museum the interior, with the exception of one lovely little marble mantlepiece, seemed drab. The excitement is out of doors. The annual drama festival takes place in July and August. Performances are given in the piazza, and a magnificent setting it is. They play native classics and Shakespeare. There is folk dancing and singing, and the New York City Ballet have been popular guests.

Concerts are held in the atrium of the palace, which is open to the sky. A beautiful staircase leads to an upper arcaded cloister surrounding it, and at ground level the most notable feature is a bronze bust dating from 1638. It is of Miho Pracatovic, known as a "worthy son of the Republic" and is the work of an earlier Giacometti, this one Pier Paolo. Mr. Pracatovic is of lean and aristocratic physiognomy, but he was, in truth, a commoner, a seaman who, in his youth, worked as a laborer on estates of the Dubrovnik nobles. He seems to have been a rakish fellow who had his ups and downs, made and lost several fortunes, was captured by pirates, excommunicated by the Pope, roundly cursed by his superiors, and pursued by the entire Turkish fleet for what must have been a noteworthy peccadillo. When the Republic of Dubrovnik was almost extinguished by famine brought on by a blockade and siege Pracatovic came through. He ran the blockade, supplied the city, and, dying fortuitously when in the chips, left his fortune to

his home town. In return they had him cast in bronze. It
was the least they could do.

Having admired this colorful citizen, we sat down to an
evening of Dvorak. The New World Symphony and Con-
certo for Violincello. We thought the local orchestra quite
good, with the exception of the French horn, a strong in-
dividualist who saw small point in collaborating with his
colleagues.

There is a night club in Dubrovnik, the Labrint, opposite
the Dominican Monastery, and I lured the doctor into it,
but we speedily departed. The noise was deafening although it would no doubt reverberate agreeably against the
stone eardrums of the young.

The next morning we woke to the continuing poetic
weather which brought much happiness to both Dr. Brown
and me. I could ramble at leisure around the walls of the
city and wind my way up and down the ancient streets
while he swam and sun bathed.

One day seeing Ahmed on the terrace I asked Norton if
our friend had been swimming. "No," he said, "there's not
much water in the Sudan, he probably doesn't know how."

"How sad. But he could go right next door to that little
sandy beach and wade in slowly. Maybe he doesn't know
about the beach."

"Maybe he knows about it and doesn't like to swim or
maybe he has cirrhosis or something and doesn't want to.
Leave the poor man alone."

"All right. I just want him to have a nice time."

I suppose Norton was right. One man's nice time is another's crashing bore. But not to take advantage of that
glorious water . . .

On one of my junkets into town, walking the walls, I
came upon a nun busy with a long stick poking garbage
between the crenelated battlements, happily polluting a
clear little stream rushing below. "Don't *do* that!" I cried,
vigorously waving my head and hands in strong negative

gestures. But she looked at me with a sunny smile and continued poking.

I had a less frustrating time in the studio of an artist, Mr. Milovan. For my taste his palette was somber and his canvases did not tempt me, but he had a charming Chinese ink and brush sketch of a little foal lying down. There was something tender and touching about it, and since it was inexpensive I bought it. It was a bargain except that back in New York the simple frame cost more than double the picture.

In the afternoon we hired a boat to take us to Lokrum, a wooded island a little over a mile long that lies just off Dubrovnik in front of the Hotel Excelsior. The boat cost about $2.40, but throughout the day regular small ferries ply the narrow strait, and the price of the voyage is a quarter.

The Benedictines erected a monastery on Lokrum in 1023 and a few fragments of wall still remain. They built another in the fifteenth century, but that was shattered by the earthquake of 1667. In the beginning of the nineteenth century they gave up and left. After Napoleon dissolved the Dubrovnik Republic in 1808 Lokrum passed into private hands and in 1859 was bought by Maximilian and Carlotta before their venture into Mexico.

Today it is a delightful public park. One can make a very pleasant little excursion by taking a picnic lunch and bathing, walking, and exploring the deeply indented bays and grottoes on the far side of the island.

It was when we were returning in our boat that one of the doctor's pet theories was punctured. As I have said, the rooms of the Hotel Excelsior all have balconies where, inevitably, people hang up bathing suits and do a bit of nude sunning from time to time.

The outer walls of these balconies are waist-high sheets of thick milky glass, which was, the doctor had assured me, opaque. Coming back, looking the hotel full in the face as we approached it and noting the attitudes of other deluded guests I am in a position to report that it is not.

If one has attained Dubrovnik another must of the Dalmatian coast is, I should say, Sveti Stevan, the tiny beach village about seventy-five miles to the south. To begin with the drive down along the splendid highway is a treat in itself.

Slavko would have interrupted the pleasure to show us the Dubrovnik airport, for which he had a passionate attachment, but we explained that over the world and over the years we had seen a good many airports and that we would be seeing his in a couple of days in any event, when we went to meet Peter, Norton's son, who was flying over from Rome to join us.

We overruled him and pushed on to our first landmark, Hercegnovi, a pleasant little community on the Gulf of Boka Kotorska. The old part of the town with its fourteenth-century fortification still stands and is picturesque and colorful. We could tell, however, that we were making no character with Slavko. All that was sleazy and jerry-built and noisy appealed to him. His instinct for it was that of a homing pigeon, and his disapproval was audible as we looked at ruins and photographed peasant women in native costume leading donkeys down narrow cobbled streets. Irena was bored too, but she simply sat in the car looking pale, pained, and patrician. Still, in fairness, one must say that she tried. Driving along a narrow road, she would remark, "This is a narrow road," or passing an electric plant, "There is a hydro-electric plant," or, as was the case with Slavko's passion, "There is the airport." Norton and I felt we were not broadening our horizons. But then we came to Kotor. Kotor is a lovable spot, and one is all the better for seeing it.

The 4800 inhabitants live mostly within the shelter of the city walls, four kilometers long, that zigzag up the mountain side. We tried climbing, but there were too many steep stone steps, and our knees and enthusiasm buckled. On the way back we passed citizens more agile than ourselves who, we were surprised to see, did not have one leg shorter than the other. One good-looking chap—we took him to be a lawyer or a doctor—came bounding home for luncheon with nary puff nor pant. Passing a vigorous-looking old woman I tossed out my one Serbian phrase: "*Kako ste* [How do you do]."

Her little grandson playing at her feet looked up quickly, telling her how to reply in English.

Kotor has been the cultural, commercial, and administrative center of Boka Kotorska for centuries and at one time was a vital port where the naval cadets of Russia were sent to study by Peter the Great. Today its marine museum is, I should say, of interest only to students of naval history, but the town itself is fascinating.

The twelfth-century cathedral harbors an extraordinary fourteenth-century altarpiece; a three-tiered octagonal pavilion, the angles formed by slim twin columns topped by standing figures. The altar is of 18-karat gold, silver washed, and the church is entered through a superb pair of carved doors.

In a flowering courtyard I spotted a lovely old stone well head and longed to own a well, wishing or not. In the main square a man was washing vegetables at the pump, and it occurred to us that probably very few of those picturesque old houses had running water. Yet, despite its antiquity, the atmosphere of Kotor, like that of Dubrovnik, is vigorous —lots of healthy-looking children running and playing in the streets.

Continuing on our way, we came to Milocer, where we had planned to lunch. Milocer is an unpretentious but attractive two-story stone villa with a broad pergola-covered terrace on the sea. Before World War II it was built as a summer home for the royal family, Queen Marie and King Alexander I, who became king of Yugoslavia in 1921. In a curious duplication of the assassination of the Grand Duke

Francis Ferdinand in Sarajevo he was shot by another terrorist, this one a member of the Croatian Ustashi society, in 1934, while driving during a state visit in France.

Milocer is now a hotel, but we could not lunch there, since the day before they had shut up shop for the season and the few remaining guests had been transported to Sveti Stevan.

The journey is not far. Sveti Stevan (Saint Stephen) is a tiny island on a reef linked to the mainland by a narrow causeway running across two crescent beaches that form little bays to the left and right.

Built on rocks and old stone walls it was a fortress in the fifteenth century and later became a fishing village. The population gradually dwindled, and shortly before 1959, the inhabitants having very nearly petered out entirely, the government removed the few who remained and transformed the whole village into a minute hotel-city. They did an admirable job. The exterior has been restored so that the houses look as they did in their prime, but inside they have been renovated and modernized into rooms that are both pretty and comfortable. There are red-tiled floors and whitewashed walls. The monastic furniture is pleasing and appropriate, the beds are comfortable, and the bathroom lighting was the best we found on the Balkan peninsula. There is no extra charge for the lovely spectacle to be seen from the deep embrasured windows; millions of light points glittering on the water like diamond-tipped javelins. The hotel can accommodate 237 guests. When leaving one's room instead of walking along miles of carpeted corridors to get to the elevator one goes up and down short flights of steps banked with flowering shrubs or along narrow twisting streets to the little bar or hairdresser or the large, newly added dining terrace overlooking the sea.

The food was good, better than the Excelsior in Dubrovnik, and the bathing superb, although instead of being sandy the beaches are composed of minute pebbles red and black and white, boulders that through millennia of being

washed by the sea have been crumbled to tiny fragments.

The romance of dinner by candlelight under the stars
was potent, diluted only by the clamminess of the chairs
and tablecloths caused by the heavy dew. We enjoyed ourselves nonetheless, for we were diverted by a praying man-
tis clinging to the stone wall beside our table. His slim, pale
green body was like faggiolini, those tender little Italian
green beans. He had four fragile jointed hind legs, two
saw-toothed front legs, and great bulging eyes in his infinitesimal triangular head with its two antennae. He
seemed a lazy creature, and Norton helped him to a flying
ant which he devoured with relish, lapping it up with a
pronged tongue like two curling hairs. When he had swallowed it, he licked his chops and his saw-tooth legs with
obvious satisfaction. He loved the warmth of the shaded
candle lamp, and after his Lucullan meal hoisted himself
up inside the shade to be nearer the source of benign heat.

By way of night life the hotel has a little band and a
little casino where foreigners may play roulette but not the
natives.

The next morning after an excellent breakfast we walked
around the island, truly a dream in miniature; terraces,
stairs, tiny squares, a little church, and all abloom with
lantana, bougainvillaea, and oleander. A lovely green glis-
tening vine whose name we did not know climbed the walls,
and there were fig trees and fragrant rosemary, sunshine,
and peace. We took photographs, but the genteel recreation
of Victorian ladies and gentlemen, sketching, would seem
the more fitting pursuit.

We were blessed by the weather but it did occur to us
that a rainy spell would be depressing for aside from bathing and the small promenade there is literally nothing to
do. For a blissful twenty-four hours or, if completely exhausted for a more protracted stay, Sveti Stevan is a world
in amber.

The rates are seasonal. July 1 to September 30th: single

rooms $11, double $18. May 16 to June 30: single $8.40, double $12.80. October 1 to October 31 and April 1 to May 15: single $7.40, double $10.80. These prices include an American breakfast and dinner.

We changed into our bathing suits and went down on the beach to loll and bathe. The spell was temporarily broken by an influx of day trippers, a busload of German tourists who, we feared, would undoubtedly picnic on the beach and depart in the late afternoon. To our selfish delight they went away after an hour or so.

I had with me a paperback copy of Helen MacInnes' *While Still We Live,* a story dealing with the siege and invasion of Warsaw by the Germans. The story is fictional, but the historical facts and background and the anguish imposed by the Germans on all conquered countries were real enough.

With all those Germans surging about, the book was an unfortunate choice, and I laid it aside, deciding there was no point in poisoning the beautiful day with bygone tragedy I could do nothing to revoke.

On our way back to Dubrovnik after luncheon we stopped at Budva, to pick up Irena and Slavko, who because of lack of accommodations in Sveti Stevan, had spent the night there. Originally a Greek colony of the fourth century B.C. Budva is one of the oldest walled towns on the Adriatic and has a beautiful beach. I am a walled-town aficionado, to me they hold endless fascination, but I can see the point of view of those who hold the when-you've-seen-one-you've-seen-'em-all philosophy. Walls and steps and huddling houses and narrow, winding streets . . . there is a similarity, but ah, the charm.

Irena had a theory about walled cities. She said, "Houses so close together because winds here very strong. In narrow streets winds can't get down, houses hold each other up." I felt her contention, while perhaps holding wind, did not hold water and I still suspect walled cities were built for economic and security reasons. Populations had to be sheltered in areas that could be encompassed by walls often speedily erected with stones brought from considerable distance by men working under threat of attack.

Back once more in Dubrovnik we joined friends of Norton's for cocktails. We had seen them lunching at Sveti Stevan. I asked if they had been into the city yet or if they were going in the morning. "Oh," they said, "we're just driving through. We don't think we'll bother."

"Not bother?" My dear husband's kick under the table told me my voice had risen ten decibels. I pulled it down to what I hoped was a normal basso profundo, but I mean to say . . . to be a few hundred yards from Dubrovnik and not *bother*.

Given the quality of the town itself the reaction, "But there have *got* to be artists," is automatic, and so there are. I have already mentioned Mr. Milovan. Acquaintances at the hotel had told us also about Jovan Obican. His studio was up the road from the Excelsior, and one afternoon I went to call on him. I climbed a steep flight of stairs and found him on a leafy sun-splashed terrace. He was most cordial and invited me inside to see his work, a personalized folk art highly colored and humorous. He works in many media—oil, tempera, ceramics, bronze—and some of his things were, he said, inspired by the carvings on tombs and monuments of the Bogomils, an ancient sect thought to have originated in Bulgaria, probably in the tenth century.

Though Christian, the Bogomils denied the divinity of Christ, declaring him to be the son of God like other prophets only through grace. A rough people, they were still fastidious, unable to accept bread and wine being transformed into flesh and blood and swallowed. Nor did they believe in the validity of sacraments and ceremonies. They considered that the miracles of Jesus should be interpreted in a spiritual sense not as literal occurrences. They thought baptism was only for adults and that religion was for everybody. They had no special priests, nor would they fast on Mondays and Fridays.

They were dedicated, widely traveling missionaries sowing the seeds of the Reformation and they suffered the persecution commonly visited on heretical spirits by the Orthodox busily saving their erring brothers' immortal souls by fire and sword and conscientiously laying about them in the name of God.

The Bogomils were of peasant stock, and all of Obican's work has a vigorous earthy quality; red cheeks, fierce mustachios, and bulging eyes. His figures are nearly always humorous and vivid.

I asked if artists in Yugoslavia were obliged to follow any party line in subject matter or treatment, and he said no. That had been the case until 1948 when Yugoslavia broke with Russia, but now artists were free to paint as they chose. Mr. Obican had been in America, where his pictures had sold well, and he was looking forward to a trip in the near future. "When we travel," he told me, "the government pays half our expenses because it considers us good propaganda."

Artists are allowed to keep the money they make from whatever source, but if they work for the state they return 12 per cent of their fee to government funds. They may do reasonably well, since the more the state pays them the more it gets back.

He also said that after a man has worked as a professional artist for thirty-five years he gets a pension equal to that received by political and government figures, the highest the country pays. Medical care for himself and his family as well as his children's education is paid by the state. Many American artists would doubtless feel that the Yugoslav way of life has a good deal to recommend it.

Slavko got his wish at last. He was able to drive us to the airport when we went to meet Peter, and we had to admit that his pride was justified. The Dubrovnik airport is a very good one, well equipped and efficient.

Peter was in luck, because while we were having tea on the terrace of the Excelsior, a young man named Otto Cimic, a friend of the far-reaching Mr. Sommerlatte of Zagreb came to call. He invited us to dine and also offered to show Pete around Dubrovnik while Norton and I packed. We were leaving the next day for Piraeus.

At eight o'clock Mr. Cimic (pronounced Chimich) and a friend of his, an alert and sparky American girl, picked us up in a taxi, and we drove for about twenty minutes along a road that spiraled up to heaven, around and around the mountain side. When you reach the threshold of the sky you find a restaurant called Zarkovoca, which means where the sun rises, and it is accurately named. It is a simple place, and we were the only people in the shadowy room, but the view of Dubrovnik and the sea are worth corkscrewing one's way up to see.

We had a local apéritif of considerable authority and a strong taste of herbs. It was medicinal in flavor but clean and palatable, and the local wine was excellent. Otto Cimic told us he was going to be in New York in the winter and we gathered that unlike other Communist countries there is no ban on foreign travel if native Yugoslavs can swing it financially.

The next morning I took Peter for the grand tour of the walls. He was enthusiastic, and I told him about Budva. We talked of the trip we had taken through France and Spain when he was thirteen and of how we had stopped to explore Carcassonne. He laughed. "If anybody ever wrote an *I Remember Mama* book about you," he said, "they'd have to call it *Mama Was a Walled City Nut.*"

On our way back to the hotel we passed an indifferent little art shop in Ulica Od Puca. They sold frames, and the inventory ran to lithographs and highly colored maidens, donkeys, and gnarled old men, but since I am incapable of passing a gallery without a mite of reconnoitering we went inside, and my eye fell upon an amusing and sprightly modern picture.

There were two men in the shop, the proprietor and a friend or customer, we couldn't tell which. I inquired who the artist was and understood from the visitor who spoke a few words of French that his name was Antun Masle and that his studio was in the neighborhood. Although I admired the picture, the price struck me as ambitious—the equivalent of $250. I wanted to go to the artist's studio in the hope of finding something smaller and less expensive. Unfortunately the French of our Samaritan did not extend to instructions for finding the street of Mr. Masle. Besides, it was then half-past ten, and we had to get to the *Istra*, the boat for Piraeus, in less than an hour.

Back at the hotel I tried telephoning Otto Cimic in the hope that he would know something about Masle, but Mr. Cimic was away and would not be returning to the Argentina until the next day. "The hell with it," said Norton philosophically, but then, he hadn't seen the picture; he didn't *care*.

We drove to the port, parted from Irena and Slavko with no great tugging of the heartstrings, and boarded the *Istra* for our overnight cruise to Greece.

The doctor is in his element on board a boat and he immediately went upstairs—topside, I suppose I should say —to organize a table and our deck chairs.

The *Istra* and her sister ship, the *Dalmatia*, cruise the Adriatic and the Mediterannean from Venice to Alexandria and Port Said. The voyage lasts seven days and while one samples a good deal of the Dalmatian coast in that time, the ship seemed to me cramped for so protracted a passage. Overnight was long enough but they punished us for our disloyal thoughts. We paid as much for our night as the other passengers paid for seven—$332. The explanation for what struck us as extortion was that although we occupied the cabins only between Dubrovnik and Piraeus they had to keep them empty the entire trip. That we questioned. Not all passengers stay on board for the whole cruise. They leave Venice and disembark at any one of several ports of call. Indeed one of the advertised advantages of the trip is that you may stay any place you please for several days, either picking the ship up on her return or waiting until she comes back on the following cruise. Furthermore, as Peter observed, "I don't care what they say about holding the cabins just for us, I had a hot sack."

There were a good many Germans on board, and the ship was run with Prussian efficiency. We were having drinks in the bar before dinner, which was announced by a trill on a xylophone, and when we did not leap immediately to our feet a steward came over to us. "Go now. Dinner."

"When we're damn good and ready," the doctor said pleasantly. We laughed about it with our table companions, a nice couple, the Paul Steikers from Laguna Beach, California. We laughed too when a tremendously fat German couple, cartoon people in the flesh, tons of it, cavorted about the dance floor after dinner. They were extroverts in brass, but they were having a good time, and the next day, splashing in the tiny deck pool, the wife looked startlingly like a happy hippopotamus.

Balancing the scales was a group of six fragile young men, three married couples, we gathered, and we wondered if at table they took care not to seat husbands and wives together, following the heterosexual convention.

After luncheon we passed through the Corinth Canal, that extraordinary slice in the earth that has been the Greek dream since the earliest days of her history, and at four-thirty on the dot, we docked at Piraeus, the port of Athens.

CHAPTER SIX

Greece

One reason we had been eager to get back to Greece, besides our affection for the country, was to see our friend, Mando Aravantinou, who six years before had shepherded us with wisdom and a humor through her native land. This time too she was, so to speak, to pick up Ariadne's thread and guide us through parts of Greece we had not before visited. To our disappointment she had a previous commitment on the day of our arrival and was not at the dock to meet us.

However, we were not neglected. A dapper and knowledgeable colleague, Mr. Dimos Vratsanos, was on hand agog to make a tour of the *Istra*, a Yugoslav ship. The reason he was curious about her was because she was The Enemy, the Greeks and Yugoslavs having for centuries been at odds over Macedonia, each claiming it as its own, with Bulgarian pretensions tossed in for good measure.

Vratsanos was willing to discuss Bulgarians, whom he considered human beings despite their Communistic leanings, but he anathematized Albanians.

Albanians he felt to be hand in glove with the powers of darkness, Russia and China. His emotions were understandable, his father and brother having been killed by Communists in Greece in the uprising of 1945 just as the Second World War came to a close.

The first time we had been in Athens we had stayed at the Grand Bretagne. This time we drove to the King George, following the way that had once been enclosed by the long walls connecting the port with the capital. The two hotels are side by side on Constitution Square and in both the rooms are quite noisy but comfortable. We thought the King George had somewhat the edge because its atmosphere is more old-fashioned, cozy, and personal.

One reason, perhaps, is that Mr. Basil Kalkanis, the owner, lives there. He is noted for his art collection, which he one day invited us to view. The gallery consists of a suite of two or three rooms, and the walls are solidly covered by many acres of canvas: large pictures and small pictures in heavy frames, mostly the work of late nineteenth- and early twentieth-century Greek academicians. A young clerk hovered discreetly in attendance and a maid with a lamp followed us about, plugging and unplugging the powerful light so we could see all the details.

Costly brands of liquor were prominently displayed on an admirably stocked bar, ice buckets and glasses sparkled, little silver dishes of nuts glittered and flashed in the light of the lamp, and the waiter who followed the maid extended a silver tray with glasses of fresh cold orange juice. I thought it delicious, but the light in my loved one's eyes faded.

The tour finished, our host spoke about the royalty that had been quartered on them at the time of the weddings of Princess Sofia to Don Carlos of Spain and of Prince Constantine to Anna Maria of Denmark.

I said that I imagined the questions of protocol must have been very delicate. Mr. Kalkanis rolled his eyes to heaven. "And not only protocol. The jewels!"

The few royal ladies left have meager opportunity for all-out display, and each, quite humanly, was trying to out-glitter the other. We gathered that Queen Juliana of the Netherlands blazed the brightest.

Athens at first glance can be disappointing. One expects so much, but the city itself has nothing like the magnificence of Paris or the appeal of certain parts of London or the beauty of Prague.

One Mr. Dicaearchus, a disciple of Aristotle wrote of Athens that it was "dusty and ill supplied with water, wretchedly laid out on account of its antiquity, while the majority of houses are mean, and very few good. A stranger at first sight might well doubt that this is Athens." More than two thousand years later it is not all that different, although we suffered from no lack of water.

Athens, I should say, is disappointing the way San Francisco is. One hears so much about it, and in the case of the latter the location *is* superb, but the houses themselves fall short of anticipation.

With the evening of the first day came Mr. Frangopolous, a vigorous, cheerful, and ebullient member of the Greek Travel Bureau and lieutenant of Dimitri Papaefstratiou, the omiscient head of the firm, known to countless Americans through his services in the New York office of the American Express Company.

We murmured something about the allure of Greece.

"No, no," said Mr. Frangopolous firmly, "never mind that. It is the Greek people, *they* are what you must see and know."

"But the art!" The splendors of the world were brushed aside.

"You'll see art in all Mediterranean countries. And ruins. They're full of Greek ruins."

"But the weather here is so wonderful."

"It's wonderful in Beirut too. No, no, it is the Greek people who are unique!"

We promised to do our best to meet as many as we could, and Mr. Frangopolous departed leaving us a bit limp from so much vigor.

We were just settling down to a drink when he whirled back again, this time with Mando in tow, our dear Mando, with soft brown eyes, soft round curves, and a pleasantly sharp tongue. We had a great reunion and learned with pleasure that since we had last seen her she had published two books of poetry. We offered her vodka, which she accepted on condition that the next day we would plunge into ouzo.

That night we dined in the hotel. There is a restaurant on the roof, and from the terrace one has a marvelous view of the Acropolis, which we also could see from our rooms. We were in and out of the city several times during our three-week visit but everytime it seemed incredible that one could look out the window and say, "There it is."

After dinner we took a cab and drove up Philopappos Hill, opposite the Parthenon. Beside the road, lovers stood embraced in the darkness and never moved when the headlights swept over them as the car rounded the curves. Bathed in the light of a full moon the Parthenon rode the height like a galleon. Norton and Peter and I stood for a long time looking at it.

The next day, for Pete's edification, we visited the Plaka, the old tiny village on the eastern slope of the Acropolis.

As those who have visited Athens know, the Plaka is a kind of Greenwich Village, although one doesn't *have* to be an artist to live there. The winding narrow streets are bricks and cobblestones, the sun-splashed walls are blindingly white, the houses tiny, and grapevines twine the trellises. It is marvelously picturesque, but housekeeping in cramped quarters cannot be easy despite the amenities of electricity and iceboxes, the latter the old-fashioned kind with the family friend delivering the ice.

Some people think that the name Plaka derives from the Greek word for slab, but Vratsanos was of the opinion that it might be a corruption of the Albanian *blaca* or holy place. It would have been holy to the Greeks as it tumbles down the slope below the Parthenon. The quarter is also known as

48   Drying squid at Thasos.

49   Mosaic at Pella. *Photo Lykides*

50   Lion hunt Pella mosaic.
      Photo Lykides

51 Statue of Poseidon in the
Archaeological Museum in Athens.

52 Kanaris Restaurant, Turkolimano in Piraeus. Greatest sea food in
the world.

53   Co-op vineyard center at Arhanes in Crete.

54   Phaestus.

55   Controversial Pantocrator,
the mosaic at Daphne.

56   Mouse Island and the monastery in the Bay of Corfu.

57   The pink house on Corfu.

Nafiotica because in the early twentieth century refugees
from Anafi in the Cyclades sought asylum there when flee-
ing from the Turks.

It would be a pity were it ever to disappear but there
is a possibility that in ten to twenty years the Plaka may be
demolished in the course of excavating for further treasures
of antiquity.

Leaving the village we drove to a very different world,
Astir Beach, a cottage resort at Vouliagmeni, about twenty-
two kilometers from the city. The grounds were meticulously manicured, green and flowery and the cottages were
really good, well furnished and designed for privacy. They
cluster around a tiny bay, but unhappily, a large, new
hotel was being erected on the opposite shore, which is
very, very near. Privacy will be abolished.

The Greeks may defeat themselves by overbuilding because they will eradicate the natural beauty and simplicity
only possible when areas are not overcrowded. For the
present, however, the financial picture is rosy and it is
understandable that the country has decided to exploit
her unique climatic and coastal resources. It seemed to us
that Mr. Frangopolous tended to belittle that bounty; the
climate and seas of Greece are marvelously in harmony with
today's passion for swimming and sunbathing. They are
magnets for tourist currency from all over the world. We
visited several of the new resorts and thought most of them
well conceived and well managed and the prices very fair.
At Vouliagmeni, for instance, the rate is $19.00 per day for
a bungalow for two, breakfast included. Prices drop
sharply in the off season between October 1 and April 1.
If you have a pet, do not take it. Usually animals are not
permitted, and parrots are not allowed into the country at
all.

Driving back to Athens we overtook a man on a motorcycle and balancing adroitly on the seat behind him was,
not the woman in his life, but the baboon, a fine chap with
little red pants on, his gray mane blowing in the breeze.

He would not have been welcome at Vouliagmeni, but he was a diverting sight. That night, pondering where we could dine we turned to Mr. Leslie Finer. Mr. Finer, a British journalist who lives in Athens and who is married to a Greek actress, has written a well documented and highly readable guidebook called *Passport to Greece*. It had become something of a Bible to us, and it came to our rescue again by recommending the Taverna Adam, 8 Makriyanni Street in the Plaka. Since it was not far from the King George, we decided to go there. It was a sound decision for the food and wine were excellent. Incidentally, I should like here to explode that myth that the only wine you can get in Greece is retsina, the brew that tastes of and I think indeed is impregnated with pine tar by way of a preservative. Finer palates abhor it—I myself on the one occasion I tasted it, didn't find it all that dismaying—but the point is that it was served on only one occasion and then we had to ask for it especially. The rest of the time the Greek wines were light, flavorful, and unadulterated.

The minute we entered we suspected the Adam was going to be good. Crowded with contentedly munching Athenians it had all the gracious atmosphere of a commuting station on the Long Island or New York Central railroads, although there was a pianist who had the sense and good taste to keep his talent pianissimo. About the most you can say aesthetically for the restaurants of Greece is that they are shelters from the elements. If the Greeks themselves have a word for them it is utilitarian. Should you find one with a pretty patio or set under the trees at the water's edge, savor it, it is a rarity. But that doesn't matter; what counts is the nourishment, and at the Adam it is very fine. We got the last table and when we left shortly after eleven o'clock it was snapped up by a party just arriving. The Athenians keep Spanish dining hours.

Our first visit to the Acropolis was in the afternoon. Threading our way among hordes of German sightseers we were picked up by an elderly guide. He imparted to us his theory that the legendary Cyclops were in reality miners who painted their foreheads with phosphorescent disks which gave them the appearance of having one great shining eye. He agreed with Homer that they lived in caves but the caves actually were mines. I hadn't heard this contention before nor have I heard it since, but I pass it on, a snippet of archaic gossip, to be hoarded or tossed aside as one chooses.

The next day we returned with Mando. We arrived at ten o'clock, when the rock opens for business, and crowds were already swarming upward.

This time we went to the museum, one of the great repositories of Greek art. All the exhibits, I believe, have been excavated in the Acropolis itself.

To my mind the most irresistible pieces are of the sixth century B.C., the archaic era. There is the Moschophoros, the calf bearer, a young man with a marble calf over his shoulders. The poor little creature is being doomed for the Greeks like all the ancient world, killed animals not only to eat, but also for sacrifice. Yet there is great tenderness in the modeling both of youth and beast and it may be that that is the statue from which the Good Shepherd of Christendom was derived. In the museum too is the archaic quadriga, four horses abreast, of striking refinement and purity of line. Not far away the headless, exquisitely draped Nike unloosens her sandal. There is the naked male rider of extraordinary beauty with beaded beard and spiral curls, and there are statues of lovely women, traces of color still remaining on their hair, lips and tunics. Finally we looked at the humorous, licentious, ogling demons who have been bursting with spontaneous laughter for 2500 years.

From this treasure house we walked down to the admirably preserved Agora. In primitive times *agora* meant the assembly of the Greek people. It was usually convoked by the king and all the citizens went, but it lacked the spirit of a town meeting, since the only people allowed to speak their pieces were the king and the nobles. *Hoi polloi* were permitted to comment, however, either by applause when pleased or, one assumes, by boos, catcalls, and hissing when the decisions of their betters struck them as less than astute.

The place where the assembly was held finally came to be called the Agora, and in the great era of the Greeks it was the market place. There were shops and law courts and cafés, and on their way to and from the temple of the goddess Athena up on the Acropolis, free men met to philosophize and converse and exchange the time of day. Slaves went to the Agora too, bent mostly on household errands, but no women were allowed and with all that life and gossiping going on the ladies' frustration must have been acute, especially when one considers that there were no modern hairdressers where they could meet and shout at each other from under the driers.

Having walked around inside the Agora we gazed out over the great open square but did not particularly care for the Stoa, the roofed colonnade which, in the original version, must have seemed indigenous to the area but which restored, as it now is, has a rather clinical antiseptic look.

One thing about Mando that had won our hearts when we first met her and which—we were entranced to find—had not changed was her interest in food. Nothing is so hunger-inducing as culture, and although we were driving out to Sounion for lunch and to see the Temple, Mando was of the opinion that a little sustenance for the road could do no harm. Besides she wanted to show us the Dionysus, a restaurant at the foot of the Acropolis from which one obtains a marvelous view and which had opened since we were in Athens.

The Dionysus is a Greek restaurant that does have style and a pleasant decor as well as extremely good food. We returned to it several times for complete meals but on our first visit contented ourselves with beer, olives, and cheese to stay us on the drive down the peninsula.

At the Sounion restaurant we were back to the no-non-sense-just-get-the-food-on-the-table approach, nor could we fault it. Everything was good and the *meses*—Greek hors d'oeuvres—and grilled sole outstanding. In *The Cartha-ginian Rose* I observed that the restaurant was mediocre. I eat those words along with that delicious meal, but in my defense as a reporter I suspect they may have changed the chef since 1959.

Sitting under the awning one has an unimpaired view of the nearby columns, all that remains of the Temple of Poseidon.

When we had been there before we had had a golden day. This time the sky was overcast, veiled in blue and gray and lavender, and Poseidon had set a strong wind blowing. We pressed into it as we mounted the headland, Mando's scarlet scarf, which she had wrapped around her head, whipping before us like a flag.

We showed Peter the column where Byron had carved his name. Ravel did the same on another. The graffiti of the famous are historic, but let poor, eager Harry Ginsberg of the Bronx commit one squiggle and it's vandalism.

Poseidon was not only the god of the sea but of all water. He was also the god of bulls and of horses, perhaps because the latter's racing manes are like whitecaps, and thousands of the fleet animals were sacrificed to him by being drowned. It is usually when men are at their most religious that they behave with the least sense and the greatest cruelty.

Back in Athens, as we were taking an evening stroll, one feature of the city that struck us as being nearly as splendid as the Acropolis was the taxicabs in all their gorgeous plethora. In the iron curtain countries they are sparse, and it was a pleasure to find them once more available.

Our friends from the *Istra*, the Steikers, came that night

to dine with us. They were staying at the Hilton and we went there afterward for liqueurs. It is supposedly the most beautiful Hilton of them all. In Istanbul and Cairo, Norton and I were guests of the ubiquitous gentleman, and sometimes his hotels are a good idea, but from preference I would not stay in the Paradise Hilton. My taste is less grandiose. I must acknowledge, however, that the ladies' room was spectacular; acres of gleaming marble, spotlessly clean.

Another Hiltonian feature was the art gallery with some nice sculpture. There are also attractive shops, but my advice is to compare their prices with those in the center of the town. There was a big, lovely woven rug for $131.50, which I thought reasonable for what it was, but in Their Majesty's Fund Shop in Voukourestious Street, the identical rug sold for $118. This is because the Fund shop is run for charity, the proceeds going to poor families of Greece. The stock is tempting: table linen, pretty necklaces, bright rugs, woven skirts, handbags, warm, light, little crocheted shawls in melting colors, everything done with taste and at reasonable prices. They accept traveler's checks or American Express credit cards and will ship merchandise around the world. Another rewarding penny trap is the Cretan Art Shop where there is gay, inexpensive costume jewelry and quite smart sports shirts from the islands.

As we would be doing a good deal of touring through Greece, we wanted to pay a visit to the travel bureau to meet those who had been so helpful in working out an itinerary in advance and to whose knowledge and advice we were to owe a great deal of pleasure. Accordingly we went one morning to the office of Mr. Papaefstratiou.

The Greek Travel Bureau is closely allied with the government and Mr. Papaefstratiou is an important man, but the luxury office as a status symbol has not yet reached Greece. Leather couches, oak paneling, acres of mahogany, and French Impressionists . . . these are not the lot of

Greek brass. Like their restaurants their offices are utilitarian. Pleasant attributes are the tiny cups of Turkish—
or I suppose, Greek, coffee—and, since it is so sweet, many
glasses of ice water.

Mr. Papaefstratiou or Papa, as in Hemingway, to his inti-
mates—glanced quickly through our itinerary, making a
few suggestions for changes to which we quickly agreed
since they would give us more time in Crete. Then he
went into conference with Mando and Mr. Frangopolous.
A torrent of Greek bounded, cascaded, swirled, and eddied
around us. It was the water coming down at Lodore. At
sporadic intervals one word that we could understand shot
out like a rocket: "Relax!"

They were, we gathered, taking pity on us. We would
travel, *how* we would travel, by plane, by car, by boat.
We would behold the art *and* the isles and the beach
resorts of Greece, but every now and then we would "Relax." That part sounded marvelous. Peter, Norton, and I
nodded at each other reassuringly and left the office to
wind up our Athenian business.

This time we had a proper full luncheon at Dionysus,
and it was delicious, as no more than befitted the god of
vegetation and wine. Under the scudding clouds we
watched the Parthenon changing in the changing light from
honey gold to rose pink; draining from lion tawny to gray.
Looking through the enormous window, we observed that
Greek flags flew from every lamppost and the waiter told
us it was because it was the eleventh of October. On that
date in 1944, after four long years the last of the Germans
were driven from Greece.

Learning that the first international Biennale exhibition
of sculpture was being held on the pine-forested slopes of
the Philopappos Hill, we went to see it after luncheon.
Eighteen countries and sixty-six artists were represented,
among them Lipschitz, Moore, Archipenko, Rodin, Picasso,
Noguchi, and Modigliani. Viewed out of doors the work

acquires a dimension and a vitality often lost in an art gallery.

Later we went to call upon friends we had met the first time we were in Athens, Mr. and Mrs. Argyropoulos. They still live in their high white house that climbs a hillside, and we sat in a beautifully proportioned drawing room while our hostess poured tea into fragile porcelain cups.

An elegant, pretty woman with soft golden hair piled on top of her head, she apologized for husband's absence, explaining that although he was at home he had work to finish since they were going to London at the end of the week. Two or three times she left us, perhaps trying to persuade him to appear, each time carefully closing the door behind her. Norton, Peter, and I sat in the great shadowy room barely daring to speak above a whisper. It occurred to me then how extremely rare it is that I ever close a door in my own house.

On her return from one of her sorties our hostess asked us about our travels through the Communist countries, especially Romania, which she knew well—her husband at one time having held a diplomatic post there.

We reported to the best of our ability but could see that she was apprehensive about Communism. She had of course suffered through the brutal 1945–47 period and was convinced that much Communist money was being poured into Greece for propaganda purposes.

Another Athenian friend, Helen Vlachos, the publisher, also suspected this to be the case, but her attitude was more carefree. One afternoon she arrived to have a drink with us, still laughing over her encounter with a young Russian. "He presented me with copies of the *Don* novels by Mikhail Sholokhov," she said. "He was very handsome, but he looked baffled. 'Everybody says I am spreading Russian propaganda, but of course I am. What should I spread? American?'"

As we were walking home from the high quiet house I

said I was sorry we had not seen our host who I remembered
as a man of great charm. "Too bad he was working," I said.

"What's *he* got to work on?" demanded the doctor, who,
like many busy professional people tends to think that
other people have nothing of importance to occupy them.

We went early to bed as the next morning we were to
be under way at 6 A.M. The flight from Athens to Kavalla
is an hour and a half, and the weather was fresh and
sunny.

Kavalla is a tobacco center. A good deal of wealth is
concentrated there, and apparently in the old days the
living was high, the young blades importing gay girls and
gypsy bands from Budapest. But Budapest is now Communist, and Communists are very moral and the happy
times have gone. Today, having not much else to do in a
provincial community, the rich burghers sit around playing
poker for large stakes.

We had arrived at half-past nine but the winter schedule
for the ferry to Thasos, our real goal, was in force and we
were obliged to hang around until one-thirty waiting for
passage.

For those who might be traveling as late in the season
as we were, it is possible, with a bit of scurrying, to make
the earlier boat and a shorter crossing, but the port is
forty-two kilometers from the air terminal, and one must
know the route.

In the course of our leisurely puttering about we learned
that Kavalla means to ride. The town is called that because
according to historical legend Alexander the Great, who
lived in Pella, had a horse named Bucephalus, and so
speedy was he that when Alexander tried to mount him
he broke away and galloped all the way to Kavalla before
his master could catch up with him. He lived to the age
of thirty, only three years less than Alexander himself, and
the emperor loved him so much that he built a city and
called it Bucephala.

There is a rather curious house in Kavalla that was at

one time the home of Mehemet Ali, and where King Farouk
of Egypt lived as a baby we were told.

The house is by no means large and today stripped of
rugs and hangings it has a ramshackle air and appears to
have been jerry-built. Yet its harem is said to have harbored
thirty women. A more sterile, confined, ignominious life it
would be hard to imagine. Nor a dirtier one! There was one
tiny bathroom with two stone sinks and one toilet, a V-
shaped hole in the floor.

We were glad to leave it and drive to the Michalis
Restaurant, where we lunched. It was only a little after
eleven, but we had been up since six and had breakfasted
on nothing but tea and coffee. Mouth-watering odors were
being wafted from the kitchen, which, in accordance with
Greek custom, we promptly went to visit. There were chickens roasting on spits and fish so fresh they all but flopped.
While waiting we sipped ouzo and with luncheon drank
an excellent white wine, St. Helena '62. The first course
was a new experience. Boureki. Triangular fragile paper-
thin crusts stuffed with cheese and popped into the oven.
The pastry is available in Greek stores in this country. It
is called phyllo and may be filled with meat or spinach
or anything one wants, but I never expect again to taste it
so perfectly prepared unless I return to Kavalla and Michalis. It is a big plain restaurant on a height overlooking
the sea, and the chef is a great man.

When Mando announced that a group of Italians was
arriving we anticipated a busload of tourists, but they
turned out to be technicians working in a nearby fertilizer
plant. Such are the mysteries and benefits of the Common
Market. Michalis only used to be open for dinner, but
now, thanks to the influx of foreign skilled labor, they do
a brisk luncheon trade as well.

Thasos lies high in the Aegean, tucked under Thrace, the
long narrow strip of northeastern Greece that is bordered
by Bulgaria on the north and Turkey on the extreme east.

It took us two hours to reach it on an American army surplus LST.

The day was beautiful and the voyage pleasant. Our companions were farmers, laborers, and technicians, virile men for the most part, dark of hair and eye with strong, often handsome faces. There is something reassuring about the peasant stock of Europe; the earth has not been leached out of them. Many Greeks have the quality of their bread, flavorful and sustaining. I used to think French bread the best there was, but this time the bread of Greece seemed even better.

Our LST dropped anchor at Limin, which means port and is indeed the port of Thasos. We went to a small waterside hotel, one of the Xenia chain run by the Greek Travel Bureau. They are simple and pleasant, with comfortable rooms always well situated, and although the caliber of the food varies to some extent from hotel to hotel, we found it for the most part very good. In Thasos I ate the freshest egg I have had since my childhood, when I once spent a summer on a farm and was allowed to gather eggs from the nests.

I ordered one for breakfast. A moment later a child Mercury took off on his bicycle for the village where he called on a co-operative hen. In five minutes he was back, and in four minutes the egg was on my plate. That's the way to do it.

On our arrival at the Xenia we had tea and then walked along the quai and followed a path winding up a hill through a pine grove. An elderly guide whom we did not need attached himself to us, but Mando had not the heart to shoo him away. "He's rather touching," she said. "He has just told me, 'Tomorrow arrives a cruise of American millionaires. I am happy.'" The prospect interested us too. A whole cruise of millionaires! Perhaps they were adherents of President Johnson's anti-poverty program and would want to help their less fortunately endowed compatriots.

The town of Thasos existed as early as the fifth century B.C., and the terraces of olive and pine trees with their stone sustaining walls seem nearly as ancient. Winding our way upward we came to the amphitheater in a pine wood on a hillside overlooking the sea. Needles cover the ground; trees rise up through the old tilting, fallen stones, and the aroma of pine hangs on the air. The stone benches have crumbled away; today they are of wood and they are in service. The year before there had been a drama festival, and the guide was enthusiastic about the five Greek classics that had been produced.

Norton and I had once been at the Epidaurus festival, and it is an extraordinary emotional experience to be sitting in the same theater, watching the same play that was performed there two thousand years ago.

In the early days Thasos was famous for its gold mines which were undoubtedly the attraction for the Phoenicians, its early colonizers. Its great exports were olive oil, honey, and marble, and today the last two are still in demand, although we could find no proof of the legend that the harbor is marble-paved. It may have been so at one time but careful scrutiny on our part failed to evoke a single glimmer and we concluded that the paving, if it existed, had long since been silted over.

Some evenings of travel are gayer than others and our night in Thasos was such a one. At first there were just four of us, Mando and Peter, Norton and I, and over our cocktails and pistachio nuts and dinner we felt very festive. Mando was amusing, outspoken, and liberal in her politics. A Greek acquaintance of hers who happened to be spending the night at the Xenia joined us after dinner, and we gathered he regarded the queen mother's forays into archaeology as something of a mixed blessing. "She gets her pictures in the paper a lot, but she is not knowledgeable, and it is hard for the real scientists."

The next morning we drove, not without difficulty, to the little mountain village of Panayia. One could truthfully say the road is paved with marble but if that evokes

visions of gleaming, meticulously joined slabs the visions
are false. The marble has long since broken into hunks and
chunks, and is larded with stones and twigs and branches
from the fir trees. The going was rough but the countryside was classic with vistas of the sea at every turn.

The village was no more than a small group of whitewashed houses with lichen covered slate roofs and three
springs of clear sparkling water that bubbled and trickled
and gushed down the gutters and across the cobbles.

We were there in October, and there was no electricity.
It had been promised for Christmas, and excitement was
already running high. We sat for a while in the tiny tree-
shaded square and then went on to visit one of the newly
opened beach resorts on the bay. The cottages were of
whitewashed cubic island architecture, indigenous and appropriate to environment and climate.

Since they were so new, the season had been shortlived,
having ended the first of October. The cottages are now
established for annual business and Thasos, sea surrounded,
with its hills and fragrant pine woods, would be a lovely
place to spend a holiday. Actually a dream vacation would
be a cruise among the Greek islands, if one had the time
and money. If not, I would suggest a little island hopping
by air, for the flights are brief and inexpensive. One could
spend a few days in various cottage colonies bathing, relaxing, and immersing one's self in sparkling waters, and in
the history and art of a fabled land.

If such is one's bent the vacation could be prolonged
indefinitely since there are 1425 islands, although, according to our friend Mr. Finer, only 166 are officially classified
as inhabited.

Our return to the mainland took much less time than
our journey out. We landed at Keramoti, picked up our
car, and drove for two and a half hours, mostly through
darkness, to Thessalonike, the capital of Macedonian
Thrace.

Our hotel was the Mediterranean Palace, an old-fashioned comfortable establishment with immensely high ceilings and balconies overlooking the waterfront. Since we were fond of Mando, the city had for us a special interest. It was her old home, where she had lived as a young girl during the war. She told us that there had been 56,000 Jews in Salonika and at first they were not treated badly by the Nazis because they were mostly of Spanish origin, descendants of those who had fled from Spain and Portugal in the sixteenth century to escape the Inquisition. In 1940 Germany and Spain were allies, but the amnesty was short-lived. Eventually the Jews were herded into ghettos and in 1943 were transported to German concentration camps. Out of 56,000 Jews, 1950 returned. After the war West Germany paid 112,000,000 drachmas to the 8000 Jews left in Greece, and the Greek government reapportioned among the survivors the land holdings of those who had been exterminated.

Thessalonike is the Salonika of one's schoolbooks, and it's an old place, too, having been founded in 315 B.C. by Cassander, the King of Macedonia who gracefully named it after his wife, a half-sister of Alexander the Great. His pleasant mood appears to have come to an abrupt end when, in 310 or 309 B.C., he murdered Alexander's wife and son. By that time the emperor himself was dead. He died, it will be recalled, in 323 B.C., at the age of thirty-three, but is that any reason to dispatch his family?

Thessalonike is reminiscent of Alexandria in that it is a great corniche, or crescent, embracing the gulf on which it lies as Alexandria embraces its corner of the Mediterranean. The inhabitants use of electricity is striking; not good but a lot of it. The Greeks are crazy about neon lights, and billboards, houses, and arcades are all outlined in luminous tubing. It is a wonder that Dr. Platon, the curator of the Acropolis in Athens, has been able to fend off his countrymen and prevent them from similarly outlining the Parthenon.

Thessalonike bristles with historic ruins, chiefly Roman and Byzantine. There are ancient fortifications, which we clambered over, and there is a fourteenth-century tower built at the time of the Crusades. It's virtually contemporary compared to a Roman arch of the fourth century, ornamented with tunicked soldiers and gracefully draped women.

Three great churches of primary interest are St. Sophia, St. George, and St. Demetrius. The first was erected as a cathedral, probably in the sixth century, and was converted into a mosque in the sixteenth. The nave is in the form of a Greek cross, and the mosaics of the dome's cupola are rich and impressive.

St. George's, probably of the fourth century, is gigantic. It too has extraordinary mosaics: saints and arches and pavilions, but the rotunda is faced with brilliantly colored squares in every one of which are centered different birds and different fruits, secular and gay.

St. Demetrius is interesting because the columns of the aisles are half the height of those of the nave, resulting in a pitched roof, the only one of its kind in classical religious architecture. The mosaic saints are tall, lean, and handsomely garbed.

The church we enjoyed most, however, was less imposing but it had a sweet private quality and seemed to be known only to Mando. It is St. David's, hidden away in a tree-shaded courtyard. It is very small, and the mosaics in the apse were only discovered after the last war. They are in charming soft colors, a figure of Christ with a lion on his left, on his right an ox, and a friendly-looking serpent rising from flowers.

We were impressed by the architectural riches of Thessalonike and also by the air pollution so reminiscent of our own dear city. Yet it must be said in defense of Thessalonike that their blight was not a permanent contribution of the Consolidated Edison Company nor of the public transportation system, belching carbon monoxide from the exhausts. It was due to the enormous amount of construction that was under way and filled the air with clouds of cement dust. Nevertheless we were glad to escape it by lunching at the seaside and going afterward to visit a rather unexpected institution, the American Agricultural School. The Americans are everywhere!

That school is a monument to faith, common sense, dogged determination, and simple guts. In 1902, at the age of sixty, an American, Dr. John Henry House, who had spent thirty years as a Congregational missionary in the Balkans, borrowed $500 and broke ground for a school he had long dreamed about. It was to provide rural Greek boys with "agricultural and industrial training under Christian leadership." He started with twelve students and fifty acres of barren ground.

Little by little small contributions trickled in, and he began construction of James Hall, which was to be the central classroom building. It was completed in 1916, but as the gutters were being soldered a spark ignited the roof and in less than an hour the work and hopes of a decade lay in ashes.

That might have discouraged most men but not Dr. House, who merely looked upon it as a challenge. With the aid of his son, Charles, he started over again and when he died at the age of ninety-one he left a growing school of 150 students and 300 acres of well-farmed land.

Charles House followed his father as director, but his own lot was not easy either. During World War II he was interned in Germany. James Hall was occupied by the Germans and nearly destroyed by bombs. Thanks to funds from America it was rebuilt and ready for occupancy in 1945, but its troubles were not over even then. Civil war erupted in Greece, and in the winter of 1949 Communist guerrillas kidnaped the entire senior class of forty-three boys and took them north toward the iron curtain. Thanks to fantastic courage, endurance, and ingenuity every single boy escaped and made his way back to school, and when the roster was called on graduation day in June, every member of the class was present.

Bruce Lansdale, who is now the director, explained to us that although they gave the boys a good general education the last thing they wanted was to make white collar workers of them. The whole point of the school is to train them in the best methods of farming, animal husbandry, and reforestation so that they may return to their villages and put what they have learned into practice.

They are taught everything they will need for village life. They can build a respectable house. They can handle simple plumbing and electrical wiring. In age the students range from fourteen to eighteen, and, "It's interesting," Dr. Lansdale said, "to see how hard they work the minute they grasp the profit system and start making a little money of their own through their own efforts. Best antidote to Communism there is."

The school, now three-quarters self-supporting, covers 400 acres, and the course takes four years. The younger boys have vegetable plots; the older ones go in for livestock, because they realize that even though it is more work it pays better. They have chickens, cows, pigs, and sheep, and President Eisenhower gave them a black Angus. "We wanted a white-faced Hereford," Mr. Lansdale said, "but it's hard to look a presidential gift bull in the mouth, so we accepted it as gratefully as we could."

The next morning we happened upon a marvel. Our goal was Volos, but making a detour, we drove to Pella where Alexander the Great lived as a boy.

Pella itself is flat and arid, but treasures are being excavated. A few rather small columns rising from a paved floor were not of unusual interest, but *then* we saw the mosaics.

Three, so far, had been dug up and an attendant obligingly opened iron doors that had been hinged onto the rough lumber frames that housed them and indicated that we could admire them at our leisure. They are of singular beauty. The mosaics are not composed of little squares of ceramic or marble as is so often the case, but of tiny subtly colored pebbles.

In one a naked youth, beribboned staff in hand, rides sidesaddle on an elegant leopard whose tail curves as gracefully as the ribbons. In another a winged chimera attacks a stag and in the third on a stony heath two male figures, naked except for short blowing capes and a curious scooped hat that one of them is wearing, menace a red-maned lion with upraised sword and threatening spear. The sense of movement and vitality is extraordinary and one of the figures is thought to represent Alexander at the hunt.

When we were there the discovery of the mosaics was so recent that some had still not been unearthed. A scaffold had been erected over one of them from which a camera could be suspended so that it could be photographed as soon as the coverings were removed.

We had learned about this incomparable find by pure fluke. When snooping around a newsstand in Thessalonike I had come upon a postcard of one of the masterpieces and asked where one could see it. On learning it was just down the road a piece, we had scurried over. More mosaics have been excavated since, and so a visit now would be still more rewarding.

Leaving Pella, we were obliged to retrace our steps a few miles and then head south, passing through the heartland of the classics, with Mount Olympus soaring on our right and the Aegean sparkling on our left. We also passed a romantic ruin, walls, turrets, and an octagonal tower, the Castle of the Fair One. It was a fortress owned by a woman who held it against the Turks. She was doing very well too, until one day a handsome young Turk disguised as a monk, pleading hunger and exhaustion, appeared at her gate. The silly creature was seduced by his pretty face and tale of woe. She ordered the gates opened. The Turks who had lain concealed awaiting the moment of human frailty poured in, and that was the end of the lady.

Less romantic but more sustaining is the Xenia Restaurant nearby, which offers a magnificent view and a good luncheon. Assured that we were well fortified and feeling we should be game for any venture, Mando decreed Ambelakia. Ambelakia has its points but she was right in sensing it should not be attempted on an empty stomach. It is a tiny village high in the mountains well away from the main highway. The road is more or less a courtesy affair, steep and precipitate, and when one gets there, there is still considerable puffing and panting to do on foot before arriving at the house our friend was determined we should see.

The house is old and in bad repair, but there are two enchanting painted rooms. On a smaller scale they are very similar to those in the rich Greek's house in Plovdiv.

We were to visit other hidden highland villages too, and we asked Mando why the early Greeks had had such a predilection for inaccessible locations. The reason, if one stops to think for a minute, is obvious. The more hidden and difficult of access for the Greeks, the more so for their enemies, especially the Turks. That is why the Greek guerrillas favored Mount Olympus as a hideout in World War II, causing the Germans no end of inconvenience and casualties.

Ambelakia had been a village of weavers, and the head man, with the un-Greek name of Mr. Schwartz, was a shrewd merchant, traveling all the way to Vienna to sell his fabrics. Like Grandpa Vanderhoff in *You Can't Take It with You*, he did not believe in taxes and was able to adhere to his principles because the Turks had an understandable reluctance to send collectors into so remote and hostile an area.

Mr. Schwartz's great-granddaughter and her family still live there. They are trying to repair the house themselves and plan to charge a modest entrance fee to those who will come to see the pretty rooms. There is always that better mouse trap but as the roads are at present it is a long and rugged way to drive for a little charm. On the other hand, if the ugly and the shoddy proliferate long enough, it is altogether possible that people will be willing to go to considerable inconvenience to look at something charming.

Unhooked from our lofty perch we drove back down the mountain and regained the main highway passing through the Vale of Tempe, where Daphne and Apollo frisked. He pursued her, but she, wanting no part of him, appealed to Zeus, who, perhaps to some degree jealous of his son's beauty and prowess, and wishing to thwart him, turned her into a laurel tree. But the god of light was not easily sidetracked. If he could not have her one way, he would another, and from her tree self he made a wreath and she was awarded as a prize at the Pythian games at Delphi, his home. The winners of the Olympic games were given wreaths of wild olive.

In the late afternoon we came to Volos, where the Xenia Hotel was specially nice. The staircase was banked with green plants, and our rooms, facing west, overlooked the Gulf of Pagasetikos and the hilly islands rising from it.

The Tzaki is an amusing restaurant a little way out of town, where one may go to dine. It is decorated with a great deal of taste, none of it very good, but it is bright and cheerful. The walls, red, blue, and green are broken by flat pilasters of painted imitation bricks. There was an open fire, welcome in the middle of October, and in front of it a cat lay curled up on a donkey saddle ornamented with gay beads and a long-haired sheepskin rug.

The thing to see in Volos is the museum with its outstanding collection of steles, the Greek gravestones. The color on the bas relief carvings is faded but in places still discernible after 2300 years. The figures and draperies recall the work of David who so many centuries later captured in his paintings that same combination of grace and solidity. The steles depicting single figures, families, and groups are beautiful. Still one cannot escape the uneasy feeling that cemeteries, bristling with tombstones all crammed together, look pretty much the same in any age and any place. I was ashamed of myself, but I could not help thinking of that ghastly Calvary Cemetery that one passes on the Expressway driving out to Long Island.

We admired the garden in front of the museum as much as we did the steles. At that season it is a riot of roses, zinnias, and pyracantha. There are also good beaches at Volos but I should not say that the town is an objective in itself. If one were cruising the islands it would be fun to put in there, not to stay, but to visit some of the villages in the Mount Pelion area which have enormous charm. Portaria, Makrynitsa, Zora, Tsangarada, Millies, and St. John are considered little stars. We ourselves went to Portaria and Makrynitsa. The latter is on top of the world overlooking hills and other mountains, the great sweeping valley, Volos, the Gulf, and the Sporades Islands.

The whitewashed houses with their roofs of split stone tumble down the mountain side, and the village square is a terrace sheltered by four gigantic plane trees and a huge ancient poplar. The tiny church is of indifferent architecture, but the carvings on the marble fountain are a delight and everywhere is the sound of running water. We sat at the edge of the terrace, admiring the panoramic view and enjoying superb freshly baked bread, sausages, ouzo, and beer.

The drive down winds between apple orchards, olive and cyprus groves until one comes to a restaurant at Malaki on the water's edge. The little waves lapped at our feet, the sea sparkled, the sun blazed, and the air was cool and fresh. After lunch, we headed back to Athens. It was a five-hour drive, but much of it was beautiful and all was history-drenched, for we were in the region of Thermopylae and Mount Parnassus with Delphi at its base, sacred to Apollo, Dinonysus, and the Muses.

I have since learned that Thermopylae means hot gates.

In today's vernacular it sounds slangy—hot sack, hot damn—
yet the connotation is not of Hades, as one might suppose,
but refers to mineral springs near the pass.

I never cared a great deal for the Spartans having always
been a partisan of the Athenians, but it is hard to reach
Thermopylae, that scene of Spartan heroism, without in-
stinctively rising—also hard if in a car—and standing for a
minute of silent tribute.

Against Xerxes' overwhelmingly superior numbers Leonidas, the Spartan general, commanded about 7000 men,
only 300 of whom were Spartans.

For three days they held back the Persians, only to be
defeated when the traitor Ephialtes led a detachment of
the enemy which cut them off from the rear.

Today, widened by deposits of the Spercheios River the
pass is nearly three miles wide, but at that time it was
a narrow defile spanning no more than fourteen yards.

Leonidas, realizing the situation was desperate, addressed
his troops saying that those who wished to might leave
without dishonor. The majority did. The Spartans, 700
Thespians, and 400 Thebans remained. It is said that the
Thebans shortly surrendered; the rest were slain to the last
man. If it was possible to escape, why didn't they all leave,
to resume the battle later in more favorable circumstances?
It seems mysterious, but perhaps Leonidas and those faith-
ful to him remained because they thought they had a fighting chance. Or, as one version has it, he may have held
the pass to permit the Greek fleet, which supposedly was
defending him from an attack by sea, to retire in safety.
Or it may have been a pure sense of what honor required.
His military strategy is perhaps open to dispute but not
his courage. He fell in the thick of battle, and Xerxes, an ex-
ponent of overkill, had his dead body beheaded and cru-
cified.

On our return to the King George, thanks to Mando and
the Greek Travel Bureau, we were lodged even more sump-

tuously than we had been before. Room 802 is a beauty
and our only possible complaint about the hotel at any time
was the room service.

That is where Aesop must have got his idea for the
tortoise in the fable except, as I recall, the tortoise finally
does reach his goal. So did the waiters. About three in
the morning even though, as was once or twice the case,
our order had been nothing more elaborate than soup and
a sandwich.

The only other trouble with the King George is the location. It is ideal, and because it is, the traveler's tasks are
slighted. Letter writing, working up the diary, annotating
film, light laundry . . . these little chores are glossed
over, thanks to the Parthenon. There it is, clearly visible
from one's window and so hauntingly beautiful in almost
every light, perhaps most of all at dawn when washed in
palest rose and lavender, that one's time is spent on the
balcony or hanging out the window simply looking at it.

I know about dawn, because Norton and I are early
risers and it gets us into a lot of trouble. When you yourself have been up since six or seven, the temptation to
telephone your friends around eight or eight-thirty is strong
and must be strongly resisted, or the friends turn to enemies.
Testy grumpy sleepy enemies who quite candidly wish you
were dead.

We did feel though that Mando had had an ample re-
cuperative spell when we phoned her at ten-thirty the
morning after our return from the Kavalla-Volos tour. Well,
she had not. She was sound asleep. We muttered hasty apol-
ogies and assured her we could manage on our own. The
doctor gave her professional orders to stay in bed and
rest, and we hung up feeling guilty.

"We must be exhausting," said my quack. He said We,
but if ever I saw a You look it was the one he directed
at me.

We missed Mando, but we had a lovely day, so much

so that we felt that if nothing good happened to us for a long time we were well ahead of the game.

The sunlight on the Acropolis had brought glory in the morning and the sense of splendor was sustained by a visit to the Archaeological Museum, which contains one of the most superb male figures ever sculpted, the Poseidon, dating from the fifth century B.C. that was raised from the sea in 1929.

We lunched at Kanaris at Turkolimano in Piraeus. The tables of the two or three restaurants on the quai jostle each other so it is hard to know where one stops and the other begins but pinpoint Kanaris. Waiters scuttle across the road from the kitchen, dodging traffic as they come, and the plates they bring are poems. Clams, oysters, crayfish, langouste so meltingly sweet no butter is needed, sole, salad of tomatoes and Feta cheese and pickled leaves of the caper plant. Ouzo and beer, watermelon, and coffee to top it off, a sustaining and memorable meal.

Mr. Kanaris has his own fleet of fifty fishing boats most of them, at that hour of the day, rocking at anchor in the little harbor. The forest of masts and rigging was in sharp contrast to the Communist countries where a private fleet, let alone a private yacht of no matter how modest dimension, is unheard of. Any yachts that one sees cruising the Dalmatian coast in all probability come from western Europe or have been chartered by Americans.

To our satisfaction the afternoon was one of those relax times that we had heard so heatedly discussed in the office of Mr. Papaefstratiou. We rested and wrote letters. In the evening Leslie Finer arrived to have a cocktail with us. He had left his wife in a theater around the corner from the hotel, rehearsing *Separate Tables,* which he had translated into Greek and was helping to direct and produce.

We asked if we might go back with him to watch for a few minutes. "Come along," said he. Norton restrained himself, but Peter and I went and were amused to see that theaters are the same all over the world. We proceeded through an alley, went downstairs, and found the company rehearsing in a set that had no bearing on the play. The action, which takes place in an English hotel, was being played out against a brightly painted farmhouse in a green field, the inevitable glaring pilot light the only illumination. To our regret, Mrs. Finer was not in the scene they were doing so we did not see her, but after listening to several repetitions of the same action Peter and I concluded that even though we vaguely remembered the plot it was still Greek to us and likely to remain so.

By air Crete lies only an hour from Athens and driving to the Xenia Hotel from the airport of Heraklion, I gazed with anticipatory pleasure at the shops with their tempting rugs and embroideries displayed on the sidewalks. The sympathetic comment I received from my male escorts, Dr. Brown and his son was: "Look at Miss Bug Eyes."

"What kind of talk is this?" cried Mando. The merchandise had caught her attention too. "The embroideries are very handsome, no? They should be looked at."

"Watch them," Norton warned Peter, "they'll have their hands in the cookie jar up to their shoulders." They maligned us, for in actuality, when we made our purchases a couple of days later, they were modest. As I have said, some of the Xenia hotels are very nice, but the one at Heraklion is not a showplace. The atmosphere is bleak and the food not first rate, but the wealth of Crete itself more than makes up for it.

Our first visit in Heraklion was to the museum. It is difficult to write about the contents of Greek museums for the adjectives are speedily exhausted. The objects *are* incomparable, matchless, breathtaking, peerless, and who is to say which is peerlesser than the other? One's favorites are due as much to personal reaction as to artistic appreciation. Vases and sarcophagi do not warm my own heart, although there are scholars to whom they are the supreme achievement of ancient art. On the other hand, I am in

thrall to nearly all the finds in the Mycenaean tombs including one recently unearthed and now in the museum at
Heraklion. This one is a vase, but exceptionally lovely, of
rock crystal, small and heart-shaped, the throat encircled by
a chaplet of twisted gold and the handles of green semi-
precious stones. There was another one too, on a different
scale, that caught my eye, or rather the contents did. A
skeleton in a fetal position crouching in the bottom proved
that the great jars were useful for purposes other than stor-
ing grain and oil and wine.

We paid our respects to further treasures, introducing
Peter to the little priestess, slim-waisted, bare-breasted, with
a long ruffled skirt, and holding a serpent in either hand.
Also to La Parisienne, the fragment of an elegant lady
lifted from the walls of the Palace of Knossos. We looked
at the slim ivory figure now brown and scored with age
that they call The Bullfighter, but I suspect he was not a
fighter in the Spanish sense but a dull dancer like the kind
one sees in the frescoes that at one time adorned the palace
walls.

Without understanding any more than scholars who have
still not been able to decipher it, we spent a long time
gazing at the Disk of Phaestos, with its spiraling inscrip-
tions, and admired another treasure, the bull's head of black
stone adorned with ivory horns. Though small in scale, it
is magnificent.

The road to Knossos passed through autumn vineyards
shimmering green and gold on the hillsides, but when we
arrived the sky had become overcast. The ruins of the
ancient palace of the Minoan kings, the abode of legend,
where Ariadne led Theseus through the maze with a thread,
seemed gray and melancholy. Yet the ruins themselves are
real enough and bear witness to the fact that the kings
and a whole coruscating civilization existed in a time of
peace and plenty, for the buildings were dwellings not for-
tresses.

In the hotel lobby was a big drawing, an artist's reconstruction of how the palace may actually have looked, and it was enormous. With wings built on varying levels it was sometimes three stories high, sometimes four and covered about six acres. Individual rooms were not large— the throne room was quite tiny—but the halls, courtyards, chambers and storage areas could well have housed several thousand people.

On the way back to Heraklion we were so seduced by the beauty of that part of Crete, the rolling vineyards, olive groves, and everywhere the sea, that we said to one another, "Here is where we should buy property." We did not do it, but the temptation was strong. Every traveler feels it, I think. Actually it is not hard for a foreigner to buy land—no law forbids it—but Mr. Frangopolous had told us: "People are always tempted, but there are reasons against it. When you are here you are enthusiastic, but do not forget—Greece is a long way from America and getting here is expensive and it takes time." He also said that most of the land is held by the government and the monasteries, which, like churches elsewhere, do not pay real estate taxes as other landowners must, regardless of how mundane their holdings.

The monasteries are sometimes averse to selling property outright but will usually grant lifetime leases. Other land can almost always be bought, provided it is not on an island the Greek government considers strategic; usually meaning islands close to Turkey and Albania.

After we had been driving for a few miles we came to Arhanes, a vineyard center. The harvest was in and two hundred girls and women were packing delicious white grapes in a big airy shed, the village co-op. They told us they shipped chiefly to Holland and Norway, but they side-tracked a few heavy bunches, urging them upon us.

Peter was all for hurrying back to the hotel, taking off our shoes and trampling out our own wine.

In the course of the evening we must have sounded as though we were doing just that. Somewhere in the day's

junketing Norton had picked up a sheep's bladder. It was
the kind the Scottish pipers use, but without a tartan sack
it looked strangely naked and shivery, like a pallid little
man in need of a hot beach and sunshine. The good doctor
was in love with this unprepossessing find, and our ouzo
hour was pierced by shrill squeals and uncontrolled laughter
from Mando and me as the lads tried their skill, passing the
instrument back and forth between them, each trill more
ear splitting than the last.

I said, "They'll put us out of the hotel."

"Not at all," said Peter, "we'll explain it's American chamber music."

"Chamber music! It sounds like stuck pigs in a barn-
yard."

That we did not wind up in the local hoosegow for
disturbing the peace I attribute to the fact that it was
late in the season and there were few guests at the hotel.

Crete was the birthplace of Domenico Theotocopuli who,
fortunately, has come down in history by the more easily
mastered name of El Greco. He died in Toledo in 1614
and is thought to have been born between 1545 and 1550.
In a church in Heraklion there are pictures attributed to
Damaskinos with whom it is said El Greco studied as a boy
before leaving Crete for Italy and eventually Spain. Just as
there are fine singing coaches who cannot sing themselves,
so let us assume Mr. Damaskinos was a better teacher than
he was a painter. Also, the cheap varnished frames surrounding his canvases do little to enhance them.

Another noted Cretan, for those who may have forgotten
their mythology, was Zeus, mothered by Rhea, sired by the
unnatural father Cronos, who ate his offspring, although
come to think of it, unnatural is the wrong word. Some
animals and many fish do devour their young. It is nature's
way.

Still, Rhea, as mothers will, took a dim view of this
habit. When Zeus was a tiny baby, she gave her husband

a stone and told him it was his son. Cronos, the clod, obviously lacking a palate and assuming it to be his own flesh and blood, gobbled it down.

All the Cretans were in cahoots with Rhea and moved the baby from cave to cave, singing and dancing and playing flutes, and undoubtedly bladders too, to drown out his cries so Cronos wouldn't hear him. The ruse worked. The god grew up, moved to Olympus and became head man.

He left behind him one of the sweet-smelling spots of the world, for Heraklion is prevaded with the fragrance of thyme; dry, sunny, delicious. It is a pleasure just to stroll the streets sniffing as one goes.

Mando told us of an episode in the last war, both comic and heroic, that had taken place in Crete. It featured an Irishman, Paddy Lee Fermore, who, with a companion, kidnaped a German general and his chauffeur in Heraklion.

As the general was moving out of the city following his troops already on the march, Paddy Lee, dressed in a German uniform and speaking perfect German, halted his car and told him that orders had just come through for him to return to headquarters. His friend, with some Cretan comrades, leaped into the car, overpowering the general and his chauffeur. With the Irishman at the wheel they made their way out of town, but the going through the narrow streets was tricky and further complicated by troops who, having got wind of a return order, were streaming back to Heraklion.

The kidnapers finally managed to get clear and sped with their hostages to a remote mountain village. For two or three months they held them captive, at the end of that time delivering them by pre-arrangement to an Allied submarine that surfaced in a secluded cove. The general and his chauffeur were transported to Cairo, where they spent the remaining months of the unpleasantness in a prisoner of war camp.

Mando told us the tale en route to Kamaris, a village where we had been assured we would find beautifully embroidered rugs and counterpanes at reasonable prices. We also bore a letter to the village president, which would give us an entree.

Our road was rugged but not impassable until we came to an enormous pile of gravel, component of a new surface they were in the process of laying. We thought we were stuck for fair, but an obliging young man mounted a bulldozer on our behalf, flattened the gravel, and on we rolled. Rounding a bend, we frightened the wits out of a donkey who shied and tossed the young girl who was riding him into a ditch. She picked herself up but seeing one of her hands bloody and swollen we piled out to ask if we could help. Norton satisfied himself that no bones were broken, the girl, although shaken, behaved I thought, with great *sang-froid*. She explained to Mando that the donkey was not hers but borrowed from a friend—"He does not know me." She remounted, gave him a sharp kick in the ribs, and trotted off.

Kamaris proved to be a tiny, rather dirty and not unduly picturesque village. The president not being present we presented our letter to the vice-president, a young man who was, we were informed, a bridegroom. He still wore his stiff store clothes, for the feasting and dancing that celebrated the wedding had lasted a week, ending only the day before. In a few minutes along came the bride. She too was in city attire—a green serge dress—and she looked peevish. I couldn't blame her. She was doubtless tired, and teetering around on the rough cobblestones in high-heeled pointed-toed shoes she must also have been miserable.

A pleasant-looking woman of middle age invited us into her house to look at some embroidery. At the door a young man involved in manufacturing araki offered us each a tiny glass of the water-clear liquid. A tiny glass was enough. Araki is distilled alcohol of high potency, and shimmering through it the bright embroidered woolens looked especially attractive. The little house consisted of two whitewashed rooms. In the living room were three narrow iron bedsteads and a couple of straight chairs, the other room contained an open fireplace with a pot cooking on the logs, and the family loom on which the rugs and bedspreads were woven.

Peter felt that a vigorous red one, gay with flowers would look well on the bed in his new apartment, but I persuaded him that I had my heart set on it. Rather like Sir Walter Raleigh tossing down his cloak and saying to Elizabeth, "O.K., then, *keep* it!" he withdrew from the competition, and a pleasure it was to see his merry face light up when I gave it to him the following Christmas.

Before purchasing it, however, we went a few yards down the street to the village café to await the arrival of the president who set the price for local products. The café was a bare room with a few chairs and tables at one of which three men were playing cards—the game seemed to be a kind of blackjack—and two were kibitzing. One of them was young and we wondered if he had no job. Small mountain villages act as magnets to travelers, but village economy is still a problem. If they do not emigrate to the cities, how can the younger generation make a living?

The clothes and faces of the blackjack group were different but still they made me think of Cézanne's great canvas, the besmocked men in the French café, playing cards.

The president's father, an amusing old rascal with legs wrapped in cloth puttees, a chaplet of twisted black cloth binding his head, offered us coffee which he brewed in a battered little pot on a battered two-burner stove behind the bar. He suplemented it with cheese, bread, and wine.

We murmured to Mando that the hospitality was unmerited and should we not pay for it? As matters developed a baby tempest was created in the coffeepot. At first the old man refused. We were travelers, it was his pleasure . . . the ancient laws of hospitality must be respected. No, no, Mando insisted, we were there on business, we appreciated his kindness, but it was only fair . . . Very well, then, a modest bit of currency might be tendered . . . "For my expenses. Cigarettes, a little glass . . ." he couldn't have been more ingratiating, nor his needs more modest. *One* cigarette, a mere *swallow* from the glass. The transfer was in progress when his son, the president, arrived and, seeing what was going on, burst into an angry harangue. A: His father was transgressing the rules of hospitality, one did not accept money from strangers and above all not from a woman, B: if any money *was* going to change hands it should rightfully come to him, the son, who having heard of our arrival in the village, had sent word to his parent to offer us refreshment as a common courtesy. We were sorry to be the cause of family conflict, but we enjoyed it very much, punctuated as it was by Mando's running colorful commentary.

Finally, having settled on prices—$20.00 for the spread, less for some bags and strips of embroidery—we gathered up our purchases and bade Kamaris farewell—not without a twinge of regret. In all probability they were glad to see the modest influx of drachmas, but for an hour we had shared a life that was as basic and flavorful as the bread they baked. It was we who were indebted to them.

Our goal for luncheon was Phaestos, a palace older than Knossos and the home of Idomeneus, a legendary king of Crete who was reputed to be of great beauty and a suitor of Helen. After her abduction by Paris he fought in the Trojan War and distinguished himself by his bravery, but as he was returning home, embraced by glory if not the girl, his ship ran into a fearsome storm. He prayed to Poseidon to save him, promising the god that he would sacrifice to him the first living thing he met on shore. This, unfortunately, turned out to be his son, and at a later date he and the Biblical chap Jephtha might have had a little discussion about the wisdom of those free-flung promises. Jephtha had rashly promised *his* god a juicy sacrifice were he victorious in battle against the children of Ammon. The victory, duly granted him, may be said to have been Pyrrhic in view of the fact that the first creature he saw on returning home was his only child, his daughter, "coming out to meet him with timbrels and with dances."

A pretty sight she must have been and a goodhearted girl to boot, because when her father said, "Alas, my daughter, thou has brought me very low and thou art one of them that trouble me for I have opened my mouth onto the Lord and I cannot go back," instead of answering, "You and your big mouth," as she well might have done, she gently acquiesced begging only for two months on the mountains that she might bewail her virginity. The request was granted, although the poor girl might better have lost it, for then perhaps her young man would have spirited her away and she would not have had to be slaughtered just so her father could keep his vow.

In any event, Phaestos on a rise of land is topped by a pavilionlike restaurant from which one overlooks the wide plane of Mesara, planted with olive groves and vines, dissolving into the misty slopes that frame it and sweep to the bay.

Just below the restaurant, with a minimum of restoration, lie the ruins of the palace. Here and there is a platform or steps, but mostly there are low crumbling stone walls, spaciousness, the plain, the sky, and stillness.

After we had chosen a delicious luncheon from his kitchen, the proprietor of the restaurant gave Norton a reproduction of the Disk of Phaestos, which he proudly displays in his office.

On our way back to town we stopped off at Gortys, where there is a tiny amphitheater—a sort of off-Broadway house, a ruined church, and a small basilica where are engraved the laws which, for the first time, gave women the right to inherit money and property.

Crete used to be famous for her windmills, and they still stand today. Occasionally one sees a few of them working, but the great wings do not flail the sky as they used to, because so much water is now pumped by electricity. A travel brochure mentioned 20,000 on the plateau of Lasithi and we were passing near it on our next day's trip to the ruins of another palace state—Malia. I yearned to go there. "They all whirl at once," I said. "It must be a marvelous sight."

From Norton and Peter I received the Oh-come-off-it family look and from Mando one of puzzlement. "May I see the pamphlet?" she said. She read it and shook her head. "I don't know what you're talking about, it doesn't say that at all."

She was right. I looked at it again. There seemed to be 20,000 of them, all right, but there was no set performance. I don't know where I got the idea unless the vision in my head transcribed itself to the page and I read what I wanted to read.

Malia belongs to the Minoan era, contemporary with Knossos and Phaestos. It is backed by mountains and overlooks the plain and gulf of Malia. In an enormous shed partially restored, hundreds of jars of all sizes that once contained grain and oil still stand in place. What happened to the inhabitants? What extraordinary catastrophe overcame them? Earthquake? Plague? Decimation by an enemy? No one knows. Civilizations seem to have vanished, rather than to have declined, although in all probability they did undergo a period of debilitation.

To reach the sea from Malia one crosses the Dhikti Mountains, an awe-inspiring range where Zeus is alleged to have dwelt. Like George Washington's night, the abodes of Zeus are claimed by every district, snippets of him partitioned out over the countryside.

Descending the southeastern slopes of the mountain we came to Minos Beach on Ayios Nikolaos. This is a group of cottages, ninety in number, white as sugar cubes, clustering on two small protected bays. It is an enchanting spot. One suns and bathes from rocks, small terraces, and a tiny sandy crescent. The water is marvelous. The cottages are two-family affairs but so well designed that each veranda-balcony has privacy.

April and May, September and October are too early or too late, since, in Greece too, the beaches are at their best in the hottest months. But even late in October, when we were there, the cottages were nearly all taken, and the water was delicious for quick dips.

Sweaters or lightweight woolen coats are prudent for evening. The resort people at Minos have really succeeded. The location is alluring, the food delicious, and the service excellent. Breakfast, served in the cottages, is hot, fresh, and instantaneous.

The main house consists of a lounge, a bar, a dining room, and a spacious dining terrace overlooking the water, and the grounds are bright with flowers.

The rates are remarkable for all the pleasure and service one receives. Eight dollars a day per person, including board. They told us, and seemed unhappy about it, that they were going to have to raise them, but the raise was to be only a dollar a day. No one, I think, will complain.

When we were there the clientele was largely Scandinavian. By and large they are a physically handsome people conforming to the popular belief of what Greeks used to look like in the days of gods and fair Helen. Today, many Greeks are handsome but they seem to have gone brunette. The Scandinavians and the few English did not appear to mind the slight chilliness in the air. Compared to home territory it probably still seemed balmy.

Relaxation is the occupation at Minos, although Mando and Peter and I went to visit a couple of old tiny churches. Cretan Tours, a small independent travel bureau, tells you in its brochure that the thirteenth-century frescoes at Krista are perfectly preserved, but don't you believe it. They are considerably deteriorated but not without charm. We bowed to passing priests looking in their long white woolen robes with rope girdles and black crosses hanging around their necks, not unlike the mosaic saints of Thessalonike. We met a pretty little ten-year-old girl helping her elderly father load a donkey with sand. Her mother, Mando learned, was dead.

I wondered what future the village held for such a child. Her face was sensitive and intelligent, and I thought, if I were a rich woman would I offer to adopt her and take her to America? Would she want to come and would her family consent and if she did and they did, who could guarantee that I would be doing her such a favor, offering her so great an advantage?

I kept the day dream to myself and we went on our way. Perhaps the child will grow up to become a famous star like the Misses Mercouri and Callas (Greek, if Brooklyn-born) or the first Greek woman premier, like Madame Gandhi of India, or perhaps she will live out her life in her native village and marry a fisherman or a good-looking young chap who will become the barman of Minos Beach and they will have ten children.

Since Norton and I had been to Delphi on our previous visit to Greece, Peter went one day to see it on his own, and Norton and I went with Mando to Marathon. The historic plain, five miles long and two wide, lies about twenty-four miles northeast of Athens. The day was chilly, overcast, and windy. Climbing the narrow steps that lead up the side of the barrowlike memorial to Miltiades and the 10,000 Greeks who defied and overwhelmed twice that number of Persians seemed to me as hazardous as scaling Annapurna. There was no railing to hang onto, and I thought I'd be swept away by the gale.

Mando and Norton sprinted up and down like human flies, but they have, if I may say so, more heft than I. Nevertheless, the climb was necessary, as I had no intention of coming to the scene of so great a battle and not having a good look at it.

It was a day in the latter part of September, 490 B.C. that

the Athenian and Plataean infantry stood drawn up in a battle formation which seemed to their Persian enemies tactically unsound. The Persians themselves had their strength in the center, but their flanks were weak. Miltiades, on the other hand, was trusting to the power of his right and left wings, knowing that his center would doubtless give way. How confident he was on the eve of battle we do not know.

The Athenians had sent Pheidippides, their great Olympic runner, to seek the aid of Sparta. Today's Marathon races of twenty-six miles, three hundred and eighty-five yards, commemorate his feat in covering that distance in two days and two nights, swimming rivers and climbing mountains in his path. Furthermore, he returned and fought beside his comrades.

Sparta had said she would march at the full moon—something to do with her religion—but the tide of battle, like that of the sea, did not wait. When the battle was joined, the Greek center was quickly overwhelmed, the Persians rushed through, and the Greek flanks closed behind them, cutting them off from their navy anchored in the bay. When it was all over 6400 Persians lay dead on the plain. One hundred and ninety-two Greeks had perished. Again Pheidippides was the messenger. He ran the twenty-four miles from Marathon to Athens bearing the shining news. As he reached the city he gasped out *"Nenikikamen!"* ["Rejoice, we conquer!"] and fell dead.

The Athenians returned swiftly to Athens to protect the city from further Persian attack and from the expected onslaught by 600 Persian ships, but the Persian fleet turned instead toward Asia. The Greek victory was complete. Oh yes, when it was all over 2000 Spartans came on the double to the rescue. Let's hear it for the Spartans!

It was at Marathon that we had the only retsina wine we drank in Greece. If you like turpentine it is not bad at all, and luncheon at Leonides a few miles away was memorable. It is a spacious restaurant and on a chilly day

the open fire was hospitable. An enormous choice of suc-
culent goodies from which to choose in the kitchen proved
to be not enough for Dr. Brown. Mando was distraught
trying to find something to please the master, but that was
the day he wanted only a small piece of broiled calf's liver.
After a few tart wifely comments he settled for grilled
steak and pronounced it excellent. I had veal stew with
spicy little onions. I was smart.

We were sorry that Peter had not been with us at Marathon. That night he acknowledged that Delphi probably
was a must but he was somewhat disillusioned, poor boy,
as on his tour the time allotted had been brief. When
Norton and I had made the trip we stayed overnight at a
mountain inn nearby, and I think it is the better way to do
it.

A much shorter junket is the one to Daphni, the eleventh-
century Byzantine church a few miles from the capital. Its
mosaics are among the most notable in Greece and the
strange commanding head of the Pantocrator in the dome
is one of the most widely discussed images of God in the
Christian world. Indeed it inspired Mr. Robert Payne to a
four-page panegyric of delirious prose in his book, *The
Splendor of Greece,* first published in 1961. The mystery,
the beauty, purity, the wisdom . . . Mr. Payne's reaction
seems to me inflamed. My own, which is perhaps devoid of
lyricism, is that the Pantocrator's expression with his turned-
down mouth and drooping mustaches is sour and suspicious,
and if he is contemplating his masterpiece, the human
race, who shall blame him? I greatly prefer the mosaics
of some of the lesser figures, especially the one of Jesus
riding a donkey into Jerusalem with a little boy watching
him from a palm tree.

Our last excursion in Greece was to the island of Corfu.
We had wanted to go to Olympia on the Peloponnesus
and I still think that in late October it would have been
the wiser goal but when we suggested it, we tangled into

an inextricable little snarl with the travel bureau, and what with errors, miscalculations and a certain stubbornness that sometimes occurs in the most flexible of organizations and with the best-arranged itineraries, we ended up following their desires rather than our own.

Not that Corfu isn't beautiful! It is one of the loveliest of the Greek islands, with a special international flavor, since it is the island nearest Europe, and a large one, with a direct jet service to and from London, Copenhagen, and Stockholm. Guidebooks pay it loving respect, the distinguished writer, Mr. Lawrence Durrell, has or had a house there, and it abounds in hotels and beach resorts.

Our mild discontent came about because we wished we were someplace else, specifically Olympia in the Peloponnesus. It quickly became obvious that we had arrived so late in the season that there would be little to do during our two full days. We were, however, comfortably lodged in the Corfu Palace Hotel, which boasts in its employ a lady of rare taste and ability in the art of flower arrangements. There were magnificent bouquets all over the hotel, but my favorite, one of my favorite things in Corfu in fact, was a tiny one in a gray pottery vase on a narrow shelf under the mirror in the elevator. Two pink carnations and one red surrounded by geranium leaves. We happily sniffed their fragrance every time we rode up and down in the little car.

On our arrival Norton and Peter immediately betook themselves to the large swimming pool, for in the middle of the day the sun was still strong enough to boost the summer's tan.

Since the hotel is on the waterfront, it is tantalizing not to be able to swim in the sea, which unhappily is polluted by sewage.

In the afternoon we drove to the Achilleion Casino, as beautifully located a gambling hell as one is ever likely to encounter. It was originally a summer palace built between 1890 and 1892 by Elizabeth of Austria, the hapless mother of the hapless Rudolf of Mayerling. One reason she may have thrown all her energies into the project was to distract her mind from the tragedy.

The taste of that period is today outmoded, sometimes laughable, but today's slot machines in the marble halls are painfully vulgar. The baccarat and roulette tables were upstairs, but the rooms were closed in the daytime, and in any event our interest was meager.

The empress of Austria, we discovered, had had a passion for Achilles, and in the garden is a marble statue of him seated, pulling that arrow from his heel, and also a great bronze statue, chest outflung, bearing shield and spear, legs greave-encased, helmet silhouetted against the sky, looking more noble than Superman. I daresay he made a nice change from the Emperor Franz Josef. Walking in the garden on a mellow autumn afternoon, thinking of the beautiful dead Elizabeth evoked a certain melancholy.

A sight more endearing than bluff Achilles was the tiny, pretty island in the bay, Mouse Island, with a church and cypress trees. Near it a long mole jutted out from the mainland boasting a monastery with white walls and brown tiled roofs.

A more worldly attraction was Miramar Beach. This is another of the Greek island resorts and the first one put up by the syndicate that built Minos. Next came Rhodes, then Ayios Nikolaos. They learned as they went along and the Cretan one is the more polished and the privacy in each cottage most complete.

Miramar was closed for the season, but we went to see it out of curiosity. The bungalows (there are one hundred) are directly on the water, which was crystalline and lovely. The disadvantage is that they all accommodate two couples, and when the louvre doors are open the mutual patio is small. They would house one family admirably or two couples if they throve on each other's companionship. Prices are $22.75 per day for two, including full board, plus a 15 per cent service charge. The place is run by Germans, who hold a ninety-nine-year lease, and the clientele, I should imagine, is largely German.

As in all these places we wondered what people did in the evening, since, for the most part, the diversion would seem slender. On Corfu of course, there was gambling for those who enjoy it.

I realize that the human race is supposedly divided into Day and Night people and that the night ones consider themselves superior and more subtle. I like to think that I too appreciate tenebrosity and can scintillate at gay nocturnal parties, but I also enjoy awakening to the wonder of dawn as we did the next morning, when the soft, shell-pale emptiness was suddenly pierced by a blinding sliver of light and the sun ballooned over the bare rocky ridge opposite our window, rose into the cloudless sky, and was mirrored in the gleaming sea.

Since neither Mando nor Peter was up yet, Norton and I breakfasted alone and then wandered into town to watch the crowds going to market. The produce all looked fresh and tempting, but the merchandise in the shops appeared rather shoddy, and despite the fact that it was the end of the season high-season tourist prices still held.

On our return to the hotel we discovered that Mando had got a permit to visit the new museum that was in the process of construction. Only a few pieces were in place, but there was a handsome seventh-century B.C. pediment, a gorgon with two serpents twined about its waist, flanked by two charming lions couchant with delicately carved designs on their haunches. I was allowed to photograph those and another solitary lioness but there were other lion pieces over which the curator shook his head. They had not yet been officially published by the official archaeological authorities.

There is also an old Palace Museum with Japanese and Chinese porcelains and an amusing scroll of Europeans in eighteenth-century clothes painted in the Japanese fashion.

We dropped into a small boutique run by two Americans and after staring at me a moment one of them said, "Aren't you Ilka Chase?" When I said I was, he said, "I knew your grandmother." He looked very young to have known my grandmother, and I said as much, adding, "How *could* you have? That seems impossible."

"I did though," said he, "my grandmother was her friend, Mrs. George."

"Mrs. George!"

The years rolled back, and there was Grandma, small determined, not in the best of humors. "I saw my friend Mrs. George this afternoon."

"Did thee, Grandma? Did thee have a nice time?"

"Ilka, thee knows quite well Mrs. George is a difficult woman. I don't think I shall see her again for a while."

Grandma was a Quaker, her opinions were strong, and she did not approve of most of her friends. Mother and I used to try to persuade her to tolerance, feeling she would be less lonely if she could bring herself to accept the glaring shortcomings, misdemeanors, and grievous faults that so obviously encumbered them and that were so harassing to a perfectionist like herself. But we could thee and thy her till we were breathless; Grandma knew right from wrong and told her friends to their faces just what she thought of them.

She and Mrs. George knew each other for years and always addressed each other as Mrs. George and Mrs. Martin. I suppose that way it was easier to withdraw into a huff under what a *blind* man could see was goading provocation, than it would have been had they been on a companionable first-name basis.

Mrs. George, like Grandma, had long gone to her long home and it seemed a curious and unlikely coincidence that their grandchildren should be meeting on a Greek island, on a mellow day in October, so many years later.

A car and chauffeur having been placed at our disposal, we decided on touring and drove across the island to a place called Paliokastritsa where, at a flyblown little restaurant on the water's edge, we ate delicious messes and *great* fresh boiled lobster with salad.

The day was an autumnal dream, but the group of Athenians sharing it with us at the next table were impervious to nature's smiles and sat throughout the meal wrapped in black woolen topcoats. Mando shrugged. "Not aristocrats," she said. Aristocrats presumably would have the wit to moult in the sunshine.

We drove up a hill to visit the inevitable monastery, and Mando told me that in Greece, unless one has been baptized in a church, he cannot go to school. The price to be paid for the vital separation of church and state is apparently the same as that for liberty; eternal vigilance. Many Greeks themselves find the situation shocking.

From the monastery the view out over the water was lovely. This is one of the bays claimed as the place where Odysseus swam ashore and met Nausicaa, the king's daughter, who brought him clothes and led him to her father's palace, where he was hospitably entertained. His wife Penelope may have had suitors, but Odysseus too had his little diversions.

The following day Mando and I left Norton and Peter to bask beside the swimming pool. Bask was all they could do, as the pool was being emptied, but they didn't seem to mind. "Our sunburns," they said, "got to keep them till we get home." Status seekers!

We lunched that day at a tiny restaurant called Pipilas. I had no complaints but the wine aroused Mando's ire. On the bottle were the words "Korasi Kakotryri." They looked inoffensive enough to me, but little did I know!

"Look at that!" said Mando.

"What does it mean?"

"It means second pressing, that's what."

"Is that bad?"

"But certainly. The first the vintners keep for themselves. How dare they?"

"Well," I said lamely, "if it's their wine . . ."

"You do not understand. How dare the landlords say, 'You, you peasants, you will drink second pressing and think it good,' and what is terrible is we do think it good."

I sheepishly agreed. "Tastes fine."

Mando growled and bit into her food. "Ah ha!" she cried triumphantly. "Him we can snobbish at least, the cook for the way he is doing his fish." The sauce displeased her, she thought it piquant and too oily, but I, with my low peesant taste, was very happy. Fish, veal, olives, superb Greek bread, and the shameful second pressing. Enjoyable, that's what!

In the afternoon we drove through little villages and in one of them stopped to watch an old woman in the inevitable black dress of the Greek peasant, making lace over a cushion stuck with countless bobbins. It was intricate work, pretty and, I should think, fatal to sight. Today, surely, the market for such talent is dwindling. How do people survive? They have orange and lemon and olive groves, small vineyards, fish, and occasionally a lamb, but their existence must be marginal.

We returned to the hotel and had a nap. In the early evening I strolled alone through the town along the waterfront. The light was marvelous, and the sea stretched without a ripple. From the third of May until the end of October Corfu had had no rain. The situation for the inhabitants was grim, but for the undeserving traveler the weather was incomparable.

There is a pink house in Corfu built many years ago by a Venetian. It was bombed by the Germans, and all that remains of it today is the charming Renaissance façade. The windows frame the blue sky, and from one of them a fig tree leans. It is like a surrealist painting.

I returned to the hotel to find my loved one in the grip of what seemed to be an acute case of asthma, caught I suspected from our driver of the day before, who had been suffering from an appalling cold or allergy of some sort.

Despite malaise, however, the doctor was very pleased with
himself.

"You remember their telling us that on some islands
foreigners couldn't buy property? Rhodes was one and
Corfu here another."

"Yes, I remember."

"Well, about Corfu I've got it all figured out."

"Oh?"

"Obvious. It's too near Albania, and with Albania in
cahoots with Communist China, a hell of a traffic in drugs
would be possible. China to Albania, Albania to Corfu
then on to Brindisi and the Mafia in Italy. From there to
the Mafia in the States."

"Very neat," I said. I thought it was too, but does Communist China want to traffic in drugs? Wouldn't they be
more interested in *suppressing them?* I am always expecting that people are going to do what would seem the
straightforward, sensible thing and then discovering the
world of codes and hidden microphones, of smuggled gold
and DOPE. I am not *with* it.

Lovely as it was, we had hoped to leave Corfu that day,
the twenty-seventh, but, unable to get transportation, we
consoled ourselves with the thought that even were we in
Athens there would be little we could do. October 28 is a
big holiday, Ochi day. This was the day the Greeks said
No to Mussolini when, in 1940 the Italians were seeking
to pass through Greece and on to Egypt in order to attack
the Allies. It is a fine day to commemorate, but remember
it and make your plans accordingly.

In almost every trip, I think there comes a time when no
matter how dedicated a traveler one may be, a tiny weasel-
ing sensation enters one's consciousness: am I resting, relaxing, absorbing new and marvelous sights and sensations,
or am I, just possibly, wasting time and money? We had
been away from home for two months and were beginning
to get restive.

The next morning when the plane from Athens, which

was on a shuttle run, was late in arriving I made inquiries
at the desk about ferries to the mainland. We were flying
back to New York the next day and could ill afford to be
stuck. Fortunately, there were several ferries, but we did
not need them. The plane did arrive and depart on the
return trip to Athens with us on board.

Our last morning we were up early, did some inevitable
last minute shopping at Their Majesties Fund Shop—"Good
Lord, I've got nothing for Helen and Nancy and Stan"—
and returned to the hotel to find Mando, who had come to
bid us farewell, arriving in a thirteen-seat bus that was to
take Norton, Peter, me, and our luggage to the airport.

Once installed in the commodious lap of TWA and recovered from the surprise of finding no duty-free shop in
the terminal we looked around at the luxury in which we
were ensconced. We tested the comfort of the seats and
leafed through the pages of the glossy magazines gazing
upon the haunts, the clothes, and the food-in-technicolor
of the affluent society. Sumptuous was the word for it, and
we were Americans, member of the club.

Why then did I feel such a sense of loss as the hard
and arid landscape of a country they call poor dropped
away and we were born for a brief span through the magical
light that enshrines the motherland of Greece?

From
New York

Frankfurt

Wiesbaden

WEST GERMANY

Prague

CZECHOSLO

AUSTRIA

Vienna

Zagreb

YUGO

CZECHOSLOVAKIA

GERMANY

AUSTRIA

HUNGARY

ROMANIA

YUGOSLAVIA

BULGARIA

GREECE

To New York